ENHANCING DIGITAL LITERACIES WITH ADULT ENGLISH LANGUAGE LEARNERS

Offering a new perspective on adult English language education, this book provides theoretical and practical insights into how digital literacies can be included in the learning programmes for newly arrived adults from migrant and refugee backgrounds.

Enhancing Digital Literacies with Adult English Language Learners takes readers inside Langfield, an adult community-based English language centre that supports the settlement and learning of this vulnerable group. Drawing on a six-month ethnographic study of Langfield's work, the book explores the approach to teaching digital literacies and presents a range of perspectives, including those of the adult learners, the teachers, and the organisation's CEO. The chapters present a holistic view of teaching digital literacies in the adult English language context by exploring: adult learners' digital literacy practices in everyday life and their learning at Langfield; teachers' beliefs and practices about digital literacies; and the support offered to them through institutional resources, leadership, and professional learning. The book identifies exemplary practices, as well as areas for further development in Langfield's work and offers a range of implications for practice, policy, and research.

Written in a detailed but accessible manner, this book contributes important insights into the strengths and needs of this unique and complex education sector. Addressing an area of uncertainty for many researchers, practitioners, leaders, and policy makers working within community-based learning contexts in Australia and internationally, this book will be an essential resource.

Ekaterina Tour is a lecturer in the Faculty of Education at Monash University. Her research focuses on the digital literacies of children and adults from refugee and migrant backgrounds. It investigates the ways in which these groups use digital technologies in English as an Additional Language (EAL) for life, learning, and employment. Her research projects in EAL contexts have examined innovative teaching and learning with technologies, in-service and pre-service teachers' experiences with digital literacies, teaching online during the Covid-19 pandemic, and technology use in culturally and linguistically diverse communities as they settle in Australia.

Edwin Creely is a lecturer in the Faculty of Education at Monash University. His research focuses on creativity, poetry, literacy, digital pedagogies and literacies, and technology in learning. He has extensive experience as an educator in schools, and has worked in community-based education for decades. Edwin is especially interested in innovation and creative practices and bringing new models and perspectives to educational research. He has published in a range of journals and is a regular contributor to research and practice in literacy, creativity, and technology.

Peter Waterhouse is a lecturer in the Faculty of Education at Monash University. His research and practice have explored literacy skills and needs, particularly adult literacy learning, across a wide range of contexts; from community settings to diverse workplaces and institutions. He is interested in how the culture and relationships within organisations shape the learning of those who live and work within them. He believes critical and creative literacies are essential to sustaining democracy and a decent life and hence provision of opportunities to develop these skills is fundamental to the ongoing quest for social justice.

ENHANCING DIGITAL LITERACIES WITH ADULT ENGLISH LANGUAGE LEARNERS

Theoretical and Practical Insights

Ekaterina Tour, Edwin Creely and Peter Waterhouse

LONDON AND NEW YORK

Cover image: © Getty Images

First published 2022
by Routledge
4 Park Square, Milton Park, Abingdon, Oxon OX14 4RN

and by Routledge
605 Third Avenue, New York, NY 10158

Routledge is an imprint of the Taylor & Francis Group, an informa business

© 2022 Ekaterina Tour, Edwin Creely and Peter Waterhouse

The right of Ekaterina Tour, Edwin Creely and Peter Waterhouse to be identified as author of this work has been asserted in accordance with sections 77 and 78 of the Copyright, Designs and Patents Act 1988.

All rights reserved. No part of this book may be reprinted or reproduced or utilised in any form or by any electronic, mechanical, or other means, now known or hereafter invented, including photocopying and recording, or in any information storage or retrieval system, without permission in writing from the publishers.

Trademark notice: Product or corporate names may be trademarks or registered trademarks, and are used only for identification and explanation without intent to infringe.

British Library Cataloguing-in-Publication Data
A catalogue record for this book is available from the British Library

Library of Congress Cataloging-in-Publication Data
A catalog record has been requested for this book

ISBN: 978-0-367-67760-2 (hbk)
ISBN: 978-0-367-67758-9 (pbk)
ISBN: 978-1-003-13268-4 (ebk)

DOI: 10.4324/9781003132684

Typeset in Bembo
by SPi Technologies India Pvt Ltd (Straive)

CONTENTS

List of figures   *vii*
Foreword   *viii*
Acknowledgements   *xi*
List of abbreviations   *xii*

1 Living and learning in digital Australia   1
   Digital Australia and newcomers 3
   On the margins of digital society 5
   Government-funded EAL programmes 7
   Focus of this book 15
   Conclusion 16
   Notes 17

2 Developing theoretical perspectives on institutional practices   18
   Socio-material theory 19
   Digital literacies 20
   Strengths-based practices 25
   Leadership for change 29
   Conclusion 35

3 Researching Langfield: Institutional ethnography   37
   Considering research design for adult EAL settings 38
   Institutional ethnography 39
   Victorian context, Langfield, and participants 44
   Data generation 55
   Thematic data analysis 58
   Conclusion 58
   Note 59

4 The digital lives of Langfield's learners 60
   Learners' digital literacy practices 62
   Learners' challenges 66
   Learners' strengths and resources 69
   Thinking about curriculum and pedagogy 79
   Conclusion 82

5 Teaching and learning digital literacies at Langfield 83
   Perspectives on digital literacies: Surviving and thriving 84
   The Techno-Tuesday programme 87
   The role of digital literacies at Langfield 95
   Teaching from learners' strengths 103
   Teachers' perspectives on strengths 108
   Exploring possibilities for digital literacies 109
   Conclusion 112
   Notes 113

6 Escaping the black hole through professional learning 114
   Teachers' experiences of professional learning 115
   Teachers' preferences about professional learning 123
   Deliberations about professional learning 131
   Conclusion 135

7 Enabling leadership for effective practice 137
   Distributed and connected understandings of leadership 139
   Envisioning change through teachers' strengths 141
   Collaboration as the core leadership value 143
   Situated difficulties of enacting change 144
   Supporting change through strategic provisioning 147
   Considering transformational leadership 149
   Conclusion 152

8 Left to their own devices: Implications for change 153
   Re-thinking curriculum and pedagogy 154
   Enhancing professional learning 158
   Developing democratic leadership practices 162
   Challenging policy positions 164
   Considering methodological and ethical issues in research 167
   Postscript: the pandemic, lockdowns, and beyond 169
   Concluding thoughts 171

References 172
Index 185

FIGURES

2.1	The concept of Sociomaterial Theory (SMT)	19
2.2	Four qualities of effective leadership	30
2.3	Scale of leadership approaches	33
3.1	Reciprocity in research design	38
3.2	The emphases in institutional ethnography	42
3.3	Conceptual framework	44
3.4	Inner urban area surrounding Langfield	45
3.5	Social housing estate in the area	47
3.6	Langfield's classroom 1	50
3.7	Langfield's classroom 2	51
3.8	Langfield's computer room	52
3.9	Classroom door with welcoming messages in different languages	54
5.1	Design of *Techno-Tuesday*	89
5.2	A shared digital literacy folder	93
5.3	Susan assisting an individual learner with an iPad	94
5.4	Reading digital books	99
5.5	Group discussion in a computer room	105
6.1	The participants' collaborative collage	124
6.2	Towards a model of professional learning about digital literacies	132
7.1	A framework for leadership towards digital literacies	150

FOREWORD

When we first came to Langfield to do what seemed to be a typical research project with some ethnographic orientations, we believed that this would be the usual exercise in collecting some data and then leaving. It has not proven to be this type of research at all. We were invited to stay longer than we planned and offered more opportunities to observe and talk to different people at Langfield. We came to know the teachers, the CEO, and the learners and began to realise that this was evolving into a full ethnographic study requiring both time and personal connection. We recognised that this is a special place in which adults from migrant and refugee backgrounds not only have a chance to learn English but are nurtured and develop other critical skills that are essential for their settlement and potential employment in Australia. We saw the importance of the work at Langfield, and we wanted to know more about what they offered and what they needed. This book reflects the length and depth of our research and professional relationships with everyone at Langfield. It also embodies the learning journey that we had with them in 2019, one that continues.

This book is emphatically about digital literacies and their pivotal importance in an increasingly digitised world. But to understand digital literacies and how they work for people, it is first necessary to understand the context for their application and use. Our context in this book is Langfield – a community-based adult EAL provider. We wanted to know how the learners used technologies and what digital literacies operated in their lives, including within their English language learning at Langfield. We also wanted to know about the teachers as professionals grappling with a changing digital world and seeking to further their practice. We understood that change must be led and managed in the challenging circumstances of community-based education providers, so connecting with leadership was also imperative.

We are three academics who work in the Faculty of Education at Monash University. This book, and research which it reports, is an outcome of a fruitful collaboration between the three of us, in simpatico with all the wonderful staff and learners at Langfield, whose voices are heard throughout this volume. While the book represents our unified voice as researchers, we had our individual motivations and inspirations driving our research and writing of this book.

For Ekaterina, the idea of a book about digital technologies in English language learning stemmed from her personal and professional experiences. As an English language teacher in her home country, Belarus, she was always interested in the use of digital technologies in language classrooms and even attempted to teach some aspects of digital literacies in the early 2000s. However, as this idea was new to her at that time, she often felt uncertain about her approach. This interest was further reinforced by Ekaterina's migration experience. She moved to Australia in 2004 and establishing a new life here often involved digital technologies. Using technologies in another language and in a new socio-cultural context for different purposes was challenging and, at times, very frustrating. This experience made Ekaterina think again about language learners' digital skills as well as teachers' approaches to digital technologies in language classrooms. As Ekaterina pursued her PhD under the supervision of a prominent scholar in the field of digital literacies, Professor Ilana Snyder, and started her academic career at Monash University, these personal and professional concerns continued to grow. They inspired generative conversations and discussions with two like-minded colleagues, Edwin and Peter. These led to the research project reported in this book.

Edwin came to this ethnographic research at Langfield and the writing of this book with a highly diverse teaching background in English, EAL, and literacy learning across primary and secondary education, and a long-time interest in the role of technologies in learning and the phenomenology of technology in human experience. His PhD focused on the experiences of PhD students and explored their use of digital technologies in their research and writing, so digital pedagogies and literacies are a core research interest. Edwin also has spent decades as a passionate voluntary teacher in adult learning contexts, working in community learning hubs and houses, and in community theatre. This experience of working with adults across many contexts and seeing their creativity and desire to learn has inspired his interest in the work of Langfield and the ways that adults from migrant and refugee backgrounds can learn and grow in a supportive community. Also, having a passion for ethnographic research, the work with Langfield has been a culmination of a range of interests and an expression of Edwin's desire to do research that has impact; research that affects things that matter. The issue of equitable and just learning opportunities, such as those offered by Langfield, is a core ethical concern for Edwin's research and practice.

Over four decades ago, as a fledgling teacher, Peter fluttered into a newly established pioneering Adult Community Education (ACE) Centre. As a student of education interested in progressive, "alternative" and community learning he was drawn to the Centre as a moth is drawn to a light. He could not know then that the Centre would have such a profound effect upon the teacher that he would become. The Centre was not Langfield, but like Langfield, it was staffed almost entirely by women, who articulated a feminist stance, and the learners were also mostly women. As the eldest child from a working-class family, with a stay-at-home mum, he had never experienced a place like the Centre; a place where "second-chance" learning was made available to adult learners, many of whom he could see had never really been given their "first chance". He was inspired by the women of the Centre. He came to see that their caring and compassion was laced with politics, passion, and activism. Their pedagogy was about making a difference in the world. Peter later became an adult educator and deeply involved in adult literacy and basic education; and an academic, researcher and consultant. He has seen ACE providers, staffed by volunteers and part-time teachers, doing important "heavy lifting" in education; often with adult learners who have multiple and complex needs. Furthermore, the essential work of ACE is often under-resourced and under-recognised. For these and other reasons, the opportunity to be involved in ethnographic research and writing about Langfield as an ACE provider was irresistible for Peter.

We hope that this book is not only an interesting read but a challenging one. It contains a rare full ethnographic study in the adult education sector. While it unfolds the experiences about digital literacies in one organisation, we believe the ideas, voices, and implications presented here can resonate with the sector as a whole.

ACKNOWLEDGEMENTS

This book was conceptualised and written in unprecedented times brought by the Covid-19 pandemic. To be honest, writing this book in 2020–2021 was not easy as our personal and professional lives were significantly disrupted by lockdowns, home schooling, working online, and uncertainty in different domains of our lives. However, there were many special people around us at that time and we would like to thank them for their contribution to the writing of this book in these challenging circumstances.

Our gratitude goes to our families for their constant support and encouragement. We would like to thank Ekaterina's husband, Andrei, whose excellent active listening skills and a systems approach to everything helped to clarify many complex ideas discussed in this book. Many thanks go to Ekaterina's two lovely children, Maxim and Veronica, who provided space and time for writing this book (to their best ability, of course). Edwin wishes to thank his wife, Trish, for her steadfast support over many years and her belief in his capacity to be an academic and to follow his dreams. Maree Waterhouse is the foundational "rock" upon which Peter's work has been built over many years. Thank you, Maree!

We also would like to acknowledge the openness and generosity of Langfield participants. The book would not be possible without the CEO of Langfield, six teachers – Tanya, Polly, Susan, Andrea, Kate, and Nicole – and Langfield's learners. They negotiated multiple commitments in their busy professional lives but still were able to find time to participate in this research.

A special expression of gratitude goes to the *Teacher Education, Language, Arts and Professional Learning Academic Community* at the Faculty of Education, Monash University, for a research grant to conduct this research project.

ABBREVIATIONS

ACE	Adult Community Education
AMEP	Adult Migrant English Program
AMES	Adult Migrant Education Services
CBD	Central Business District
CEO	Chief Executive Officer
DET	Department of Education and Training
EAL	English as an Additional Language
ESL	English as a Second Language
ICT	Information and Communication Technology
OECD	The Organisation for Economic Co-operation and Development
SEE	Skills for Education and Employment
SMS	Short Message Service
SMT	Socio-material Theory
TAFE	Technical and Further Education
TESOL	Teaching English to Speakers of Other Languages
UNESCO	The United Nations Educational, Scientific and Cultural Organization

1
LIVING AND LEARNING IN DIGITAL AUSTRALIA

FIELD NOTES

Langfield[1] is a small but sprawling organisation with learning spaces spread over several distinct sites. As a not-for-profit community-based adult education organisation, Langfield utilises existing community facilities and does its best to provide quality English language education within the obvious constraints of a limited budget. It has a unique geography, built in an inner-city landscape of high-rise housing and streets consisting of closely packed residences – with the old and new together. This place has a large migrant and refugee population, some of whom attend Langfield as part of government-funded programmes for settlement and English language learning.

It was through this rich and diverse landscape that the CEO of Langfield took us on a literal and explanatory journey. It was our first meeting as researchers with her and we chatted as we walked – asking her about the area, the various sites for teaching and learning used by Langfield, its learners, teachers, and her work as a leader. Clearly, her passion was for her learners and her teachers above all else. There was an excited tone in her voice when she spoke about both groups.

The central topic of conversation was emphatically about the importance of digital literacies for adult learners from migrant and refugee backgrounds as they settle in Australia. As we chatted and walked, she spoke about initiatives to bring these understandings to learners. We recall her affirmation of a group of three teachers at Langfield who had initiated a more comprehensive approach to using digital technologies in the teaching and learning of English and were modelling this approach for their colleagues. Even at this point, it was evident to us that Langfield was developing some highly promising pedagogical

DOI: 10.4324/9781003132684-1

practices, but (as later we discovered) they struggled to see the significance of what they were doing and saw themselves as somehow missing the mark.

The CEO was keen to hear what we thought about digital literacies. As part of the conversation, she explained that they had tried to develop a bank of digital devices such as desktop computers and tablets to facilitate change. However, she felt that the use of these technologies was limited by the skills that teachers were able to bring to teaching digital literacies. She knew that Langfield's teachers needed professional learning, but she lamented that little of this was currently offered in a formal sense. For her, this was of the highest priority as she understood the overwhelming significance of digital literacies for adult learners. She knew that Langfield's learners need the ability to survive in an increasingly digitised world and their teachers need the wherewithal and scope to integrate digital literacies into the heart of their English language teaching. From her perspective, digital literacies cannot be hit-or-miss but have to be centralised in pedagogical practice and in the curriculum. However, the CEO was uncertain about how to achieve this conceptually and logistically in this complex teaching context.

June 18, 2019

This opening vignette developed from our field notes draws attention to the importance of digital literacies for adult language learners from migrant and refugee backgrounds as they settle in a new country. The most significant insight, however, is Langfield's genuine attempts to help adult learners to develop digital literacies and its significant difficulties associated with establishing a comprehensive, consistent, and, importantly, effective approach for this. This challenge is not limited to Langfield. Teaching digital literacies is an area of uncertainty for many institutions and practitioners in the English as an Additional Language (EAL) sector, both locally and internationally, regardless of the numerous calls for the inclusion of digital literacies in the curriculum and a growing body of relevant research, teaching resources, and policies that have emerged in the last decade.

To understand why teaching digital literacies in the EAL adult context represents a challenge for institutions such as Langfield and what can be done to enhance institutional and practitioners' approaches, it is important to understand the broader social context. This context includes the communities within which Langfield's learners live and learn. It also includes the organisation where teachers work and engage in professional learning. More broadly, the socio-political and economic context impinges on what is possible and shapes leadership decisions. In this chapter, we explore this rich context with a particular focus on the complex and dynamic transformations that have taken place in Australia over recent decades and how such transformations have shaped the communication patterns of everyday life within the Australian community. In particular, we draw attention to the crucial role of digital literacies as we discuss the digitalisation of all life domains in Australia in recent years and the implications of this for multicultural and multilingual newcomers from migrant and refugee backgrounds as well as EAL programmes.

Digital Australia and newcomers

The 21st century has been marked by the unprecedented global emergence and spread of digital technologies. In many contexts, including Australia, in the last 20 years we have seen the rapid growth in the use of mobile devices, complex computer networks, broadband Internet, a diverse range of information and communication technology (ICT) applications and systems, virtual and augmented reality, cloud-based computing, the "Internet of Things", digital data, artificial intelligence, digital twins, automation, and robotics (Broadband Commission for Sustainable Development, 2017). These technologies have become central to Australia's growing digital governance, economy, business, health system, transport and logistics, agriculture, education, tourism, and leisure.

In different sectors and domains of life, these technologies have altered (and continue to alter) the ways in which people live, learn, work, and socialise. They have also changed how essential services are delivered and how information needed for day-to-day tasks is accessed. Australian vital public services are now predominantly online, including Medicare,[2] Australian Taxation Office, Centrelink,[3] MyHealth, job search, child support, housing services, aged care, disability services, and others. The utility services, such as water, electricity, gas, telephone, and internet, as well as payment services, are also online. Workplaces are increasingly digitised as Australian industries, similarly to many other economies in the world, are under competitive pressure to adopt technologies to offer faster, cheaper, and more convenient services and communication (Morrison, 2021). Educational institutions, including universities, TAFEs, schools, childcare providers, and others have their own digital platforms for teaching, learning, and communication.

At a cultural and community level, digital technologies are central to keeping in touch with families, friends, and different networks locally and globally. Digital technologies are also pivotal to leisure activities, including engaging in hobbies and accessing movies, music, games, reading, and other digital content. In other words, digital technologies are not a simple "add-on" to people's activities but have become integral to people's everyday experiences in Australia.

Everyday life, work, and learning now often involve complex interactions based on engagement with sophisticated digital texts, exchanges between people in digital spaces and also communications between humans and machines (Broadband Commission for Sustainable Development, 2017). Smythe (2018) points out that the digital era governance, in particular, repositions people significantly:

> When automated or "zero-touch" technologies such as sensors, cameras, algorithms, "chatbots," Automated Tracking Systems, scanners, and automated phone systems/interactive voice response systems (IVRs) are coordinated,

they form an assemblage of machine learning that can replace human intermediaries in key government services; automated technologies take queries in service call centers, track the activities of users of government services, and issue fines and pay checks.

(p. 199)

This shift to more digitally based services, information, and activities has been somewhat gradual over the last few decades. However, as we write this book in the middle of the Covid-19 pandemic, we observe an acceleration in the use of digital technologies, both locally and internationally, due to the restrictions aiming to slow the spread of the coronavirus. The pandemic not only increased the use of what has been available online already but has also prompted the development of further online provisions, including activities and events that were less common in digital modes at the beginning of 2019. Schools and universities had to embrace fully online learning; doctors started offering, in some cases requiring, phone and video appointments; sports providers organised remote sessions; music, dance, and cooking classes were delivered online; concerts, exhibitions, conferences, and sporting events were live-streamed; people were having virtual dinners and parties. In challenging times, digital technologies played an extremely important role and became a necessity, rather than an option, in the lives of people in Australia across different age groups.

While the benefits of digitalisation of society, government services, education, and industry cannot be denied, it is also important to understand that accessing and making use of a full range of opportunities afforded by technologies requires very sophisticated skills, knowledge, understandings, mindsets, and critical dispositions in relation to the interplay of the digital, social, and language. In this book, we refer to these as "digital literacies" and we further explain and theorise this highly contested concept in the next chapter. Digital literacies are essential for all Australians, not only to fully unlock the communicative potential of digital technologies but also to enhance effective participation in an increasingly digitised society. For adults moving to Australia through different migration, asylum, and humanitarian programmes, this ability to engage digitally is essential for their wellbeing and settlement.

Upon arrival to Australia and its intensely digital environment, being able to engage in digital practices in English, which is usually a new language for many new settlers, is a crucial necessity. To organise their lives, they need to be able to access vital services and information, find a job or enrol in learning, join and participate in new communities, establish new networks, reconnect with families and friends, and engage in independent English language learning (Chapman & Williams, 2015; Hafner, 2019; Kenny, 2016; Shariati et al., 2017). In other words, for adults from refugee and migrant backgrounds, digital literacies provide empowerment for successful settlement in the host country. However, as Zaidi and Rowsell (2017) argue, "when people 'go global', they do not pull their former lives by the roots but instead integrate, mediate, even disrupt aspects of their environments, reimagining familiar contexts where they have come of age through a global lens" (p. 1). Successful settlement, thus, means that new arrivals can find their feet in a new place without losing (and, in fact, building on) their unique identities, cultures, languages, and other strengths.

Australia has a long history of accepting people through its migration, asylum, and humanitarian programmes. These are quite distinctive groups of people with often complex backgrounds and particular needs. In this research project, we were especially interested in the vulnerable learners who came to Australia as part of the Refugee and Humanitarian Program and associated family visas because their needs are very different from often highly skilled and educated people entering Australia as skilled migrants. The Refugee and Humanitarian Program was established in 1977, and it allows people who need protection from persecution in their home country to come to Australia and stay permanently (Refugee Council of Australia, 2020). This programme has two parts: "offshore" (for those who claim protection while being overseas) and "onshore" (for those who claim protection while being in Australia on a valid visa). Most people have come through the "offshore" stream which accounts for 523,790 newcomers since 1977 (Refugee Council of Australia, 2020). The exact number of people who have come through the "onshore" part is difficult to calculate due to the changes in the government policy over many years and consideration of the number of "boat arrivals" and the type of protection offered to them.

There are annual caps on these types of visas and so the demand is very high. For example, while 100,222 applications (both onshore and offshore) were lodged for the 2018–2019 Humanitarian Program, only 18,762 resettlement visas were granted (The Department of Home Affairs, 2019a, 2019b). According to the Department of Home Affairs (2019b), the majority of offshore applications in the 2018–2019 programme came from the Middle East (58% of all applications lodged), followed by Asia (26.2%) and Africa (14.9%). The majority of applicants were under 30 years of age (62%), but there was a consistent gender balance in the applications (49% of female applicants). In 2020, however, consistent with other decisions of the government regarding Covid-19 within Australia, the granting of all humanitarian visas was suspended. Clearly, the need for protection is very high and the number of newcomers entering Australia before the pandemic was significant. This demand is likely to re-commence post-pandemic.

On the margins of digital society

Resettlement experiences in a highly digitised country are challenging because they involve the use of sometimes unfamiliar digital technologies in a new language and in a new socio-cultural context. Thus, it is not surprising, perhaps, that people from refugee and migrant backgrounds often find it difficult to access all the benefits (and often the basics) of digital services and resources in Australia. There is significant evidence that these groups of Australians often find themselves on the margins of the digital society as compared to other population groups who have the ability to access and then confidently use digital technologies (Thomas et al., 2019).

The notion of a digital divide, coined by Lloyd Morrisett in 1998, is often used to describe this inequality. Initially, digital divide mainly referred to inequality in physical access to the devices and the internet (Valadez & Duran, 2007). More recently, the notion has been redefined to offer a more nuanced understanding of the spectrum of digital experiences (Alam & Imran, 2015; Rowsell et al., 2017). Ritzhaupt et al. (2013) conceive the digital divide as a "multilayered" (p. 293) phenomenon that "includes several related dimensions of computer access, usage, and skill" (p. 293). This definition highlights that, in addition to differences in access to digital technologies, people have different repertoires of digital practices, levels of expertise, and motivation to engage in digital experiences. Furthermore, the notion of digital divide includes access to learning opportunities to develop digital literacies: while some people have access to relevant learning programmes and skilful teachers, others may lack such opportunities (Valadez & Duran, 2007).

In Australia, the digital divide is evident in many communities. In particular, people from refugee backgrounds may experience digital exclusion as they often have limited physical access to technologies and few opportunities to learn about digital technologies (Alam & Imran, 2015; Batalova & Fix, 2015; Kenny, 2016; Reichel et al., 2015). The Australian Digital Inclusion Index (Thomas et al., 2019) survey suggests that digital inclusion among recently arrived people under the humanitarian immigration programme is lower than the national average. Affordability or, in other words, the impact of internet access expenditure on limited household budgets was identified as the key barrier. On average, 3.83% of their household income is spent on access as compared to the national average of 1.18%. This is significant given that this group often comes from disadvantaged socio-economic backgrounds. Furthermore, due to socio-economic factors, many people from refugee backgrounds rely solely on a mobile phone connection, not broadband Internet, which may limit what they can do online (Alencar, 2020). Upon moving to a new country, people from refugee backgrounds do not always gain immediate access to quality devices and Internet access and, thus, they may experience limited opportunities for digital literacy practices within their communities (Alam & Imran, 2015; Colucci et al., 2017; Kenny, 2016).

In addition to the barrier of physical access to technologies, this group of arrivals often finds it difficult to use technologies. This is, perhaps, not surprising because many of them are unfamiliar with digital technologies due to their life experiences: they often spend years in refugee camps or come from countries with poor access to technologies due to wars and conflicts (Leung et al., 2009; van Rensburg & Son, 2010). For example, Alam and Imran (2015) identified "digital skills" as a key barrier to digital inclusion of refugee groups (aged 18–64) in regional Australia. Van Rensburg and Son (2010), exploring experiences of five Sudanese women in rural Queensland (Australia), found that they were not familiar with main computer parts (e.g. monitor, keyboard, etc.) and had "no idea of any activities that could be done on the computer." (p. 73). Similarly, Kenny (2016) reported that many newly arrived young people (aged 14–25) had "poor knowledge and familiarity in basic digital skills and online safety" (p. 2). They "were not aware of key privacy functions and were unable to set basic privacy settings on popular social media platforms" (p. 19).

On the other hand, it is important to avoid deficit thinking in considering the needs of this group and the labels we apply to them. Indeed, it is a very diverse group and their repertoires of digital literacy practices vary. For example, Peromingo and Pieterson (2018) argue that people from refugee backgrounds might have well-developed operational skills. This is an important skill set, but the use of technology, as we suggested above, also requires knowledge of language and social and digital contexts in which this language is used. This often represents a significant challenge for those who are at the beginning of their English language learning journey.

The Australian Digital Inclusion Index (Thomas et al., 2019) survey found that lower digital inclusion levels among people from refugee backgrounds were attributed to print-based literacies in English and other languages. In particular, 39% of the survey respondents (N = 146) did not read well in English. Furthermore, many (27%) were also unable to read in a home language. Research literature highlights the same issue: limited literacies in home languages became a significant barrier in engaging in and mastering digital literacies in English (Alam & Imran, 2015; Leung et al., 2009). In addition, language learners usually have to learn how to re-appropriate their technologies and adjust their practices in response to a new socio-cultural context and its dominant discourses. This learning requires time and relevant scaffolding.

Thus, these issues have had significant implications for EAL education in Australia and worldwide. The importance of digital literacies for language learners has been widely recognised and it has been acknowledged that digital literacies need to become an integral part of the language programmes (Godwin-Jones, 2015; Hafner et al., 2015). English language providers and teachers are often encouraged to extend their curriculum to include digital literacies (Kenny, 2016; Smyser, 2019; van Rensburg & Son, 2010).

Government-funded EAL programmes

There are several post-arrival programmes available in Australia to assist people from refugee and migrant backgrounds to learn English and navigate their new lives in Australia as part of their settlement. Australia has a long history of teaching English to newly arrived migrants and refugees. It was the first (and, for many years, only) country in the world that offered a fully funded English language programme to newcomers (Scanlon Institute, 2019). Established in 1951, these programmes started in Nissen Huts in northern Victoria with the hundreds of teachers volunteering their time to help thousands of post-war migrants from Europe to learn English to settle in Australia (AMES, 2020).

Today, post-arrival programmes are offered in elements of the Humanitarian Settlement Strategy, Adult Migrant Education Services (AMES), and Settlement Grants Program (Refugee Council of Australia, 2019). AMES is a government "leading provider of humanitarian settlement, education, training and employment services to refugees, asylum seekers and newly arrived migrants in Australia" (AMES, 2020, n.p.). AMES manage a number of federal and state government contracts including the Adult Migrant English Program (AMEP), the Skills for Education and Employment (SEE) programme,[4] and The Skill First programme[5] (AMES Australia, 2020). Langfield's learners were enrolled in one of those three accredited programmes. However, the programmes were seen as funding streams. Thus, the learners were usually grouped by their abilities rather than by a programme type. Due to the scope of this book and its focus on digital literacies for settlement, we provide only relevant background information about the AMEP.

Adult Migrant English Program (AMEP)

The AMEP provides fully funded English language classes to eligible migrants, humanitarian entrants, and their families to develop foundation English language and settlement skills for life, work, or further education in Australia (Department of Home Affairs, 2021a). According to a recent report (Tynan et al., 2018), family visa holders represent the highest proportion of AMEP learners, followed by humanitarian migrants and a small percentage (less than 4%) of eligible skilled migrants. Recently, the Australian Government announced major reforms within the AMEP which removed the previous 510-hour limit on free English tuition and extended eligibility from the need for basic functional English to include vocational English. This is significant as more learners are now able to access extended free English tuition till they reach higher levels of proficiency. To be eligible, an individual needs to be a permanent resident or hold an eligible temporary visa and have little or no English. Although the programme targets adults, young people (aged 15+) from refugee backgrounds who have disengaged from school are also eligible.

Learners entering the AMEP are assessed using the four levels of the Australian Core Skills Framework: (1) Pre-beginner: Unable to communicate in English language; (2) Level 1: "Works alongside an expert/mentor where prompting and advice can be provided"; (3) Level 2: "May work with an expert/mentor where support is available if requested"; (4) Level 3: "Functional" English – "works independently and uses own familiar support resources" (Centre for Policy Development, 2020). Depending on their levels of language proficiency, in Victoria, learners are offered a range of courses: from the course in initial EAL for learners who have experienced disrupted schooling and limited literacy, to Certificate IV in EAL (Further Study) (State of Victoria, 2018). A national curriculum, known as *The EAL Framework* (State of Victoria, 2018), will become compulsory for all AMEP providers in 2023 (Department of Home Affairs, 2021b).

AMEP courses are taught by qualified teachers who must have the requisite curriculum licensing qualifications to deliver the curriculum and also meet the trainer and assessor requirements set by the *Standards for Registered Training Organisations* 2015 (Tynan et al., 2018). Many teachers have postgraduate qualifications in TESOL (Teaching English to Speakers of Other Languages). Furthermore, many providers have their own volunteer programmes which train volunteers to provide language assistance (Scanlon Institute, 2019).

Adult Community Education (ACE)

The delivery of AMEP sits under the umbrella of adult education and is administered by a range of providers. For example, most AMEP courses are provided by TAFE Institutes since 2017, but a significant proportion are also delivered through Adult Community Education (ACE). Langfield was one such ACE provider. In this research, we were specifically interested in the community-based sector for a number of reasons. First, we found it intriguing that this adult education setting often appears to be more popular than TAFE institutes among learners from migrant, refugee, or asylum seeker backgrounds (Scanlon Institute, 2019). Second, as we explore below, the setting of ACE is quite unique in being independent and community-based, which we thought may be significant for teaching digital literacies. Finally, given that over half of the AMEP entrants are assessed at the "pre-beginner" level of the *Australian Core Skills Framework* (Centre for Policy Development, 2020), we anticipated that teaching digital literacies in this context may be especially challenging.

ACE is defined as "organised adult learning in community settings" (Clemans et al., 2003, p. 7). This definition signals that such providers are community-owned, community-managed, and not-for-profit (Government of Victoria, 2008). Their programmes are delivered in the community at education centres, community neighbourhood houses, public housing estates, libraries, churches, and in the facilities of a range of other non-government organisations. Victoria's ACE sector is currently the largest, most diverse, and most active provider of adult community education in the country (State of Victoria, 2019). In 2019, there were 272 registered adult community education providers across Victoria, catering annually for 28,000 learners in small institutions, larger organisations, and non-educational community services (State of Victoria, 2019). Receiving funding from various private sources and government funding from local, State, and Commonwealth governments, their offerings range from basic education to certificates and diploma-level qualifications.

The central feature of ACE is accessibility to learners, especially to those from educationally and socio-economically disadvantaged backgrounds who are unable to access and/or participate in more formal education experiences (Government of Victoria, 2008). In particular, some programmes, such as the AMEP, are free for the learners or the cost of the course is significantly lower than formal educational alternatives. There are often minimal pre-requisite requirements for entering a programme. ACE programmes are local, so easy to get to, and have a certain degree of flexibility (State of Victoria, 2019). They are "place-based around the learner" (State of Victoria, 2019, p. 7) to meet the needs of learners, employers, and communities in specific locations. Many educators working in the sector are passionate about their work and its potential to make a difference in the lives of their often disadvantaged students. Rappel (2015) points out that,

> [t]hese adult educators were more interested in the intrinsic value of work rather than in aiming for elevated professional status or substantial monetary benefit in their professions… [E]ducators who gravitated to this type of work appeared to be motivated through a need to empower self or others, holding an interest in improving the lives of others as a way to contribute to society in positive ways.
>
> *(p. 320)*

Thus, teachers in the ACE sector are likely to be ones with a transformational approach to their pedagogies and motivated by a belief that they can create positive change in the lives of their students.

AMEP challenges

For more than 70 years, the AMEP played a very important role in helping newcomers to learn English, which is central to a successful settlement. However, currently, the AMEP faces a number of significant challenges and dilemmas which, of course, have important implications for institutions, its leaders, teachers, and learners (Scanlon Institute, 2019).

Some of these challenges, which are still evident in the sector today, have been brought about by economic changes, including funding requirements linked to training output, that began in the 1990s. One of the earliest changes was associated with the National Training Reform Agenda of 1995. Reflecting a shift to employees with higher levels of literacy and qualifications, the reform emphasised the need for Australia to respond to the demands of global competition by generating a highly skilled flexible workforce (Foley, 2005). As Foley (2005) noted,

> learning through ACE is no longer constructed through the discourses of 'individual empowerment' promulgated in the 1970s, but rather, is now in line with the notion of education being an investment in 'human capital' which leads to greater economic returns.
>
> *(p. 3)*

This appears to be at odds with the teaching philosophy of educators in the sector.

This shift to industry-oriented training overlapped with new trends in migration: migrants started to come from Asian countries, especially China and India, rather than Europe, as in previous years. Additionally, Australia has increasingly started taking refugees from countries such as South Sudan, Somalia, Myanmar, and Nepal. These trends continue today. As a result, the AMEP has to cater now for learners who come from contexts with diverse linguistic traditions. Furthermore, many learners have little or no schooling experience and literacy education even in their home languages, or their education has been disrupted by war, trauma, or life in refugee camps (Rose, 2016; Scanlon Institute, 2019).

More recently, the challenges in the AMEP sector were associated with the introduction of a New Business Model by the Department of Education and Training in 2017. The model intended to improve student participation and English language proficiency through offering additional tuition hours for eligible students, enhanced monitoring of student progress, and improved assessment and streaming processes (Tynan et al., 2018). The model also aimed to simplify accountability processes and improve the efficiency and accountability of funding. While there were certain advantages of the new model, there were many strategic, structural, and operational challenges affecting AMEP programmes and settlement outcomes of AMEP learners (Tynan et al., 2018; Refugee Council of Australia, 2019). One of the most profound issues was related to an increased focus on employment rather than on settlement, thus weakening AMEP providers as places that embrace migrant settlement. This shift was consistent with earlier changes in the ACE policy.

The government put more pressure and elevated the demands on the AMEP "to show it was providing clear pathways for students into jobs or training, and delivering perceived value for money" (Scanlon Institute, 2019, p. 29). This, in turn, led to a reduction in settlement topics, fewer excursions to community sites, more onerous assessments, extra unpaid work for teachers, more students in the classroom, compromised working conditions, cutting of classes, less teachers' preparation time, declining teacher enthusiasm, employment of less qualified teachers, and stressful new audit requirements (ACTA, 2019; Rose, 2016; Scanlon Institute, 2019; Tynan et al., 2018). This affected both teachers' work and wellbeing as well as learners' engagement within the programme. The AMEP sector is not seen as an attractive workplace by experienced teachers and learner enrolments and course completions have dropped (Scanlon Institute, 2019; Tynan et al., 2018). In its recent review, The Australian Council of TESOL Associations (2019) support this conclusion:

> current DET policies aligning the AMEP with the SEE Program show no understanding and appreciation of the AMEP's unique, vital and longstanding role as a program that is central to the settlement of newly arrived migrants and refugees in Australia. These policies are seriously undermining the AMEP and have plunged it into crisis.
>
> *(p. 11)*

More recently, in response to some of these issues, on the August 28, 2020, the Australian Government announced a major AMEP reform aiming to "drive better settlement outcomes for refugees and migrants with a focus on employment, English language acquisition and community integration" (Department of Home Affairs, 2021b, para 8). Starting from April 2021, the following changes took place: (1) removing the previous 510-hour limit on free English tuition; (2) extending eligibility from functional English to vocational English; and (3) removing the time limits for registering, commencing, and completing English tuition for eligible visa holders and citizens in Australia on or before October 1, 2020. These changes were seen as positive in the field because they offer more learning opportunities to AMEP learners to develop the level of language and literacies required for full participation in the society. Being proficient in English is not simply a matter of developing discrete language skills; it is about having enough time for these skills to be embedded in a new culture as part of the settlement.

In addition to these recent reforms, the AMEP business model has been revised and a new model is offered by the Australian Government for implementation in 2023 (Department of Home Affairs, 2021b). As we are writing this book, the field is engaging in a debate in relation to one of the key components – the outcome-based payment model proposing that 67% of funding to AMEP providers is contingent on students' achievement of competencies identified in the new common national curriculum, *The EAL Framework* (State of Victoria, 2018). The interim response of the Australian Council of TESOL Associations (ACTA) states:

> Outcomes-based funding for the AMEP will damage the Program more fundamentally than did the disastrous 2017–2020 contract. It will completely negate the positive and long-overdue reforms instituted on 19 April 2021. It cannot "make English tuition more accessible, ensure better quality outcomes and encourage greater participation" (Discussion Paper, p. 6). Its inherently perverse and unethical incentives will directly and potently undermine the conditions necessary to achieve any such outcomes.
>
> *(p. 6)*

This assessment by the ACTA goes to a fundamental question about the efficacy of English language education: that the learning of a new language is not just about modules or concepts completed and competencies reached; it must be contextualised within a new cultural setting and be enacted through a range of engagement and participation practices that are engendered by AMEP providers.

Digital literacies in the adult EAL settings

It has been widely acknowledged, both in the research literature and policy, that language learning programmes, including the AMEP, need to prepare learners for the demands of the settlement in the digital society and need to include digital literacies in their curriculum (Godwin-Jones, 2015; Hafner et al., 2015; Kenny, 2016; Smyser, 2019; van Rensburg & Son, 2010). For example, Godwin-Jones (2015) argues that, "[a] likely stated goal of many language programs today is 'digital literacy'" (p. 10).

Reflecting these important calls, *The EAL Framework* makes quite explicit references to digital technologies, digital texts, and digital skills across a number of EAL courses. For instance, there are specific learning units dedicated to some aspects of digital literacies. *Course in Initial EAL* includes a unit under the title "Identify common digital media" (VU22383).[6] *Certificate I in EAL (Access)* offers two units: "Use basic digital technology language and skills" (VU22596) and "Operate a personal computer" (BSBITU101). *Certificate II* has "Access the internet and email to develop language" (VU22606). The curriculum describes each unit outlining the knowledge and skills that EAL learners need to develop in the context of the learning units. The curriculum provides a very detailed overview of what should be taught. However, there is a strong focus on learning how to make technology work which is evident in the unit titles and learning content.

Some aspects of digital literacies are incorporated into other non-digital learning units in a more seamless way in the curriculum, reflecting the ideas of the socio-cultural theory of literacy and positioning digital literacies as new forms of literacy, closely connected to social purposes and contexts. The curriculum often refers to "printed and digital texts" in a tandem as well as encourages consideration of audiences, purposes, and contexts. For example, the unit "Read and write short simple messages and forms" (VU22593) includes a range of traditional (e.g. print-based) and digital short messages: handwritten notes, lists, SMS, email messages, social media posts, cards, letters, comments on a petition or noticeboard. The unit "Explore current issues" (VU22609) suggests digital sources of information such as websites, blogs, social networking, alongside the traditional sources (e.g. newspapers, posters, petitions, etc.).

While this reference to diverse digital texts within the curriculum is important, there seems to be limited guidance and details in terms of *what* should be taught when learners engage with digital texts, navigate digital platforms, and communicate with audiences in digital spaces. The digital literacy practices may have some features of print-based literacies but, as we discuss in Chapter 2, their nature is very different and they require more sophisticated skills, knowledge, and understanding (Jones & Hafner, 2012; Lankshear & Knobel, 2006; New London Group, 1996). For instance, the framework suggests using non-text elements in multimodal texts as "cues" (State of Victoria, 2018, p. 352) for reading rather than teaching learners how to decode and interpret multimodal texts. Furthermore, there is no reference to the critical dimension of digital literacies in *The EAL Framework*. There is no focus on problematising digital platforms, texts, spaces, relationships, and power in order to understand how people are positioned in digital literacy practices and the implications of such positioning. This is important in terms of not only effective participation in Australia through digital spaces, but also for security online and for developing a sense of digital citizenship. To sum up, *The EAL Framework* includes some aspects of digital literacies required for settlement and employment in a new country. *The EAL Framework* is a very important starting point, but it may not be enough for the demands of the highly digitised life in Australia.

The EAL Framework has just become compulsory for all providers (Department of Home Affairs, 2021b) and its effect on the integration of digital literacies in English language teaching is yet to be seen. Traditionally, "the introduction of current and emerging forms of technology in adult English as a Second Language (ESL) education has not been widely embraced" (McClanahan, 2014, p. 22). Thus, what is currently known about digital literacy practices in the adult language learning sector is limited, and the research literature is scarce. In particular, there is very limited knowledge about how formal learning programmes, especially in the AMEP context in Australia, include and teach digital literacies. In the literature review conducted for this research, we identified only two brief examples.

Van Rensburg and Son (2010) describe a community programme piloted with five female learners from Sudan aiming to teach "basic computer literacy skills" (p. 72). Two-hour contact sessions per week over a period of 12 weeks focused on the introduction of computers and computer-related terms, including turning computers on, using a mouse and keyboard, typing; using the URLs of target Web pages, and creating, saving, and printing a document. The main pedagogical approaches used in this programme were repetition, Content and Language Integrated Learning (CLIL) and computer-assisted language learning (CALL). Another example described by Rose (2016) is a 20-hour module focusing on how to use language learning programmes which, in addition to language learning, help learners to develop discrete digital skills. Rose (2016) does not specify what exactly is taught in relation to digital literacies but she explains that while the learning module is broadly informed by the four A's approach (anchor – add – apply – away), "in terms of mastering the computer and the software, there are aspects of the mechanistic tradition at work" (p. 28). These programmes are, of course, useful because they provide important foundational learning opportunities for adult learners and focus on some aspects of digital literacies (van Rensburg & Son, 2010). Furthermore, adult learners often feel motivated and excited about learning with technology as they see its immediate relevance to their personal lives in a new country (van Rensburg & Son, 2010).

However, these digital programmes are relatively short and, thus, they are limited in what content they can include and how much time learners are given to consolidate and apply the skills. This is likely due to the limited funding and short timeframe but such "one-off" short programmes are obviously insufficient for developing repertoires of digital literacies required for successful settlement in Australia. From this perspective, these examples of programmes cannot be used as a model for the sector that needs a systematic approach to digital literacies.

Existing research also reports a number of challenges that often constrain the successful development and delivery of such programmes. For example, Traxler

(2018), analysing current digital education policy in the countries hosting the Palestinian refugee community, argues that there is a "lack of any currently adequate policy, strategy, resources or curriculum to develop or deliver a digital literacy curriculum" (p. 17). Lack of these systemic resources, or frameworks, definitely affects the design and implementation of these programmes both in terms of content and pedagogy. Peromingo and Pieterson (2018) emphasise that, if learning programmes aim to empower people from refugee backgrounds, they should "go beyond pushing buttons" (p. 33). This argument illuminates the danger of conceptualising digital literacy within a narrow set of technological and mechanistic competencies – as a checklist of skills that can be easily transferred from one context to another. Furthermore, critiquing existing models and practices, Traxler (2018) states that "there is clearly a gap between what is provided (by educational systems and policies) and what is needed (by people and communities)" (p. 17).

Teaching with and about technology is further constrained by other factors. McClanahan (2014) argues that the inclusion or quality provision of digital literacies within adult language learning programmes is affected by educators' and managers' concerns for the perceived complexities of technology integration into their classrooms as well as their assumptions about their learners' age or access to technology. Limited professional learning has been also often identified as another obstacle (Murray et al., 2006). While there is some research on professional learning in relation to digital literacies (Knobel & Kalman, 2016; Skinner et al., 2014; Tour, 2017a, 2017b), very little is known about the opportunities for professional learning and experiences of EAL teachers working in a community-based setting with its unique nature and challenges. This knowledge is central to understanding how the provision of digital literacies can be enhanced in complex teaching and learning environments.

To sum up, in spite of an increased interest in digital literacies in language learning contexts in recent years, EAL programmes within the adult community sector remain under-represented in larger public discourses about education and under-researched. There is a lack of clear and, importantly, holistic guidance around the inclusion of digital literacies as a part of the English language curriculum for newly arrived adults from refugee and migrant backgrounds. Furthermore, narrow definitions of digital literacy are often used to inform learning programmes and there is limited knowledge about teachers' professional learning needs. The sector has clear challenges, not the least being learners' limited pre- and post-migration experiences with technology and learning about digital literacies. Thus, it is not surprising that digital literacies are an area of uncertainty for many practitioners, leaders, and policymakers working within the sector in Australia and internationally (Traxler, 2018).

Focus of this book

The discussion above suggests that there is an urgent need for empirical research as the basis for innovative approaches to digital literacies education within adult EAL learning. This book aims to contribute much-needed knowledge by exploring, documenting, and sharing how one adult community EAL centre in Australia, Langfield, is responding to the demands of the digital society and the digital needs of its adult learners from refugee backgrounds within EAL programmes. To develop a detailed and nuanced understanding of how digital literacies are taught in this adult EAL community setting, and how this teaching might be enhanced, this research, and the book reporting it, takes a unique conceptual approach to the research issue.

First, we adopt a holistic perspective on the institutional practices with digital literacies which, using institutional ethnography, draws on and intertwines voices and experiences of different stakeholders within one institution: the adult learners, the teachers, and the CEO. Second, to conceptualise institutional practices with digital literacies in a way that accounts for the totality of this institutional setting, we draw on a number of contemporary theories that are discussed in a more detailed way in Chapter 2. These theories allow us to move beyond the narrow deficit thinking used in much previous research. In particular, we view digital literacies as situated social practices rather than as a discrete skill set that can be transferred easily from one context to another. We also take a strengths-based approach when exploring experiences and perspectives within Langfield and, while still being critical, we focus on "workable" practices, positive mindsets, and needs as articulated by the participants themselves. This strengths-based approach is used to explore the experiences of different participants: the learners, the teachers, and the CEO. Finally, to appreciate the complexity and challenges of this leadership work, we draw on the notions of distributed, democratic, and feminist leadership models.

Understanding the range of experiences and perspectives in relation to digital literacies within Langfield provides insights into the ongoing needs and new possibilities for supporting learners. More broadly, we contend that such understanding is central for advancing institutional approaches to digital literacies within other EAL contexts, including how learning digital literacies might be envisioned, organised, and sustained in the adult EAL sector. With increasing global movements to the digital and rapid development in digital technologies, high-quality digital literacies programmes that effectively scaffold digital learning of adult EAL learners are central to the successful settlement (Alam & Imran, 2015; Kenny, 2016; Smyser, 2019). Thus, we believe that this book can be especially important for policy-makers, institutional leaders, practitioners, and researchers in the field.

Conclusion

In this chapter, we set up the background of the research reported in this book which, we think, is important for understanding why and how this research was conducted. We introduced the broader social context in which Langfield operates which includes the increased global mobility of people, advances of digital technologies in different domains of human lives and the crucial importance of digital literacies for people from refugee and migrant backgrounds. We argued that the complex and dynamic processes of digital change have important implications for adult EAL programmes, including ones in adult community-based EAL settings. This chapter also provided an overview of the relevant literature to explore what is currently known about the implementation of learning for digital literacies in other settings. The literature suggests a number of practice and policy issues and emphasises the need for substantive research that addresses these issues in a nuanced and sensitive way. This book contributes to this debate by providing a systematic ethnographic account of Langfield, its work, and practices within the larger cultural and policy setting in Victoria (Australia). It offers both an intimate study of one organisation but also important implications for the wider adult educator sector.

Notes

1 A pseudonym.
2 Medicare is Australia's universal health insurance scheme which offers all Australians access to a wide range of health and hospital services at low or no cost.
3 Centrelink is a service provided by the Australian Government. It delivers a range of government social security payments and services for different groups such as retirees, the unemployed, families, carers, parents, people with disabilities, Indigenous Australians, students, apprentices, and people from diverse cultural and linguistic backgrounds. These are mainly delivered through the online platform www.servicesaustralia.gov.au
4 The Skills for Education and Employment (SEE) Program helps eligible job seekers to learn the skills they need to get a job (Australian Government, 2020).
5 Skill First is delivered with Victorian and Commonwealth Government funding that provides training to eligible students to get them ready for jobs (AMES Australia, 2020).
6 A unit code in *The EAL Framework*.

2
DEVELOPING THEORETICAL PERSPECTIVES ON INSTITUTIONAL PRACTICES

In this chapter, we explicate the theoretical ideas that are used to understand the rich data generated from this ethnographic study of Langfield and also to provide a conceptual foundation for the findings offered in the chapters to follow. We aim to give the reader a sense of the totality of Langfield as an institution and educational practice setting that embodies many complex aspects. This requires a number of theoretical perspectives to do justice to this complexity.

When exploring human experiences with digital literacies in an institutional setting, the material dimension of these experiences and human interactions with the material objects are important to consider. Institutional spaces, used for teaching and learning digital literacies, have an array of whiteboards, digital projectors, laptops, tablet devices, display materials, and furniture. There are also the artefacts that teachers and learners bring into the space such as personal smartphones. In this sense, the learning space is not just populated by humans but also infused with the materials in which humans move, interact, and learn, and includes the design of the space itself.

To understand these interactions with the material and their implications for teaching and learning digital literacies, we selected socio-material theory (SMT) as an important theoretical lens. The key concept of this research – digital literacies – is understood from a socio-cultural position in this research. A socio-cultural theory of literacy, offered by Literacy Studies, views digital literacies as social practices and allows for an exploration of both learners' everyday digital literacy practices and literacy capabilities taught in the classroom.

A strengths-based approach is used alongside this socio-cultural perspective to explore how digital literacies can be taught in an adult classroom by utilising the existing personal resources and strengths of students as well as building opportunities for teachers' professional learning through reflexive practice. Finally, to understand how leadership in promoting the integration of digital literacies into

DOI: 10.4324/9781003132684-2

teaching and learning is enacted in Langfield, we critically engage with the principles of educational leadership by drawing on the notion of distributed, democratic, and feminist leadership models.

Socio-material theory

SMT affords an understanding of the material and the agency of all human and living and non-living entities that exist in interactional spaces. It was used in this research for understanding the interconnections between the various materialities, including diverse digital technologies. Rather than focusing on individual and socially oriented interactional experiences, SMT is about the complex meaning spaces, tensions, and intersectionalities that are created as the material, individual, social, and institutional agencies come into relation with one another. Agency is taken to mean the ability to affect change and impact on decisions. Thus, SMT is about understanding these complex relationships and intersections between the social and material worlds, especially as enacted in everyday life in institutions and organisations (Orlikowski, 2007, 2010; Sørensen, 2009). This set of relationships is illustrated in Figure 2.1 which is designed to illuminate how SMT positions social, institutional, and material agencies as having relatively equal force and how these can exert comparative agential power, which is expressed at institutional sites as these agencies come into play.

Clearly, there is a greater focus on the agency of the material in SMT, and a recognition that there are powerful material agencies, which include all the

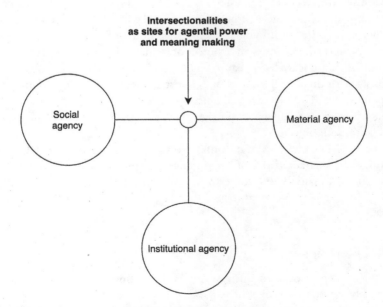

FIGURE 2.1 The concept of Sociomaterial Theory (SMT)

objects and technologies in the lives of people that shape how we conduct our lives, make decisions, and interact with the world. By contrast, in other broad theoretical areas such as linguistics and social and cultural studies, there is a stronger focus on human interactions, communications, and language, and agency is a very human phenomenon expressed in particular social and institutional settings. In SMT, the agency also intrinsically comes with non-living entities (including technologies). The important point to note in Figure 2.1 is that meaning-making does not just involve individuals and how they relate to each other but includes the objects (and technologies) that populate our worlds and connect closely with us as we work in organisational settings. It is at these points of human-technology-institutional connection that digital literacies are vital to effective meaning-making.

According to SMT, professional and social interactions and activities within a variety of contexts (including educational contexts) are constituted in institutional life and shaped by the policies, procedures, processes, and values of an institution. However, these are not the only factors that shape them. Importantly, the theory emphasises that a central concern in the work of professionals is the material dimension, which includes digital technologies and all the objects and physical spaces that agentially shape human practices, processes, and decision-making. Far from being peripheral, or sometimes not even considered as being important, the material dimension is viewed in SMT as critically important, and impacts directly on the agency (the ability to affect change and be self-determining) of individuals within an organisation.

In terms of the materiality of technologies, there is a recognition that in the software and interfaces of technologies, there is explicit and implicit influence on the choices and experiences of human agents (Hayles, 2009; Orlikowski, 1992). In other words, the technologies themselves, both software and hardware, are influences on the behaviours and choices of humans. For example, as we will see at Langfield, adult learners appear to engage relatively easily, naturally, and spontaneously with their own smartphones but struggle with desktop computers in a computer room. The two material objects that require different ways of engaging from users have no doubt affected usage behaviours and the contrasting meanings attached to both objects.

In sum, SMT conceives of meaning creation beyond just the social, cultural, and linguistic characteristics of organisations. It positions the material and the human in an essential confluence from which meaning emerges. The implications of this perspective are further illuminated and discussed in our findings chapters.

Digital literacies

Another concept central to this research is the notion of digital literacies. This is a highly contested term which is often defined and understood in a range of ways in different academic and practice contexts. Since digital technologies have become prevalent in a range of domains of life, there have been numerous attempts in research and policy to articulate what it means to be literate in the so-called Digital Age. This has resulted in a set of overlapping concepts: digital literacy, ICT literacy, digital competence, digital skills, electronic literacy, technoliteracy, and new/digital literacies. There are also many definitions that vary in detail, scope, meaning, and conceptual underpinnings. Pangrazio et al. (2020) argue that this definitional debate is still unresolved in the research literature and policy documents. However, the ways in which "digital literacy" is conceptualised has significant implications for pedagogy as well as for researching digital literacies. This contestation continues in relation to literacy in a broader sense as well. Thus, the debates about digital literacy can be seen as yet another manifestation of the continuing debate about what it means to be "literate".

One of the most prominent understandings of digital literacies, often evident in policy documents, conceives it as an individual's ability to use digital tools within a number of competence areas. For example, a UNESCO framework (Law et al., 2018) refers to digital literacy as "the ability to access, manage, understand, integrate, communicate, evaluate and create information safely and appropriately through digital technologies for employment, decent jobs and entrepreneurship" (p. 6). Similarly, OECD (2015) uses the concept of "digital skills" and defines them as "the capacity to use ICT devices and applications to access and manage information and solve problems" (p. 1). Such definitions are often driven by the attempt "to standardise the concept of 'digital literacy' to ensure its definition could be measured and compared in an increasingly globalised educational setting". (Pangrazio et al., 2020, p. 443).

Such definitions may be a useful starting point to understand what skills and knowledge people may need to be able to use technology. However, these functional approaches to digital literacy are often viewed as too narrow and, thus, problematic because they tend to ignore the complex settings in which people engage in digital literacies. According to Knobel and Lankshear (2006), such definitions often conceive digital literacy as a "unitary phenomenon" (p. 8) and "an autonomous entity" (p. 12). From this perspective, digital literacy is a list of "abstracted skills and techniques" (p. 12) that people need to develop and, once they develop them, it is assumed they can use them in different contexts. In other words, such definitions often simplify digital literacy to a set of monolithic, fixed, and universal skills which are by their very nature transferrable. This unitary perspective has been criticised by socio-cultural scholars who argue that these skills and ways of knowing cannot be easily and successfully transferred from one context to another because the ways in which people read, write, and communicate in digital spaces are shaped by culture and context, history, and circumstances (Gee, 2015; Jones & Hafner, 2012; Knobel & Lankshear, 2006; Tour, 2020). Hence, there is not just "digital literacy" as a singular skill, but many digital literacies for multiple contexts. This socio-cultural perspective or lens, widely accepted in the field of language and literacy education in recent years, informs this research and our understanding of the data.

This socio-cultural perspective, known as Literacy Studies, emerged in the early 1980s in relation to print-based literacy (Barton & Hamilton, 1998; Baynham & Prinsloo, 2009; Rowsell & Pahl, 2012; Street, 1984, 2009). This influential body of work drew attention to "everyday practices" – what people do with literacy in their lives – and facilitated the "the social turn" (Rowsell & Pahl, 2015, p. 6) in thinking about literacy and language. It challenged a purely linguistic perspective on language as an abstract system and literacy as a set of decontextualised and generic reading and writing skills. From a socio-cultural perspective, "reading and writing can only be understood in the context of social, cultural, political, economic, historic practices to which they are integral, of which they are a part" (Knobel & Lankshear, 2007, p. 1). Thus, literacy can be understood as "social practices that vary from one context to another" (Street, 2009, p. 21). This means that literacy is always plural – literacies – taking multiple forms and modes, and requiring different understandings, competences, and skills (Gee, 2015; Rowsell & Pahl, 2015).

Starting from the mid-1990s, Literacy Studies scholars observed that print-based literacies were only a part of contemporary literacy practices as many people engaged actively in literacy activities in digital spaces. These observations facilitated another significant shift in thinking about literacy – "the digital turn" (Knobel & Kalman, 2016, p. 5). For example, Snyder (2008) describes the changing nature of literacy and argues that digital literacy should be viewed as a new form of literacy:

> [l]iteracy [is] inextricable from the changes that have taken place in communities, societies, nation states and the global domain, both in recent time and over the centuries. Literacy is ever-evolving. Today, as much as in any historic period, new literacy practices are emerging and the concept of literacy continues to change as it has always done.
>
> *(p. 216)*

Indeed, some significant changes were observed in literacy practices associated with digital technologies (New London Group, 1996; Snyder, 1997; Warschauer, 1999). One of these changes is associated with the increase of digital texts consisting of several semiotic systems (e.g. multimodal) that require new ways of meaning-making. The New London Group (1996) identified five different modes of meaning-making: linguistic, visual, aural, gestural, and spatial. While meaning-making has always been multimodal and involved more than just words (e.g. the use of colour in writing, the use of tone in speech), digital technologies gave rise to a wider range of texts which can be very complex semiotic entities.

Another change, noted by The New London Group (1996), is the advent of greater access to cultural and linguistic diversity due to increased migration but also due to the affordances of digital technologies to connect people. Different communicative activities, including reading and writing online for social or business purposes, often happen across different geographical locations, cultures, and languages. Interestingly, while The New London Group pioneered the discussion of diversity and its impact on literacy, García and Kleifgen (2020) argue that these ideas were not in the focus in research and practice to the same extent as multimodality until recently. In recent years, however, there has been a shift in thinking from the L1/L2 dichotomy to understanding language and literacies as diverse but interrelated, flexible, and fluid, especially in practices afforded by digital technologies (García & Kleifgen, 2020). Concepts such as multilingual literacies (Martin-Jones & Jones, 2000), pluriliteracies (García et al., 2007), and translanguaging (García, 2009; Turner, 2019) are increasingly used to illuminate that all literacy practices have value for the meaning-making of multilingual speakers. Similarly, the ideas of transculturalism and cosmopolitanism have only recently become central to literacy and language research (Zaidi & Rowsell, 2017). Many digital spaces are dynamic multilingual and multicultural spaces where people use different languages and engage in translanguaging practices – combining features of different languages to communicate meaning and experience from the perspective of the speaker (Lees, 2019).

Another important way in which digital technologies alter literacy practices is related to what is often called "digital cultures" (Tour, 2020, p. 3) or "online culture" (Jones & Hafner, 2012, p. 116). The notion of "culture" has a broader meaning in this context and it is not limited to a particular geographic location or ethnic group. Rather, digital/online cultures are "discourse systems made up of ideologies, norms of communication, ways of conducting social relationships and practices of socialisation which people participate in" (Jones & Hafner, 2012, p. 116). From this perspective, different digital spaces have different cultures or, in other words, their distinctive – "ways of acting, interacting, valuing, believing, and knowing" (Gee, 2015, p. 44). These norms determine what counts as appropriate or inappropriate, natural or unnatural, right or wrong in these spaces which, in turn, shapes how people engage in literacy practices in these spaces. For example, Twitter culture is different from Facebook culture. Twitter emphasises the importance of ideas and topics, while Facebook emphasises the importance of networks and communities. Both platforms have their distinctive assumptions about how meanings are made. Valuing the informational function of language, Twitter limits its posts to 280 characters. In contrast, Facebook allows users to share long posts drawing on the relational (rather than informational) value of language for establishing and maintaining social relationships (Jones & Hafner, 2012).

As evident, literacy practices in digital spaces are very different from conventional print-based literacy practices, although they often overlap and share common language skills and cultural understandings. They are often multimodal, multilingual, shaped by distinctive digital cultures, and influenced by broader social contexts with their audiences and goals. However, despite acknowledging the pervasive nature of digital culture, we do not subscribe to the perspectives of social determinism. As we discussed in the previous section, the important role of materiality (e.g. the type of digital device) in shaping the practices should be considered as pivotal to digital literacies and complementary to socio-cultural theory. Similar to print-based literacies, there is no one universal form of digital literacy. Rather, there are multiple practices of reading, writing, communicating, and being in digital spaces. For example, writing an email is different from writing a text message. Creating a profile on Facebook is different from creating a profile on LinkedIn. Sending a text message to a manager is different from sending a text message to a partner. Reading a recipe online is different from reading a research report online. Doing something with the help of a desktop computer can be different from doing it on the phone. Thus, in this research, digital literacies are understood as practices of reading, writing, communicating, relating, thinking, and being in social and digital spaces for specific purposes in specific contexts (Hafner et al., 2015; Jones & Hafner, 2012; Kalantzis et al., 2016).

To engage in digital literacy practices, individuals need more than just technical skills to make technology work or navigate the platform. They need a wide range of sophisticated skills, semantic knowledge, cultural understanding, and a disposition to be able to engage in these social practices in meaningful, contextually, and socially appropriate ways. To be digitally literate means to have a rich repertoire of digital literacy practices. As there is a myriad of digital literacy practices and new practices emerge all the time, there are challenges in predicting what digital literacies learners will need in the future. However, as Rowsell et al. (2017) argue, "the more exposure and practices students have with multiple genres and registers…, the more likely they are to gain both competency and confidence in dealing with 21st-century texts in an ever-changing world" (p. 158).

Exposure to different technologies and contexts can provide rich opportunities to read, write, and communicate for different purposes and with different audiences. In turn, this will assist learners in extending their knowledge, understandings, strategies, ways of thinking and attitudes needed for meaningful, appropriate, and critical digital literacy practices. The richer their repertoires of practices are, the more comfortable they will be to develop new digital literacies. Research in the field suggests that everyday digital literacy practices often provide opportunities to develop digital literacies (Barton, 2012; Marsh et al., 2017; Omerbašić, 2015). However, educational institutions still play an important role as not all learners have adequate access, individual capacity, and relevant support to develop and extend their repertoires of digital literacies in everyday settings.

The perspective of Literacy Studies has profound implications for practice. As new forms of literacy, digital literacies may be challenging to develop without relevant teaching, guidance, and scaffolding. This is especially true for language learners from refugee backgrounds who are usually unfamiliar with new social (and digital) discourse systems, their social norms, rules, and ways of doing (Murray, 2008). Thus, over the last decades, there have been numerous calls to rethink what it means to be literate in another language, how technology is positioned in language learning contexts, and to what extent digital literacies are included in the language curriculum and classrooms practices across different language learning contexts (Hafner, 2019; Hafner et al., 2015; Lotherington & Jenson, 2011; Murray, 2008). Thus, this socio-cultural framing of digital literacies is used in this research to explore how digital literacies were taught in Langfield and how learners' everyday digital literacy practices can be used to further enhance these approaches.

Strengths-based practices

Another lens for understanding Langfield and its learners, leaders, and teachers is that of strengths-based practices – a perspective that focuses on what is provided by learners, not what is absent. That is not often considered in the discourse associated with people from refugee and migrant backgrounds. In many countries around the world, people from refugee and migrant backgrounds are frequently positioned as ethnic minorities and learners with limited or low literacy in the mainstream language, both in policy, public media and scholarly work. Shapiro and MacDonald (2017) and Roy and Roxas (2011) discuss the dominance, and the destructive consequences, of what they describe as a deficit discourse that defines and positions many learners as lacking or deficient in a range of core linguistic, social, and digital skills. It is, as Shapiro and MacDonald (2017) note, a discourse that

> tends to emphasize what students *lack* more than what they *bring* to their U.S. schooling experiences. This trend is particularly salient with regard to students who came to the United States through the processes of displacement, asylum seeking, or refugee resettlement. Key words such as *trauma, victimization, limited (or interrupted) education, and preliteracy* [emphasis in original] are prevalent in discussions of refugee-background students and their families.
>
> (p. 80)

The social and political pervasiveness of the dominant deficit discourse is such that it may be still considered normative in many contexts. That is to say, it is a "common sense" taken-for-granted understanding that learners in English speaking countries without strong English literacy and language skills are disadvantaged. By default, they are deemed to be problematic and have little to bring to their learning. Indeed, in many contexts, they are defined as "the problem" and "having needs" and this understanding is reflected in policies, learning programmes, and the classroom experiences of learners. Interestingly, this often happens without awareness and is not without good intentions (Roy & Roxas, 2011; Ryu & Tuvilla, 2018). However, as Ryu and Tuvilla (2018) argue, "these practices inadvertently perpetuate the idea that refugees are helpless victims who need extra help" (p. 541). The issue is that this dominant deficit narrative can become the only learning story (Adichie, 2009).

We are well aware of the fact that even by referring to and discussing the dominant discourse, we are using it and therefore reinforcing it (Lakoff, 2010). Furthermore, it is not easy to shift from these entrenched ways of naming and framing to positioning the capacities of learners from migrant and refugee backgrounds differently. The stereotypical language is pervasive and strong. Similarly, Roy and Roxas (2011) report that even when teachers are aware of the dominant deficit discourse, they are unsure how to address it. It is entirely appropriate to talk about needs and challenges. In fact, consideration of needs is a cornerstone of any education design. However, it is important to talk about these needs without falling into the deep well of the deficit model where the existing capacities and agencies of learners are not considered. Vella (2002) argues that the key question should be: "Who needs what as defined by whom?" (p. 5).

There are two essential points to draw from Vella's (2002) insights here. First, this provocative question is fundamental to designing for democratic education because it considers if the needs are determined by the teachers, by the adult learners themselves, by prospective employers, by policy and prescribed programme outcomes, or by "society" at large. There are multiple possible and legitimate answers here – and they may not always be in alignment. Engaging with alternative perspectives about needs and managing the tensions that come from differences are part of the educator's challenge. Second, Vella (2002) stresses the importance of the genuine "listening effort" (p. 6) that is necessary for teachers to solicit learners' articulation of their needs. Such listening can help to build an adequate understanding not only of the learner's needs but, importantly, the *resources* and *strengths* that the learners bring to learning.

Vella's (2002) emphasis on the personal resources that learners bring also resonates with the work of some other scholars who suggest that searching deliberately for strengths rather than perceived deficits is more productive (Ryu & Tuvilla, 2018; Shapiro & MacDonald, 2017). In recent years, in Australia, learner descriptors, by default framing learners as lacking or deficient, shifted to more inclusive conceptions offering more positive frames about the rich resources that learners can bring to their learning and to the learning context. For example, terms such as Non English Speaking Background (NESB) and English as a Second Language (ESL) have been replaced by Culturally and Linguistically Diverse (CALD) and English as an Additional Language (EAL), respectively. Furthermore, in the research literature, some scholars deliberately use "people from refugee backgrounds" (e.g. Tour et al., 2021) rather than "refugees" to signal that this identity is neither fixed nor attached to people forever.

Finding strengths can be an excellent source for creating "counter-stories" to dominant deficit narratives (Roy & Roxas, 2011). Importantly, as Waterhouse and Virgona (2008) discuss, "working from strengths" can make a significant difference in learning and teaching. In recent years, there have been many important calls for strengths-based education for learners from refugee backgrounds across different age groups (Ryu & Tuvilla, 2018; Shapiro & MacDonald, 2017). Empirical research with this focus is limited though (e.g. Hayward, 2017; Whitley et al., 2016).

To conceptualise strengths-based education for this study, we referred to a wider body of literature. A central assumption of strengths-based education is that "every individual has resources that can be mobilised toward success in many areas of life" (Lopez & Louis, 2009, p. 2). It attempts to discover the best qualities of learners, believing that capitalising on them, rather than trying to overcome personal weaknesses, will lead to more successful learning. The approach explores ways to empower individuals and enable them to thrive rather than simply survive (Liesveld & Miller, 2005). It is a learner-centred approach aiming to help learners to become "confident, efficacious, lifelong learners whose work is infused with a sense of purpose" (Lopez & Louis, 2009, p. 2).

The notion of "resource" is central to this perspective and it is often interchangeably used with the concepts such as an "asset" and a "strength". Previous texts documented the extraordinary, unique, exceptional, and inspiring stories of people from refugee and migrant backgrounds (Aden & Hillman, 2015; Brierley & Buttrose, 2013; Do, 2010; Fu & Fox, 2012). They demonstrate remarkable human capacity, resilience, and repertoires of strategies that can be employed towards educational goals. Relocation experiences, home languages, cultures, different intellectual, physical and interpersonal skills, capacities, dispositions, interests, and motivations are all valuable resources that provide strong foundations for further learning.

Lopez and Louis (2009) propose five principles of strengths-based education which together provide a useful framework to explore teaching practices. Their first principle refers to *measuring strengths*. While we find the word "measuring" too prescriptive, we interpret this principle as being about awareness of individual strengths. The second principle is *individualised learning* meaning that educators attempt to personalise the learning experience by helping learners to set personal goals drawing on their strengths and supporting them in using their strengths in learning. The third principle is about *networking*. This principle suggests that one's weaknesses can be managed by leveraging other people's strengths. Thus, building strengths-based collaborations allows learners to learn and meet their needs with the help of other learners' talents and personal resources. This, in turn, has a transformative effect on learners, whose agency is activated. The fourth principle refers to the *deliberate application* of strengths within and outside of the classroom. In other words, educators create opportunities for successful use of strengths in the classroom and help learners "to translate" this experience to other domains of life. The fifth principle is *intentional development of strengths*. To maximise learners' strengths, it is important to engage in new experiences rather than recycle existing strengths all the time. Educators play an important role in offering such experiences in a safe way as well as helping learners to develop a habit of proactively seeking new experiences. This is significant for being adaptive in changing environments. This framework seems to be a valuable lens for this research aiming to understand how digital literacies are taught in the adult EAL setting.

Interestingly, in their discussion of strengths-based education, Lopez and Louis (2009) state that "strengths-based education begins with *educators* [our emphasis] discovering what they do best and developing and applying their strengths" (p. 2). From this perspective, educators need to be well aware of their own talents, strengths, and resourcefulness and, importantly, consciously use them in teaching and professional development. If they work from their personal strengths in their own teaching, then they are better positioned to help learners to identify, use, and extend their strengths in and out of the classroom.

This body of work offers valuable insights into how to make teaching and learning of people from refugee and migrant backgrounds more meaningful, engaging, and, thus, effective. These ideas are new for the field of digital literacies which, as we discussed above, is currently in search of suitable classroom approaches, especially for language learners. To our best knowledge, this perspective has not yet been adopted to research classroom practices. The research reported in this book is pioneering this important work in an attempt to understand what can be learnt from this perspective and how "strengths-based" education might look in relation to teaching digital literacies in the adult EAL context.

In considering the strengths inherent at Langfield, we are compelled to note here that these are overwhelmingly the strengths of women. The teachers at Langfield are all women. The CEO is a woman, as is the Education Manager; and most of the students at Langfield are also women. In short, Langfield is, in effect, a community-based organisation run by women, essentially for women, although there are also some male students who are made to feel very welcome.

Such women's organisations have a proud history and heritage in adult community education and in adult literacy education in particular (Campbell, 2009; Macrae & Agostinelli, 2002; Sanguinetti, 1994). Furthermore, this alignment between women, community education, literacy, and empowerment is not unique to Australia. Researchers have also written about the feminist influence in adult community and literacy education in the context of the United Kingdom (Duckworth & Smith, 2018) and Canada (English & Irving, 2015). Maber (2016) reports on similar themes emergent in Myanmar, and Bracken (2010) explores the same sorts of issues in Latin America.

Yet despite the importance of this work, domestically and around the globe, researchers have also noted that the contribution of women and feminist thinking in this domain has been substantially downplayed, under-researched and undervalued. For instance, Norton (1994) decried and theorised "literacy work as women's work" (p. 71) to help explain the gender politics and the lack of recognition. More recently in our own Australian and Victorian context, Clemans (2016) reports,

> [d]espite the rhetorical location of adult community education in Victoria as a legitimate and important sector of post compulsory education and as part of the platform on which the government's lifelong learning agenda is realised, perceptions held of it continue to devalue the significant educational work that is done within it and the outcomes it achieves.
>
> (p. 156)

Hayes (1992) considered British and American literature and noted that despite its potential significance, the feminist influence in adult education was under-researched and under-documented and she commented on the factors that "inhibit the integration of feminist perspectives into adult education publications" (p. 125). A parallel concern is noted more recently by researchers undertaking a national and international policy document analysis in South Korea (Lee & Kim, 2018). Similarly, in their substantive book on *Feminism in Community: Adult Education for Transformation* (English & Irving, 2015), the authors reflect on the research and note they could find "none specifically on women's learning in non-profit organizations" (p. 129).

Given these apparent "blind spots" in the research literature, our work with Langfield and documentation of their pedagogical practices emerged as perhaps even more significant than we had anticipated. It begs important questions about the extent to which the pedagogies at Langfield might reasonably be characterised as feminist. It also invites questions about the nature of the leadership within the organisation – leadership of women, by women. We return to these sorts of questions in subsequent chapters on pedagogy and leadership, respectively.

That said, however, the discourses of feminism and women's studies are extensive and contested and the scope of our work in this study, focussing on digital literacies, does not enable deep and comprehensive engagement with these issues. Notwithstanding the limitations, however, we do have a considerable affinity with the stance of provocation and "stirring" advocated by English and Irving (2015) who note the following:

> If we are working in an NGO dedicated to pre-employment training for women [such as Langfield], we might think about how workplaces are structured against family life and indeed privilege white males who may not have the "burden" of childcare. Or, if the training centres on ICTs, [or digital literacies] we might look at how women are usually only considered as end-users and not designers of the technology (Foroughi & English, 2013). Feminist pedagogues have a responsibility to provoke, to stir, and to challenge the status quo.
>
> (p. 112)

Leadership for change

Challenging the status quo requires leadership. So, as we have noted above, another important theoretical perspective adopted in this research is considering leadership styles, notions of democratic, and distributed leadership to support the learning in the adult EAL sector. Exploring leadership practices and understanding the leadership culture was seen as central to develop a holistic perspective on how digital literacies were taught at Langfield, and, most importantly, how change might be instantiated. To conceptualise leadership practices, in the sections below, we critically engage with the principles of educational leadership by drawing on the notion of distributed and democratic leadership models.

30 Developing theoretical perspectives

The importance of educational leadership is emphasised at the local, state, and federal level, and is viewed as increasingly important internationally (Antonakis et al., 2004). Effective contemporary leadership across all sectors in education is considered in the literature to be a major factor in the success of an organisation and its long-term growth and viability. Effective leaders set the direction and tone of an organisation and, through supporting the development of staff and learners, assure sustainability (Hargreaves & Fink, 2006). Successful leadership is inclusive of four important qualities (Centre for Creative leadership, 2021; Northouse, 2010; Rudnitski, 1996) that we illustrate in Figure 2.2. These qualities are not mutually exclusive but should be seen as interconnected in leadership practice.

First, educational leadership, to be effective, requires the setting of *a vision* that points to the direction and purpose of an organisation (Sarros et al., 2011). This vision is widely shared but also subject to change, depending on need and feedback from stakeholders. A vision is only useful as it sets the scope and values of the organisation. A successful vision is transparent and regularly articulated within and outside the organisation.

Second, effective leadership embraces *inclusive people management* within an organisation which means that everyone's input and agency is valued (Hollander, 2009). It has often been stated that the greatest resource of an organisation is its people. Leadership that acknowledges and actively engages with the views, skills,

FIGURE 2.2 Four qualities of effective leadership

and interests of those employees is pivotal to both the climate of an organisation and its potential for development. This includes investment in the relationships that undergird the work of an organisation and the wellbeing of people who carry out its vision. This investment in relationships might include, for instance, team building, acknowledgement of successes and effective work, and utilising the knowledge of people in the organisation to create innovation. It also includes prioritising the professional learning needs of people in the organisation.

Third, effective leadership is best informed by *grounded knowledge* of what is happening within the organisation, including its policies, communications, practices, relationships, and actions. For leadership to be responsive and adaptive, there is a need for an ear-to-the-ground, practical/pragmatic knowledge-based approach in terms of the day-to-day life of an organisation (MacGillivray, 2018). This would include the effectiveness of governance processes within the organisation such as a sound management structure and articulation of rights and responsibilities. In practice that means formal and informal regular communication with staff and all stakeholders and, in an educational setting, visits to teaching spaces to connect with teachers and learners. The so-called ivory tower approach to leadership or consistent disconnection between leaders and staff within an organisation is not conducive to effective organisational outcomes. Such grounded knowledge is only possible in circumstances where leaders listen (with intentional concern) to all stakeholders within an organisation.

Fourth, *an evidence-based approach* to leading change and innovation is strongly supported in the literature (Scott & Webber, 2008). This means that there is a need for a direct connection between current thinking, empirical research, and the decision-making of educational leaders. This evidence can come from formal academic research as well as it might be gathered internally within an organisation through methods such as surveys, reflection on and accounts of effective practice, needs-analysis investigations, action research, and the sharing of successful teaching ideas and strategies. The work of associations within an educational sector can coordinate and distribute evidence based on the experiences of different settings and provide a way of efficiently sharing information about practice, governance, sector-wide needs, and innovations (including digital innovations).

A related aspect of effective leadership is strengths-based approaches to leadership. Figure 2.2 depicts these practices as being foundational to, or the ground upon which, effective leadership in education is constructed although literature about strengths-based leadership practices has only emerged in recent times (Welch et al., 2014). Consistent with our discussion of strengths-based education and the strengths of women in the section above, strengths-based leadership refers to an orientation towards a positive view of the people within an organisation and their potential to be active and agential in the success-making. Strengths-based leadership is about making decisions and innovations on the basis of three interconnected aspects of organisational life: (1) achievement orientation, (2) promoting participation and agency, and (3) professional learning as extending existing skills and competencies.

Achievement orientation. Strengths-based leadership in education is about building institutional systems, culture, and criteria for success from the existing valuable resources and achievements of an organisation. In other words, the foundation for leadership is grounded on current successes, rather than looking for deficiencies. Thus, this achievement orientation is about actively looking for success and developing awareness of the effective practice. It also involves leveraging and publicising success and broadcasting this success to the broader community involved in the educational organisation.

Promoting participation and agency. A strengths-based educational leadership approach is one of encouraging educators to fully participate in the success of an organisation, rather than being peripheral to it. It is a recognition that educators have skills and capacities that can add to the success of an organisation. Thus, leadership with an orientation to people's strengths is active in recognising these skills and capacities. This might involve, for instance, assessing what current staff in an organisation can provide for the needs of an organisation. Part of this orientation to strengths is about enabling the agency of educators in their active participation in change and innovation and the provision of resources.

Professional learning as extending existing skills and competencies. Professional learning from a position of strength means that instead of positioning professional learning as satisfying the perceived deficiencies in an organisation, there is an active appreciation of existing skills and competencies as a starting point of learning and the evolution of an organisation. Further capacities are built upon existing skills and known resources. The focus is on the development of those already in the organisation, based on an intimate knowledge of what they can do rather than what they cannot. As such, professional learning becomes strategically oriented to the sustained development of staff and driven by the collective vision of an organisation. This, we believe, is especially important in times of substantial change, including the ongoing movement towards the digitisation of society.

An approach to leadership, or a type of leadership style (Berson et al., 2001; Hersey & Blanchard, 1982), is created by the (often) implicit perceived understandings about the role of leadership that are the foundation for how leaders behave, as opposed to the more overt expressions of leadership (qualities). Approaches to leadership can be considered on a scale, from low intervention (laissez-faire) to high intervention (autocratic) (Figure 2.3). All educational leaders would fall somewhere on this scale in terms of overall style, but they would likely vary the approach, depending on the circumstances, people, and the issues involved.

A laissez-faire leadership approach and style is based on an understanding that leadership should have low intervention and high consultation, and only intrude when needed or at a macro (large picture), not micro level. In the extreme form of this approach, an organisation is more or less left to fend for itself. This approach may mean that there is a lack of clarity about both the process and the chain of command in making institutional decisions, depending on the ways in which

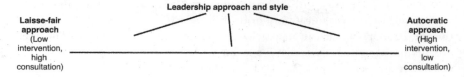

FIGURE 2.3 Scale of leadership approaches

the leadership structure is organised. On the other hand, an autocratic leadership approach is strongly interventionist and often operates at both a micro and macro level within the work, practices, and structures of an organisation. It is characterised by a high level of control and low levels of consultation in terms of decision-making. The autocratic approach and style tend to diminish the involvement and agency of most stakeholders in an organisation.

As part of a consideration of leadership approaches and the level of intervention and agency that operate within an organisational setting, it is important to discuss a democratic approach to education, which is inclusive of leadership and the type of intervention style employed. Democratic education is a global approach to education that includes democratic values and ideals and an egalitarian approach to methods of delivery within educational settings. Democratic education is generally taken to mean a deliberative blending of teaching/learning and the development of curricula with the values of a democratic society (Biesta, 2015). This means esteeming self-determination and respect for each person, and the facilitation of an active creation of meaning involving leaders, teachers, and learners, which is likely to be significant for organisations where the relational connection is pivotal to their core business. There is an openness to the contribution of all stakeholders in the educational process and mechanisms for encouraging input for everyone involved. A democratic leadership approach would fall somewhere in the middle of the scale and include a flexible approach that might be consultative at times and more directive at other times. A democratic approach would likely take into account the limitations of either end of the scale and there would be adjustments of approach and style to meet the needs of an organisation.

There are five key aspects of democratic leadership and these key aspects should be seen as highly interconnected (Choi, 2007; Klinker, 2006). Democratic leadership might also contain a strength-based approach to building an organisation and its staff through a climate of affirmation and locating effective practices. One aspect of democratic leadership is *involvement* by all staff and stakeholders in the critical decision-making of an educational organisation. This comprehensive involvement of the community assures that what is provided is linked to the perceived needs of all those in an educational community. Another aspect of democratic leadership is the *transparency* of decision-making within the organisation. The basis for the decisions that affect all stakeholders in the organisation is communicated as a matter of priority. This can be linked to an *openness of communication style*, in which leadership decisions and policy positions are shared informally and formally within the organisation. It is also important that there is a *consultation at the grassroots level* prior to decisions being made or new initiatives being adopted. Such an approach enables disclosure, ownership, and broader organisational goals as far as that is possible within an organisation.

All five aspects of democratic leadership point to a broader question about the disposition of the management structure that supports leadership. Top-down, rigidly hierarchical approaches to management structure are unlikely to engender democratic ideals or at least make a democratic approach problematic to implement. A more distributed approach to management structure is consistent with democratic leadership and would involve both a senior leadership team and middle management (Spillane et al., 2001). This approach fosters decision-making and problem-solving across a larger group of people within an organisation, and also promotes leadership across different levels of operation so that decisions for change are not solely the responsibility of one person or even a small leadership team.

However, there are some issues with a democratic leadership approach (Starrat, 2001). First, making decisions can be delayed by layers of consultation. At times fast decision-making is imperative, especially in organisations subject to market forces or the need to adjust deliverables in line with funding requirements of government and other bodies. Second, the need for the efficient processes possible in a well-constructed chain of command may conflict with being representational and fluid in leadership.

The ideas presented in this section are conceptual and, perhaps, aspirational and provide the ground from which effective leadership in education can be evaluated; but it is clear that leadership in education across all sectors is subject to significant issues that can be small or large in scope, involving both internal and external factors. Even the best educational leaders experience difficulties and thorny problems, including ones related to material resources, outside organisations, policy frameworks, and human resources. In terms of human resources, the individuals within organisations have diverse opinions and beliefs. This can and does lead to conflicts, not only between teachers and management over process, policy, governance, and vision but also between colleagues about personal as well as professional matters. Resolution of conflict and satisfactory outcomes can be tricky and, on some occasions, unresolvable.

Effective leadership in education is thus deeply connected to ethics and values – to informed decisions about what is best for the organisation, for the welfare of the people who work in it, the learners it serves and for the sector as a whole (Ciulla, 2002). This connection is also about the personal values of a leader, including values that lead to appropriate personal conduct and awareness of issues to do with duty of care and fairness in all matters. At the heart of a vision of an organisation is also an ethical outlook and a sense of the shared common good. In education, this ethical outlook has to concern the primary business of the organisation: the teaching and learning, students' success, and their care. That ethical bedrock is often essential in difficult times of threat, change, and dealing with issues such as misconduct or inadequate performance. It provides the foundation for resolving conflict and bringing focus to the purpose of an organisation.

The developments in digital technologies in recent decades have shaken the pedagogical foundations of many educators and presented challenges for educational leaders in managing change. Educators are looking to their leaders for personal support, professional learning, and the provision of resources that enable the articulation of successful teaching and learning. One of the most significant issues for using digital technologies in education is operationalising technologies to suit the situated needs of an organisation, ensuring that the logistic and training support is provided (Beaudoin, 2015; Sow & Aborbie, 2018). This has been as significant in adult education contexts as in other educational sectors; arguably, more so. It has also brought to the forefront the existing need for digital literacies, both for educators and the learners with whom they engage (Frank & Castek, 2017; Selwyn, 2002).

However, there are specific areas of concern that relate to leadership in regard to digital literacies in adult EAL education which we explore in this book. First, adult EAL education in Australia is often delivered through specific community-based providers that tender for the work to governments. They often manage on smaller budgets than other sectors and, thus, they do often have limited resources for technological change and the professional learning of teachers to deal with such change. Moreover, given that many of the teaching staff are part-time or casualised in the adult EAL education sector, consistent implementation of comprehensive change about digital literacies in the programmes is more difficult. Within these circumstances, leaders have to prioritise resources. Second, as it is argued throughout this book, digital literacies are pivotal to and need to be prioritised within the settlement and employment programmes for people from refugee and migrant backgrounds. Digital literacies are emphatically becoming a priority area in adult EAL education to which leaders need to assign resources.

From this perspective, leaders' understanding of the needs within the institution is central to enhancing the provision of digital literacies. Understanding the needs is done most effectively in the context of the principles of democratic leadership discussed above. This involves a more distributed approach to leadership and an openness to an extensive consultation that involves both learners and teachers. There may be a danger in conceiving "need" from a deficit perspective – that is in assessing need, there is an undue focus on what is missing and not what is working. In this book, we have affirmed the place of strengths-based approaches to pursuing change in terms of digital literacies. From this point of view, "need" is not a deficit but more akin to opportunity. It is about finding points in pedagogy and practice that can be strengthened.

Conclusion

In this chapter, we presented a number of important theories that informed this research and established connections between them. We argued that to develop a holistic understanding of how digital literacies are taught within one institution, there was a need for a multifaceted conceptual framework as there is no single theory that is sufficient to illuminate, explore, and conceptualise the complexity and totality of institutional experiences with digital literacies. It is also important to appreciate that this conceptual framework is only one way of understanding our research phenomenon and making meaning from the data, and clearly, every framework has its own affordances and limitations. In the next chapter, drawing on the ideas discussed here, we present our conceptual framework and explain how it is related to our research design alongside the description of Langfield and the broader social context in which it was located and had to operate.

3
RESEARCHING LANGFIELD
Institutional ethnography

This chapter discusses our thinking about and selection of an appropriate research design and methodological approach to the research project reported in this book. This discussion is woven together with rich descriptions of the context of the organisation as a beginning point of our ethnography of Langfield. From our perspective, there always needs to be a match between the methodological approach adopted and the setting for the research.

The research was conducted over a period of six months in 2019. In order to develop a holistic understanding of the role of digital literacies within the teaching and learning at Langfield, we were regularly on site and engaging with the learners and the teachers, as well as the leadership. Our concern was to understand the pedagogical approaches of the teachers, their professional learning experiences, the strengths and needs of learners, and the leadership practices. To do this, we required a close and supportive relationship with the organisation and we needed a research design that would enable us to understand the inner workings of Langfield. Thus, the project was designed around the idea of reciprocity and the ethical processes of establishing a research collaboration that was sustainable.

To support this design, we selected institutional ethnography as the preferred methodological approach, especially as embodied in the ideas of Dorothy Smith, a prominent Canadian sociologist. In this chapter, we consider this methodological approach as one among a number of ethnographic approaches and justify its selection. In response to the widely accepted position that institutional ethnography "rejects the dominance of theory" (Smith, 2005, p. 49), we engage critically with this perspective and explore the value of additional conceptual underpinnings within this research perspective. We also provide a detailed overview of our data generation methods and explain the ways in which the data in the project was analysed using the conceptual framework presented in Chapter 2.

This chapter also introduces the research site, Langfield, and begins with a rich description of the wider context and community within which it sits – an inner-urban area of Melbourne with an active cosmopolitan community of nearly 100,000 people from diverse cultural and socio-economic backgrounds. We explore how Langfield's work is framed within government policy priorities and imperatives as well as how it sees its role in the lives of people from refugee and migrant backgrounds, including in relation to digital technologies and digital literacies. In this instance, we believe that in juxtaposing these aspects of the research together, a more nuanced understanding of the alignments between research design, methodology, and context can be forged.

Considering research design for adult EAL settings

We started this qualitative research project with a view that the design of the study should fit the organisational context in which the research is to take place (Marshall & Rossman, 1995). This context would include the type of organisation, its stakeholders, and its purpose. The design should accommodate the interests of researchers and what an organisation and its members can offer. As researchers, we planned to come to this research context with our specific research agendas and interests. At the same time, we recognised that an organisation may have its own needs. From this point of view, we believed that there should be *reciprocity* in terms of what different parties can and want to offer each other (Maiter et al., 2008; Tour et al., 2020; Trainor & Bouchard, 2013). In designing this research, this reciprocity, built on common conversations about mutual benefit, was very important to consider as part of the process of conducting a dyadic (university-industry partner) study, as depicted in Figure 3.1.

The diagram presents the mutual recognition and equivalence of needs in strong research partnerships. This recognition emerges in the negotiation process (preferably early) and through the ongoing fluidity of the organisation-researcher relationship (Harrison et al., 2001; Tour et al., 2021). This fluidity and interdependency include the evolving nature of shared concerns, the capacities to do the

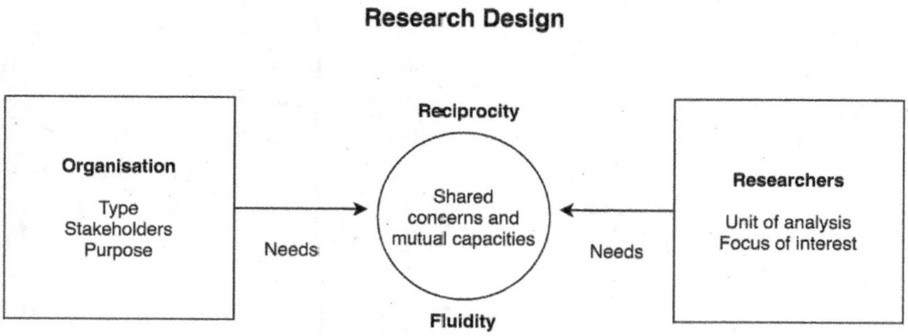

Research Design

FIGURE 3.1 Reciprocity in research design

research, accommodation of changing circumstances, and the desire to nurture these relationships over the longer term. Such an overarching approach to designing research that accounts for the participant organisation as well as the researchers provides the basis for sustainable research that can have longevity, and also research that would be useful for all parties involved (Bstieler et al., 2017). This sustainability is especially important for research involving the community-based sector because the financial resources available to this sector and, thus, consulting opportunities are often limited (Adult Learning Australia, 2015).

Langfield is a distinctive learning community and institutional setting for EAL learning. Reflecting this distinctiveness, the design of the research needed to embrace this uniqueness and be sensitive to the situated organisational needs in negotiating the direction of research on digital literacies. The research design necessarily leads to selecting an appropriate methodology that supports the design principles (Carter & Little, 2007; Perri & Bellamy, 2012). To appreciate the ways that digital literacies were embodied in the practices of teachers, learners and supported by the CEO at Langfield, we had to negotiate both emic (insider) and etic (outsider) positionalities as researchers (Beals et al., 2020). Emphatically, what evolved in our negotiations with Langfield was the need for an ethnographic study in which the researchers came into the lifeworlds of the participants and participated in close fieldwork as part of the ethnography. At the same time, we needed the "distance" to view the work at the institution from the broader perspective of what is happening in education more generally, especially in the community-based sector, and as part of a body of empirical research about digital literacies in educational contexts. Institutional ethnography embodies this approach to research and accounts for the institutional setting, the work and experiences of individuals in that setting, and the reciprocity of the research relationships.

Institutional ethnography

Ethnography is a research tradition that has its origins in social anthropology. It goes back to the early 20th century and the work of scholars such as Margaret Mead, Bronisław Malinowski, and the Chicago School of ethnography that had a strong emphasis on understanding what is there in a research context (Crang & Cook, 2007; Scott Jones & Watt, 2010). In social research, researchers often come into particular communities (sometimes living within the communities) to understand their social ways, values, and traditions first-hand, with a focus on subjects and subjectivities. So, one of the cornerstones of ethnography is an intimate interconnectivity with a community and its members. This connectivity has the purpose of understanding what participants in a community do and why they act as they do in order to provide rich insights through holistic engagement within a sociocultural setting over time (Hammersley & Atkinson, 2019).

Another important aspect of ethnography is detailing of the connections and understandings between researchers and participants through the production of various texts that unfold the nature of the community in co-subjectivities and collaborative meaning-making (Lassiter, 2001; Richardson, 2000). These texts might be produced within the community, by the researchers or through collaboration between the researchers and community members. Indeed, the origin of the word "ethnography" comes from "ethno" (race, culture, distinct community) and "graph" (writing, communication). In a contemporary context, the production of research texts might also include interactions and communications from digital and online environments, social media, and virtual worlds (Kaur-Gill & Dutta, 2017).

An ethnography of a site is an overt set of communications (including texts) about a discrete context that has its own culture, subjectivities, and practices. However, what should not be forgotten in ethnography is also the *materiality* of the context in which the research is being undertaken – the "siteness" of the site (Roehl, 2012). The ontologies of a site might include the geographical location and relationship to place, buildings, physical structures, or virtual spaces with their affordances and limitations, technologies, artefacts, significant objects, and patterns of using the material to create meaning. In this sense, there is some layover of ideas from archaeology that focus on the material that might be useful for conceiving the purposes of an ethnography (Henare et al., 2006).

There are different forms of ethnography that share general characteristics of ethnography as a methodology (as described above) but also have specialised features or particular applications to a certain context. These forms of ethnography embody different positionalities for researchers and epistemological understandings.

- *Ethnographic realism*. In this form, the ethnographer takes a strongly etic or abstracted position (an out-of-sight stance) towards a community and participants. From this perspective, the researcher observes and analyses the participants' experiences without much or any participation in the context (Maxwell, 2012). One variant of this ethnographic approach is the emerging use of *quantitative ethnography*. This approach is about documenting a site, organisation, or context statistically to establish patterns, specific content, or trends (Williamson, 2017).
- *Relational ethnography*. The ethnographer looks at fields, rather than defined contexts, and critically examines the boundaries between contexts, as well the cultural conflicts and intersections. Thus, the ethnographic approach is across sites and contexts (Desmond, 2014).
- *Participatory ethnography*. This is a methodological approach in which the researchers are immersed to some degree in the context of the research site and, thus, they can offer emic perspectives about the relationships, rules, and practices within this community (Blomberg & Karasti, 2012).
- *Critical ethnography*. This approach to ethnography might be considered not so much a form of ethnography but a stance within ethnography that turns to criticality, to the uses of positionality and power within and across settings

in relation to different dimensions such as gender, ethnicity, religion, and age (Madison, 2012).
- *Institutional ethnography*. It is oriented to the constitution of an organisation and what makes it function through the interconnections of people with each other and with the practices, policies, and understandings that operate at an institutional site (Kearney et al., 2019).

In considering our methodological needs in researching Langfield, we looked at all these ethnographic possibilities and came to three conclusions. First, we needed an ethnographic approach that would help us in understanding the constitution of the relationships, pedagogical practices, technologies, and textual artefacts that impinged on the use of digital literacies in English language teaching. Second, we also wanted involvement and agency from the stakeholders (teachers, learners, leaders) because they are central to the teaching and learning at this site. Finally, we hoped to develop personal interconnections to and an ongoing relationship with the organisation to reflect our professional desire for reciprocal research design considered above (Figure 3.1). To address these intentions, the best fit, from our perspective, was an *institutional ethnographic* approach.

Institutional ethnography is a form of ethnography that contains some elements of the other types listed above (including, especially, critical ethnography). It is an approach to qualitative inquiry that considers how the ordinary experiences of people are organised or put together by both the shared texts and disposition of relationships within organisations, including the power relationships and ways of ruling (Campbell & Gregor, 2002; LaFrance, 2018). So, institutional ethnography is emphatically about the sociality of an organisational setting in juxtaposition to its policy statements and textual outputs, and how such sociality and textuality shape individuals' experiences and practices within the institution (Smith, 2001).

There are three emphases in institutional ethnography as illustrated in Figure 3.2. First, institutional ethnography has a strong social focus. In other words, it focuses on the nature of the relationships in an organisation as well as the tensions, alignments, and ways of working that go with this social focus. Second, institutional ethnography draws attention to the ontological constitution of the institution and how the organisation is put together in terms of all its facets that impinge on individuals within it. This amounts to a set of situated understandings on the ground. Third, institutional ethnography is about critical analysis of both the social focus and the ontological constitution. This might involve consideration of the operation of power and hierarchies, as well as the ascriptions applied to people within the organisation such as gender, ethnicity, and other broad categorisations.

Institutional ethnography is generally associated with the research and writing of Canadian sociologist and feminist writer, Dorothy Smith (2005), who stressed the importance of professional relationships within institutional settings in juxtaposition especially to the texts that are operational within that setting.

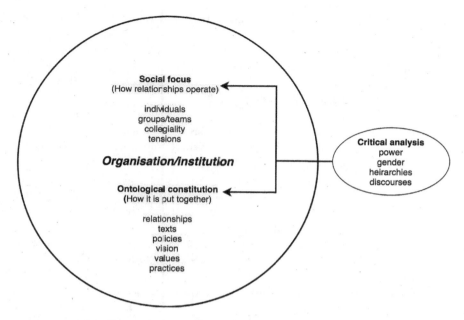

FIGURE 3.2 The emphases in institutional ethnography

She also drew attention to how the nexus of texts coordinates the disposition of people and their relationships within a setting and a location or place. Smith (2005) describes institutional ethnography as sociology of people, but people are never inert, so there is politics and ways of ruling within organisations. For Smith (2005), institutional ethnography "proposes to enlarge the scope of what becomes visible from that site … making visible how we are connected into the extended social relations of ruling" (p. 29). Smith was especially interested in women: their voice and their sense of empowerment at a site and within the scope of an organisation and its texts and social relations.

Smith (2005) implies in her writing that there is a deep and important interconnection between the individuals (and groups) within an institutional setting and the effectiveness of the institution, including its values and mission. These relational interconnections become the organising principle that shapes an organisation and how people feel and function within it. According to Kearney et al. (2019), "institutional ethnography orients to exploring and explicating the social relations that organize… experience in the institutional setting or settings in which they exist" (p. 18). From this perspective, the emphasis in institutional ethnography is on how an organisation comes to be the way it is (in all its ontological dimensions) because of the people in it and the social forces that constitute it. The researcher using institutional ethnography, thus, becomes interested in what is *experienced*, what is *done*, what is *documented*, and the *nature of the professional relationships* that afford or constrain practice and collegiality within an institutional context.

Institutional ethnography was selected as the core methodology for this study for a number of reasons. First, the research design, built around reciprocity, necessitated an approach that is strongly inclusive of relationality. We wanted to build an ongoing and close connection with Langfield. Thus, it was important that the relational constitution of the organisation was understood in detail. Institutional ethnography afforded this possibility. It also points to the ontologies of power and positionality that operate, sometimes implicitly, within a setting. Second, we aimed to gain insights into the relational processes (manager-teacher/s, teacher-teacher and learner-teacher) that are at the heart of the teaching and learning. Institutional ethnography allows for doing this. Next, given our interest in policy documents, curriculum documents and resources that are pivotal to teaching digital literacies, the pervasive influence of texts in shaping the nature of both the organisation and relationships emphasised in institutional ethnography is significant. Finally, there is a strong ethnographic tradition in the field of Literacy Studies – the body of work that this research draws on in conceptualising digital literacies. There has been a range of ethnographic studies of literacy over the past 40 years – both full ethnographies and studies drawing upon ethnographic approaches (Barton, 2013). Although these studies often had a focus on everyday life of people, they provided many important contributions in many areas as many of them are rooted in educational concerns. Similarly, understanding the "everyday" concerns that may exist within a specific institution is essential for effective pedagogy. Such understanding can best be developed through ethnographic research, especially, in the context of Langfield, institutional ethnography.

Despite the affordances of institutional ethnography as a research methodology, this approach is not without its critics and its issues. There were two issues that needed to be accounted for in our thinking about researching Langfield. In particular, we do not agree with the disavowal of theory as part of ethnographic research. Whilst in accord with the Chicago School, it is important to comprehend "what is there" at a site, theory becomes important for later reflexivity and understanding of the broader meanings that participants and researchers attached to the data collected (Wacquant, 2002; Wilson & Chaddha, 2009). This is especially important when a research phenomenon, such as digital literacies in the adult EAL contexts, is complex, multifaceted, contested, and cannot be explained by the conceptual underpinnings of the institutional ethnography. Figure 3.3 illustrates our thinking about the intersection of a number of theoretical perspectives and intuitional ethnography that guided this research.

Furthermore, as Dorothy Smith envisioned a broader perspective when looking at meaning within an organisation, we believe that there needs to be greater accounting for the macro environment outside the immediate organisational context. For instance, globalisation and the movement of peoples, and the larger national and international policy frameworks can and do impinge on work and practice at the local level. This provides a tension between the local and the global, but it is a productive tension between the objective of ethnography to look at the local in juxtaposition with the politics of what is beyond.

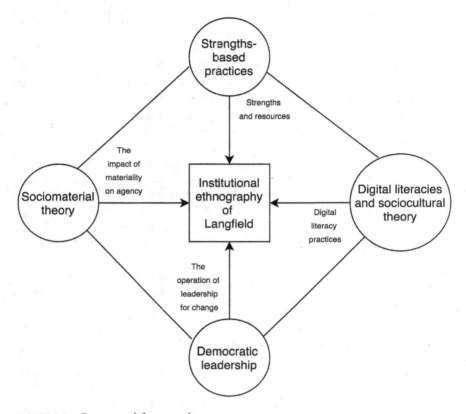

FIGURE 3.3 Conceptual framework

Victorian context, Langfield, and participants

As we discussed throughout the beginning of this book, our research focused on one institution – Langfield – a registered government-funded ACE provider of English and employment programmes for adult learners in several different locations in Melbourne (Victoria). However, educational institutions do not exist in a vacuum. They are always part of larger social systems. Thus, to fully understand Langfield's practices and experiences, it is important to consider the broader context in which it operates. In this section, we offer observations about various contextual features of the organisation built from our ethnographic field notes, on-site photographs, relevant policy documents, and demographic sources.

Victorian context

Victoria is one of the eight states and territories of Australia. It is the most densely populated state in Australia as well as one of the most culturally diverse states. According to the 2016 Census, Victoria's population was 5.93 million with 28.4%

of Victoria's total population born overseas in over 200 countries; 49.1% born overseas or born in Australia with at least one parent born overseas; 26% speaking a language other than English at home; 59% followed one of more than 130 different faiths (State Government of Victoria, 2021). While the majority of the overseas-born Victorians came to Australia as skilled migrants, a large number of overseas-born Victorians came to Australia as refugees from conflicts in the Second World War in Europe, Indo-China, the republics of the former Yugoslavia, the Horn of Africa, the Middle East, and Afghanistan. Melbourne is the capital city of Victoria. Focused around a central city, the area of Greater Melbourne is made up of many suburbs – each with its own distinctive character – that spread 30 to 40 km north and south, east and west of the central business district (CBD).

The setting for Langfield's inner-urban main base is cosmopolitan and diverse (Figure 3.4). Walking the blocks around Langfield, one might see parks, gardens,

FIGURE 3.4 Inner urban area surrounding Langfield

tree-lined residential streets, and construction sites. There would be cranes on the skyline and urban graffiti on walls and fences, churches, childcare centres, a theatre, a dance studio. A metropolitan train line runs through the area and on the busy arterial roads private vehicles share the lanes with trams and buses – all shuffling thousands of commuters through this area every day into the Melbourne CBD, a short journey away and out to the distant suburbs. Within a short stroll from Langfield one might also find the municipal library, schools, a hospital, and many different services. One could also easily find a fingernail parlour, aromatherapy and massage services, hair salons and tattoo shops, a news agency and a printing press provider. There would be many small retail outlets as well as restaurants, bars, and cafes with food inspired by almost anywhere in the world, from Thai to Turkish, Indian to Italian.

On average, Langfield sits within a relatively affluent area. Based on Australian Bureau of Statistics data, from the 2016 national census, average incomes in the Local Government Area are approaching $2000 per week, which is higher than the average for the greater City of Melbourne overall (Australian Bureau of Statistics, 2016). Across the municipality, unemployment is also relatively low, at approximately 5% which is lower than the Greater Melbourne average for unemployment. However, statistical averages can be deceptive. There are significant communities in this municipality that do not share this affluence and relative advantage. The Index of Relative Socio-Economic Disadvantage (IRSD) reflects indicators of disadvantage such as unemployment, low income, and education levels and lack of internet access. Within this municipality, the scores of the IRSD vary from 1,123, reflecting a relative lack of disadvantage, to 341, reflecting a high proportion of households experiencing significant disadvantage (Australian Bureau of Statistics, 2016). For instance, within a short walk from the Langfield centre, there are neighbourhoods where over 50% of the households have an income of less than $650 per week from their combined sources, including pensions and allowances (Australian Bureau of Statistics, 2016). There is a significant number of residents living in "the estates" (Figure 3.5). These are high-density, high-rise, government-sponsored social housing estates where unemployment rates may be much higher and internet connectivity is much lower than the average across the broader municipality.

Langfield and research participants

It is within this vibrant, yet heterogeneous setting, that Langfield sits with its several learning sites spread around various locations in this inner-urban area. It delivers a range of accredited English language classes from pre-Certificate I to Certificate III that are free to eligible learners as they are funded by different government initiatives. Langfield also offers many programmes that assist newly arrived learners with settlement, educational, administrative, employment, and cultural issues in Australia.

FIGURE 3.5 Social housing estate in the area

At the time, when the study was conducted, Langfield catered for 200 learners, mainly coming from Vietnam, China, Thailand, Somali, Ethiopia, and South Sudan. Their ages ranged from the early 20s to 80s and they were predominantly female. The majority of Langfield's learners were not employed at the time of the reported research and lived in social housing estates. However, they were no longer homeless or stateless and were building cultural and language foundations for the future. Many learners had little or interrupted schooling; however, they remained committed to education despite their difficult histories and traumas.

The linguistic and cultural diversity at Langfield was extensive. The languages spoken by learners included Vietnamese, Mandarin, Arabic (African region), Oromo, Somali, Amharic, Dinka, Tigrinya, Cantonese, Indonesian, Cambodian,

Portuguese (Brazil), Thai, Tibetan, Turkish, Farsi (Iran), Tagalog, and French (African region). While some learners could not read and write in their home languages, they embodied important cultural and linguistic understandings and resources that may richly inform learning, including the development of their digital literacies. Twenty learners participated in this study.

There were 15 EAL teachers at Langfield: one teacher was working full-time and 14 working part-time, ranging from one to four days per week. The CEO and six EAL teachers volunteered to participate in the study: Kate, Andrea, Susan, Polly, Tanya, Nicole (pseudonyms). All teachers were qualified to teach English as an Additional language. Andrea, Susan, Tanya, and Nicole held Master of TESOL degrees while Polly and Kate held the Graduate Diploma in TESOL and the Graduate Certificate in TESOL accordingly. Three teachers (Susan, Polly, and Tanya) also had a Bachelor of Education and taught previously in Australian primary and secondary schools. As a Vietnamese-Australian, Nicole was bilingual; the others were monolingual, of Caucasian heritage.

Langfield's governance and funding

Langfield's work is funded through Commonwealth and State government funds accessed through competitive tendering processes. In recent decades many governments have shifted from being direct service providers to being purchasers of services on behalf of their constituents. Service provision is outsourced to contractors which may include traditional public institutions such as TAFE colleges who compete for the funds with private organisations that are both for profit and not-for-profit community-based organisations. They are all seen to be operating within the same market and also a regulatory framework which also includes some quality assurance and compliance mechanisms (Hodge et al., 2020).

Thus, Langfield is positioned within this competitive market as a community-based *Learn Local* provider. To be eligible to tender for government funds the institution must be:

> able to demonstrate that adult education and vocational learning is a key focus of their business… community owned and managed and operate on a not-for-profit basis… [and] able to deliver and govern programs that meet the Board's quality standards.
>
> *(ACFEB, 2019, p. 3)*

The criteria to be met for registration include providing evidence that "the governing body draws the majority of its members from the community where it operates or the community of interest it serves" (ACFEB, 2019, p. 8). As a registered provider, the organisation becomes eligible to use the *Learn Local* brand to support marketing and promotion of programmes. Some limited support from the state is also provided for system wide professional development activities and to subsidise some business-related software. Registration lasts for up to five years. However, registration in itself is no guarantee of funding.

Typically, government funds for projects or service delivery are allocated to the service providers on the basis of competitive tendering processes. They are usually funded for a limited contract cycle – perhaps, a year or two. The nature of these competitive tendering processes means that the work of the organisation must be framed within government policy priorities and imperatives. As we discussed in Chapter 1, these policies have been increasingly shaped by a focus on vocational outcomes and a preference for formal competency-based qualifications (Bowman, 2016; Foley, 2007; Hodge et al., 2020). This puts Langfield in a somewhat challenging position as its learners are not ready, at least initially, for vocational education. They are still seeking reassurance, support, and guidance as well as building their confidence and their skills to be able to take the next step into a more formal learning setting. They may be quite daunted by the thought of undertaking a certificate course as the possibility of undertaking such a course may never have occurred to them. However, there may not be funding for places to consolidate their resettlement. As such, there are concerns about whether these adult learners will ever engage meaningfully with a vocational component of these programmes. Langfield often had to negotiate these tensions in their learning programmes.

Learning spaces and access to technology

Langfield delivers its programmes across several locations across an inner Melbourne suburb. Trying to reach learners, the classrooms were often located in the social housing estates and in easily accessible public spaces such as libraries and community houses. With limited funding, the classrooms just had basic furniture and resources (Figures 3.6 and 3.7).

Within its sites, Langfield had two dedicated computer rooms with internet access, several sets of iPads, as well as projectors and teachers' laptops in some classrooms. Computer rooms were set up in a traditional way: each computer room had eight to ten desktop computers facing the walls as captured in Figure 3.8 below. Most of the devices worked, although some of them were slow, according to the teachers – probably due to the age of the equipment.

Importantly, the institution and its teachers often relied on learners' personal mobile phones. The learners were allowed and actively encouraged to use their mobile phones in the classrooms for learning purposes. The CEO and teachers seemed to be satisfied with the range and number of devices, although some stated that the internet connection on iPads "drops a lot", affecting the flow or even disrupting learning with technology. There were no technical support staff at Langfield which meant that teachers had to troubleshoot all the technical issues, whether in the computer room or with phones, iPads, or projectors in class.

At the beginning of the project, our research attention was immediately directed by the participants to a programme specifically dedicated to learning digital literacies – *Techno-Tuesday* (pseudonym). From our first day at Langfield, it was obvious that this programme was positioned by everyone in the institution as the main venue for learning digital literacies and the teachers working within

FIGURE 3.6 Langfield's classroom 1

the programme were seen as digital literacies experts. The programme was initiated and developed in 2017 by three teachers participating in this project: Tanya,[1] Nicole, and Polly. It was specifically designed to address learners' needs in relation to digital literacies and it was co-planned and co-taught by this team of three teachers. This programme, of course, attracted our research interest and it will be further explored in Chapters 5 and 6.

Langfield's mission

The urban context of diversity and disadvantage presented challenges to Langfield and its educators. Writing from the US urban context, Rogers and Hansman (2004) suggest that one of such challenges is addressing the needs of low-income urban participants. Similarly, Benseman (2014) notes that adult refugee learners with limited education present as learners with "substantial and distinctive

FIGURE 3.7 Langfield's classroom 2

educational, social, and psychological needs" (p. 93). Like other ACE providers across the nation, addressing these needs was central to Langfield's mission.

One of the main educational goals at Langfield was providing safety, care, and belonging in learning programmes. The institution positions itself as a safe place for initial access, engagement, social connection, and learning. For adult learners, who may have experienced war, dislocation, and trauma, this sense of safety and security is especially important and becomes a crucial prerequisite for their learning. Institutions such as our research site play an important role in rebuilding trust and social connections with adult learners (Miralles-Lombardo et al., 2008). Langfield's mission reflects these ideas and is centred around the importance of making connections, forging new friendships, and providing opportunities for social interaction. It is worth noting that this sense of feeling welcome and safe is often seen as especially important for women to transcend their difficult domestic circumstances and gain new skills and a new identity as a learner. The majority of Langfield's learners are female, so this learning centre became a sanctuary for them.

FIGURE 3.8 Langfield's computer room

Langfield's programmes are offered with particular sensitivity, reflexivity, and care. This is important because adult learners can "vote with their feet". They have the option to discontinue their engagement, or simply not turn up to classes if they are perceived as not meeting their needs. To address this challenge, the staff showed a deep level of commitment, engagement, and, what Wilkinson and Kaukko (2020) call, "pedagogical love" (p. 1). As Sanguinetti et al. (2004) argue, "teachers and learners do not merely work, or learn, or visit, at the ACE centre, they *belong to it* [our emphasis]" (p. 57). Indeed, there was a sense of mutual ownership or connection at Langfield: the people belong to the centre and the centre belongs to the community. This sense of belonging relates to the "bonding" or belonging dimension of the social capital generated through ACE (Falk et al., 2000).

Another important aim for Langfield was to represent and encourage its learners' engagement in local community forums, assist with everyday communication, administrative, and employment issues and provide assistance to new arrivals with settlement, including language learning, digital literacies, and cultural issues. As a non-for-profit educational organisation, Langfield did more than just offering English language classes to these learners. The CEO noted that while the organisation is small and lean, it also has the capacity for "thinking big". Mindful of the circumstances of adult learners they are trying to reach, the Langfield's team attempted to remove barriers and connect with hard-to-reach learners, particularly those on "the estates", through their outreach programmes.

While Langfield intends to help its learners to settle in a new country and learn a new language, it also aims to support cultural and linguistic diversity. Langfield's learners are linguistically diverse. Amongst our participants, only one teacher, Nicole, has a shared language (Vietnamese) with some learners. In this context, the complexity of students' linguistic profiles can be difficult to navigate. However, during our visits we noticed that the CEO and teachers attempted to create a multilingual environment. They seemed to appreciate this linguistic diversity and, importantly, saw home languages as an important resource for learning. For example, Figure 3.9 is a photograph we took of a door to the classroom with welcome messages in different languages, suggesting that home languages were valued and celebrated within the centre environment at the time of our visit. This reinforces the message that learners are welcome. During our visit to the classroom captured in Figure 3.9, we noticed a poster in the corner of the board in which classroom instructions (e.g. find your group) are written in three languages. This suggests that learners' home languages were centralised in classroom activities and routines. For learners still at the beginning of their English language learning journey, this seemed a useful strategy for ensuring that they participated in classroom activities as well as enhancing their linguistic awareness which is important for language learning.

We also observed that Langfield's teachers, even though the majority of them were monolingual, actively incorporated home languages in their curriculum. Most especially, Nicole – a bilingual teacher – often offered explanations of the content and instructions in both English and Vietnamese. Other teachers actively used Google translate in their instructions and supported peer interactions for learning purposes in home languages. One of the teachers, Susan, even reported buying a smartphone with a bigger screen to be able to use Google translate in the classroom more effectively. It was clear that the teachers welcomed, supported, and, in fact, actively employed the cultural and linguistic capital of their learners.

A feminist perspective about Langfield

As we noted in Chapter 1, Langfield is a predominantly female organisation: it is led by a female CEO, has only female teachers and has predominantly female learners. In this respect, this institution reflects the mostly female constituency of the ACE sector for teachers, learners, and leaders (English, 2005; English & Irving, 2015; Golding & Foley, 2017). In her history of adult literacy and basic education in Victoria, Campbell (2009) discusses the significance of female

FIGURE 3.9 Classroom door with welcoming messages in different languages

narratives in this context and she argues that such narratives counter normalised patriarchal views widespread through other sectors in education.

For teachers, the feminist perspective points to the highly gendered nature of the workforce; dominated by women doing work that is characterised as caring, or "heart work"; teaching and nurturing responsibilities carried by women, often as volunteers. While we do not subscribe to gender stereotypes, we observed that the leadership and teaching practices at Langfield were informed by care and empathy for vulnerable and often traumatised learners. Another example of highly gendered nature of work in the sector that we observed at Langfield was related to the employment type: there are mostly part-time, limited tenure, contract, or "casual" positions – something very typical for the sector as noted by Macrae and Agostinelli (2002). There was only one teacher working full time; other teachers, regardless of their preference, were working part time. For learners, the feminist perspective is often associated with empowerment and the critical-emancipatory tradition of adult education (Campbell, 2009; Klenk, 2017; O'Grady, 2016; Shan, 2015). There was a strong orientation and commitment to empowerment for and of learners at Langfield.

Data generation

Data generation for this research fitted the broad scope of ethnography and was especially oriented to the institutional ethnography approach described above (O'Reilly, 2005). There were four methods of data generation in the study which were used for what Richardson (2000), drawing on postmodernist thinking, calls "crystallization" (p. 13). Metaphorically speaking, we were using different methods as crystal prisms to gain a deep, complex, and thorough understanding of our research phenomenon.

Participant observation, field notes, and video recording

One of the methods employed in this research was participant observation which has a long tradition in ethnographic research. It represents our emic embeddedness within the research context that is significant for deep and complex understanding (Diamond, 2006). In total, we conducted four extended observation sessions. We started this research with the observation of the physical spaces at Langfield as part of an extended tour of the facilities led by the CEO. During this two-hour tour, we visited three different learning sites to see administrative offices, learning spaces, and computer rooms. We also met several teachers and students as well as observed the neighbourhoods in which the learning sites were located. In addition to this introductory tour, we conducted three observation sessions (90 minutes each) focused on the learning programmes that attracted our research interest, such as *Techno-Tuesdays*. We focused both on teachers and learners within the programme. Furthermore, we made numerous incidental visits to Langfield over the course of the project which allowed us to observe the institution in a more informal way and provided additional insights into its work and life.

Our observations were recorded with the help of detailed field notes, photography, and video recording. Our purpose in observations and field notes was to capture the immediacy of the setting as a phenomenon. The field notes taken during classes included references to oral exchanges with both the teacher and the student *in situ*. In the field notes, ontological attention was especially given to:

- The structural features and sequencing in the lessons
- The use of digital devices during the lesson
- The interactions of teachers and learners with these devices
- Practices with technologies in relation to digital literacies
- Hierarchies and ways of ruling relations

Often in the notes, more interpretive and explanatory asides were added to do with pedagogy or to identify strengths, affordances, and effective practices, as well as challenges and limitations within the teaching and learning about technologies.

Individual interviews

This research employed one "walking" interview and several traditional semi-structured interviews. A walking interview with the CEO occurred as she took us on almost a two-hour tour around the neighbourhood area and teaching spaces at multiple sites during our first visit. In other words, this walking interview entailed us (the researchers) and the CEO talking while walking together and it was employed concurrently with ethnographic observation (King & Woodroffe, 2017). This type of interviewing was spontaneous, flexible, dynamic, and less structured in terms of topics discussed because our conversation was closely tied to the locations that we visited, people that we met, and things that we observed. It appeared to be a valuable multisensory method of data collection which helped to deepen our understanding of Langfield's lived experiences.

Semi-structured, individual interviews, which are commonplace in qualitative and ethnographic research, were also central to this research. They were seen as a specialised discursive space for eliciting personal voice and allowing it to be evident in the research data to establish the situated personal experiences and intersubjectivities that constitute being in the organisation (DeVault & McCoy, 2006). We conducted two sets of semi-structured interviews. The first set included individual interviews of 40-60 minutes with the CEO and all six teacher-participants. The interviews focused on the broad experiences of being in the organisation, its mission and policies, resources, collegial relationships, work with learners, issues and problems encountered, and professional learning needs to do with digital literacies and pedagogies, among many other themes explored. The second set of interviews was conducted with the teachers whom we observed in the context of the *Techno-Tuesday* programme. These were de-briefing 15-minute multiple individual interviews with Polly (three interviews), Susan (two interviews), and Nicole (one interview). They were conducted straight after the classes that we observed and they focused on what was observed.

Artefacts

In this study, we recognised the significance of objects and artefacts in mediating human activity and experiences within organisations (Miettinen & Virkkunen, 2005), reflecting also the sociomaterial theory employed as an interpretive lens. These artefacts included the learning spaces, physical resources, computers, mobile devices, and other technologies. In addition, the participating teachers shared some artefacts related to digital literacies such as teaching resources or materials used for professional learning. In documenting and recording these artefacts, we employed photography and videography to capture the materiality of the setting for later analysis (Schwartz, 1989). We generated 50 photos and 270 minutes of videos.

Focus groups

This research included the use of focus groups. The purpose of focus groups as part of ethnographic research was to understand collective experiences and appreciate the interconnections between people within a setting, including the similarities and differences in regard to their values and perspectives (Agar & MacDonald, 1995). In addition, focus groups enabled meaning-making through socially shared knowledge that comes through the dialogic exchange of individuals within a group setting. They also facilitated some potential understanding of how hierarchies and power operate within groups and the larger organisational setting (Marková et al., 2007). Given that a focus group is a more-or-less artificial type of group, care needs to be taken to see this data set in relation to the findings of other data sets (Reed & Payton, 1997).

In this project, we conducted two types of focus groups. The first type was an activity-oriented focus group with five teacher-participants. The participants were asked to create a collaborative collage which we pitched as "My perfect professional learning about digital literacies". This activity enabled meaning-creation performance using a visual modality, which included participatory design and visual play (Lee & Tan, 2013). Once the collage was created, the teachers explained their visual representation to the research team. The collage was used to stimulate discussion of the participants about their professional learning needs in relation to digital literacies. All interactions between the participants and with the researchers (during both designing and discussing the collage) were audio recorded.

The second type was focus groups with adult learners from the learning programme, *Techno-Tuesday*. There were two 30-minute focus groups that had four participants each. The focus groups were conducted with Vietnamese-speaking learners in their home language. A Vietnamese-speaking research assistant facilitated both focus groups. The group discussion was conducted in a somewhat informal way to ensure that the learners, who were not familiar with research practices, were not overwhelmed by this activity. The conversation was structured around a set of themes to do with everyday digital literacy practices and *Techno-Tuesday* programme. The research assistant translated and transcribed the data generated in the learners' focus group.

Thematic data analysis

This ethnographic research generated a substantial amount of data coming from different sources (e.g. interview and focus groups transcripts, observation notes, artefacts, photographs, video-recording). To code and analyse the data, we employed a thematic approach. This hybrid approach, incorporating both inductive and deductive processes, to understanding the data was selected as it best fitted the complexity of the unit of analysis (digital literacies) and our holistic way of understanding of Langfield from an institutional ethnographic perspective. This approach was conceived in collaborative discussions and in consideration of the approach of other researchers (Braun & Clarke, 2006; Brooks, 2015; Swain, 2018). The hybrid approach had the following elements:

1. *Level: 1 Inductive coding.* There was initial inductive reading of the data to identify any patterns or regular occurrences within the data. We read the data independently, and then met to discuss these patterns, paying attention to what was important to participants. This was an opportunity to come to consensus about what was important in terms of the focus of this study, collaboratively finalise a priory codes, based on the conceptual framework (Figure 3.3), and generate codes.
2. *Level 2: Deductive coding.* Using collaboratively generated codes, the researchers coded the data and developed several categories individually. Rather than being a set of static categories for analysis, our theoretical ideas and conceptual understandings were applied contextually and holistically to tease out the relationships between different aspects of our research phenomenon – institutional experiences with our unit of analysis, digital literacies.
3. *Data analysis.* Having conducted two levels of coding and generating major categories individually, we then compared our categories and discussed discrepancies in analysis until a consensus was reached. This process helped us to refine, revise, and merge these categories into themes.

In the next chapters, we present the main themes that emerged in this study of Langfield in relation to the role of digital literacies in learners' lives, teaching practices with and about technology, professional learning, and leadership.

Conclusion

This chapter has provided an overview of the research design, detailing, and justifying our choice of methodology, methods of data generation, and approach to thematic analysis of the data. These methodological considerations have been juxtaposed with an introduction to our research site – Langfield – and the research participants, touching upon how the institution frames its work within government policy priorities as well as the needs and strengths of the community. We believe that our description of the broader social context surrounding the institution, and details about Langfield as a situated organisation, offers the essential understandings that informed our methodological choices and provides an important and useful backdrop to the discussion of the findings in the upcoming chapters.

Note

1 Tanya was the lead teacher of the programme. Tanya participated in the first part of this research project that involved interviews and focus groups. However, due to changed circumstances in the second part of the research, we were unable to observe her teaching practices. As Susan replaced Tanya in the programme we observed her classes.

4
THE DIGITAL LIVES OF LANGFIELD'S LEARNERS

FIELD NOTES

We met EAL learners who participated in this research for the first time on a Tuesday afternoon as we arrived at Langfield for our very first observation session of *Techno-Tuesday*. While Langfield's CEO and teachers agreed to participate in the project, we were yet to invite the learners. Such invitation usually involves a brief introduction of the project, reading explanatory statements and signing the consent forms. This may seem to be an easy task for many researchers and potential participants. However, it appeared to be a different but very thought-provoking experience for us.

We came to this meeting prepared: bringing image-based PowerPoint slides to talk about our research, having all paperwork translated in Mandarin, Vietnamese, and Arabic and significantly simplified forms in English. The group of 20 friendly learners seemed to be curious about our visit and listened carefully to our introduction. The teachers – Polly, Susan, and Nicole – occasionally inserted a word or two to support learners' understanding of our talk. The introduction went well but as we proceeded with the paperwork, the classroom dynamics changed dramatically and suddenly became very hectic.

The idea of signing a form almost caused panic among the learners from refugee and migrant backgrounds. It disrupted the somewhat quiet classroom atmosphere within a few seconds. Some learners started talking to their peers to check their understanding of the documents; some were reading the documents with great attention; a few approached us to clarify different questions;

> some learners took their phones and started translating; one took a photo of all the documents using her mobile phone; some chased their teachers for help. This took almost 20 minutes but all learners returned their signed consent forms to us indicating their willingness to participate.
>
> August 27, 2019

While the vignette above describes some typical issues which may emerge in the process of getting an informed consent of potentially vulnerable research participants, what stood out for us in this first meeting was the ways in which Langfield's learners navigated what was for them a new experience. All these learners were at the beginning of their English language learning journey and, of course, even our simplified language might have been difficult to fully understand. Furthermore, the idea of participating in research, giving informed consent, and understanding the concepts of privacy and confidentiality were new to them. It is possible that they were apprehensive about signing our paperwork, perhaps fearing different legal and financial consequences related to their residency status in Australia. These are all valid concerns, and the easiest way out would be to decline an invitation to participate which we would understand and accept. However, Langfield's learners obviously looked beyond the challenges and concerns that they had. Within a few seconds after the forms were distributed, they mobilised all existing resources to deal with new information and decision-making. While our initial reading of the class was "hectic", we soon understood that, in fact, it was "proactive" as the learners eagerly sought assistance from peers, teachers, us as researchers, and, of course, their personal digital devices. They seemed to be motivated and determined to overcome the challenges and they had strategies to do this.

Such proactive attitudes appeared to be central to their other experiences, including those with digital technologies within and beyond the classroom at Langfield. This idea of positive and resourceful learning engagement is central to this chapter, in which we report our first set of research findings about the digital lives of the Langfield's learners. We begin by considering the learners' previous experiences with digital technologies before analysing their practices with technologies necessitated by the new digital landscape in Australia.

Currently, there is relatively limited published research about digital literacy practices of adult language learners from migrant and refugee backgrounds. Our study suggests that digital literacy practices, especially those involving mobile devices, are central to their lives and aspirations and an important learning resource. In this chapter, we also challenge the deficit discourses in policy, public media, and some research that tends to frame these learners as helpless victims, emphasising dependency, and what they lack and cannot do. Adopting a strengths-based perspective, the chapter identifies a number of important resources that the participants drew on when navigating the complex digital landscapes of their lives in Australia. We also consider the needs of the adult learners; but, in contrast to a deficit perspective given from outside the context, we embrace the perspectives of the learners themselves and focus on their voices and their understandings of what they did to address these needs. By exploring what participants said about their needs, we position learners' agency as an important aspect of decision-making in terms of teaching and learning about digital literacies.

Learners' digital literacy practices

During the focus group, the majority of learners reported that they did not use technology in their home countries, while some said that they had access to phones but they mainly used them for making phone calls rather than for using other digital applications:

> In the past, I knew nothing, nothing at all [about technology].
>
> Previously, I knew how to use the cell phone. I had never accessed email. You know, that is common in Vietnam.

It was apparent in the focus group discussion that they had very limited direct experience with digital technologies before arrival due to different pre-migration histories. However, they all noted that this dimension of their lives had changed in Australia. Indeed, all of them reported active technology use in their everyday lives, as well as within the learning context of Langfield. Hence, living in a new country presented both opportunities and challenges in terms of developing their digital literacies. It also shaped their digital literacy practices in unique ways as is evident in the data analysis to follow.

Everyday digital literacy practices

There was a strong preference for mobile hand-held devices such as smartphones and iPads for the everyday activities of all learners participating in this research. Three focus group participants offered these comments:

> There is no computer at home. I only have a cell phone and an iPad.
>
> I only use an iPad at home.
>
> I don't use an iPad. I only use the mobile phone.

For some participants, mobile devices were the only technologies they owned and they did not have a desktop or a laptop at home. All of the participants had mobile phones connected to the Internet, while others used iPads alongside their phones as complementary devices. There were several participants who reported that they owned a desktop computer but did not use it, preferring their mobile devices. Two participants stated this unequivocally:

> I do not use the computer very often.
>
> I have a computer at home, but I do not use it.

Only one out of eight focus group participants reported occasional use of a desktop computer, while still preferring mobile devices. She stated: "I mostly use [my] mobile phone and iPad, sometimes I use the computer". To explain their preference for mobile devices, they mostly referred to convenience of usage as evident below:

> I use my cell phone most frequently because it is portable, so it is convenient.
>
> I can use the iPad well because it is easier to handle, just touch.

In these quotes, the participants refer to the materiality of the mobile devices such as their small size, portability, and potential for easy haptic manipulation. Sociomaterial theory suggests that the materiality of the device itself plays a pivotal role in shaping and directing the meaning-making processes. Mobile devices move with a person physically across locations and facilitate easy and regular communication (such as messaging), consumption of media, and searching for information, including translation and access to services where needed. Thus, the device becomes integral to the navigation of many life choices because of its proximity to the everyday actions of a person. In addition to the mobility of the device as the user carries it across many settings, the device itself creates a direct connection between the natural propensity to touch objects in the world and the functionality afforded through interaction with the touch screen. This is clearly not the same level of interaction as experienced with other computer devices. Finally, because of its small size and mobility, a mobile phone provides a means of connecting and integrating the various meaning spaces in a person's life, be it their place of learning, their home, or their community. In this way, a mobile device becomes a technology for converging the disparate worlds of a person.

The focus group participants reported a number of digital literacy practices that they engaged in with the help of their mobile devices on a regular basis. Many of them regularly accessed the online news about Australia, home countries, or other places globally. They watched the news on YouTube or other platforms and/or read the news using their devices. For two of the participants, accessing the news was their favourite activity:

> I use the Internet very often, addicted to it. To see the news, like the news about Hong Kong, Canada, Russia. The news is great!
>
> I often use an iPad and YouTube. To read or watch the news.

Googling information related to everyday activities was another practice reported by the participants. While one participant described this experience in a somewhat generic way, another provided a more specific example of how she often used Google to find recipes:

> When I need to search something, I can use Google, everything will appear. It is a great device to use in our life.
>
> For example, if I want to cook something, I just type, and it appears immediately. I do not use the computer at home, I just use the iPad to search for things I want.

Langfield's learners also reported using their mobile devices to engage in communication with family members, friends, and teachers, mainly through messaging. One participant reported the communicative potential of mobile devices, while another used messaging to manage her small business and communicate for work purposes:

> I often use an iPad because it has many functions. For example, I can send messages.
>
> I have Facebook, Messenger, email, Zalo accounts. I have to use Zalo for managing my business. It is like a group of people... When I send a message, everyone gets it: some do management, and some execute the assigned tasks.

Although it was less common, some also mentioned email as an important communication channel. This included communication with government services, such as Centrelink:

> I use the cell phone to check mail.
>
> All information that Centrelink sends me, I use the cell phone or the iPad at home.

Other participants referred to leisure practices as another example of what they do with technology.

> I often watch YouTube, to watch comedies or soap operas [on the iPad].
>
> There are many games that we can both play and learn English.

The participants often used technologies for independent English language learning. These were self-initiated practices. One participant described her use of language learning applications, another named Google and YouTube as useful platforms for language learning, and the third participant referred to translation tools:

> I have downloaded some applications to learn English. I often get online to use them. That application is amazing. It teaches me an English word, then it asks me to check the equivalent in Vietnamese or vice versa. That helps me remember the word very well... When I search for it [a word], I see it, but I actually do not know how to read it out, but now I open in the application, it reads, and I repeat and read the words more correctly.

> I often use mobile phones to access Google or YouTube to get information related to learning English.
>
> When getting home, I use the iPad or cell phone to translate words and learn a little further. They serve as translators very nicely.

These examples illuminate a number of digital literacy practices that were central to the participants' lives such as accessing different types and sources of information, interacting with different people via different platforms, spending free time, and engaging in self-initiated English language learning. The above examples were not unique or unusual: such experiences can be found in repertoires of practices of everyone who carries a digital device. However, what was notable about these participants is the way in which they engaged in these practices. The participants' digital literacy practices almost always involved checking the meaning of the new words or phrases with the help of their mobile devices.

The participants reported that if they, for example, watched YouTube or read news and came across unfamiliar English words or phrases, they usually translated the words and checked their meaning with the help of dedicated apps on their mobile devices in the context of their digital literacy practices:

> Whenever I do not know an English word, I need to check it on my mobile phone.
>
> For example, if I do not know a word, I can search to learn its meaning. I think here I use my cell phone most frequently because it is portable, so it is convenient: whenever I do not know something, I can take it out and check right away. I just type in keywords and search it out.

Again, the utility of the device-in-the-hand is evident here in its proximity and availability, and these participant descriptions suggest that in their digital literacy practices, they often moved between the text content and the language itself. Indeed, vocabulary plays an important role in meaning-making and understanding a text. Without knowing what most of the words mean, it can be difficult, even impossible, to participate in a digital literacy practice and achieve its social purpose. The participants used the same approach even when digital texts drew on several modes of meaning-making (such as visual and video materials) which could help infer the meaning.

This strategic use of digital devices suggests that they were deliberately taking up opportunities for language learning offered through their everyday digital literacy practices. Rather than seeing these participants as passive learners, we regard them as aware and active language learners, keen to gain proficiencies that will facilitate their participation in Australian society. As we discuss later, in the conventional parlance of adult education, they might be described as self-directed language learners. Digital devices and everyday digital literacy practices may be seen as identity resources which teachers can utilise to develop language interactions, networking into community, and self-directed language learning.

Learning with technologies at Langfield

As briefly introduced in Chapter 3, the use of digital technologies was central to teaching and learning at Langfield. The *Techno-Tuesday* programme offered at the institution was specifically dedicated to learning about digital technologies and provided further opportunities for learners to develop their digital literacies. While we discuss *Techno-Tuesday*, its design and pedagogies employed in the programme in a more detailed way in Chapter 5, in the context of this chapter, we explore the learners' experiences with and perspectives on this programme to fully understand the repertoires of their everyday and institutional practices.

The participants had a very positive opinion about the digital dimension of their learning at Langfield and they especially enjoyed the *Techno-Tuesday* programme. Within this programme, they appreciated its three-fold focus on mobile phones, iPads, and desktop computers providing an opportunity to learn about and with different technologies. As one focus group participant observed: "Both iPad and computer, or even the phone is good. They are all good". It seems that the learners were receptive to a range of digital technologies within their learning programmes. Reflecting the opinion of all focus group participants, two learners further elaborated on why they enjoyed these classes:

> I like this class [*Techno-Tuesday*] because the teacher teaches in a way that facilitates my understanding. I can acquire the knowledge and skills faster. I've learned a lot.
>
> When we study here, the teachers train us in using emails, how to get to YouTube. She teaches us enthusiastically... I really like the class.

The learners stated clearly that they enjoyed the *Techno-Tuesday* programme because they felt they were able to develop new skills, knowledge, and understandings in relation to digital technologies. They felt that they were learning "a lot" and this made the programme effective and, thus, enjoyable for them. Importantly, they referred to the most essential aspects that, indeed, can determine the success of the programme: the range of technologies available, the learning content, and pedagogies used by their teachers. This data suggests that they were well aware about what makes learning effective and relevant for them. Reflecting their everyday experiences identified and discussed in this chapter, the central finding here is that these EAL adults from refugee and migrant backgrounds unequivocally viewed and positioned themselves as learners. In other words, they were active in their learning, drew on a range of resources to support their learning and enacted a strong learner identity across different domains of their lives.

Learners' challenges

When asked about the challenges that the participants faced in their experiences with technologies, their responses varied depending on the context of technology use. For example, in reference to technology use at home, all of them described themselves as "confident" and "fairly confident" in their ability to use mobile devices even if they faced difficulties. Interestingly, describing their digital experiences, participants said that they "have a lot of difficulties" but they did not seem to feel very stressed about these difficulties with mobile devices in the home settings. At the same time, some of them realised that not all activities can be accomplished with mobile devices. One participant reflected on her desire to search and apply for a job:

> I want to learn to use the computer so that I can write email, search information and all things that I need there. I also want to learn [how to use a computer] so that I can look for and apply for a job in Google. It is easier [with a computer]. For every job, I need to submit my resume. People have asked me to do so, but I did not know how to. I had never done it, so I couldn't figure out how to do this. I felt so lonely because nobody helped me. Well, my English was not so good… so I felt stressed. I wanted to show my pride by doing it by myself, without begging people for help.

As this participant clearly articulated, practices such as searching and applying for a job and writing a resume can be performed more effectively with the help of a computer and also through engaging with relevant online platforms. However, she saw her knowledge and familiarity with computer technologies and online platforms as well as the level of language competency required for these digital practices, as insufficient, and thus she felt challenged by this experience. Her use of phrases "felt lonely", "stressed", and "begging people for help" illuminates the sense of frustration and disempowerment associated with limited digital literacies required for finding, applying for, and getting a job.

These different responses suggest that the level of participants' digital literacies varied. They were comfortable and familiar with some everyday digital literacy practices (e.g. finding a recipe online with the help of a mobile device) and had relevant knowledge skills and understandings to engage in them confidently. However, there were also practices that they were less familiar or even unfamiliar with, as evident in the quote above. For this participant, searching and applying for a job as well as writing a CV were not a part of her previous life experience, even in a home language, which was further limited by her English language difficulties and unfamiliarity with a desktop computer.

Another important insight offered by the participants during the focus group was related to their experience with digital technologies and computers in public spaces. One participant said:

> You know, when I go to some council's office, I see them use the computer. I feel curious and want to learn to use it. Sometimes the officers there use "heavy" words with me, but I did not know how to talk back. You know, many of them look down on me, they criticise me, and use bad words with me… I hate them. I do not know how to talk back. I just follow whatever

> they want me to do. And then they often say this and that. Honestly, I am upset. I want to learn.

In this reflection, the participant referred to her challenging experience of using a computer in the local council office to access government services online. She could not figure out how to do what she needed to do on the government platform and requested assistance from the office worker. Indeed, these platforms are often complex and heavily rely on understanding the English language and knowledge of specific social practices such as claiming Medicare benefits or getting Centrelink payments. Furthermore, the stakes of "getting it right" are high as completing forms incorrectly may have serious (often financial) consequences.

The digital literacy practices required for successful use of these platforms were not yet a part of the participant's repertoire of practices, but she understood their relevance and importance and, thus, wanted to learn them. With this strong motivation and desire ("I wanted to learn"), she needed appropriate linguistic, social, and technological scaffolding to develop skills and confidence. People who have skills associated with accessing, navigating, and understanding government services are best positioned to scaffold such learning. However, as evident in the quote, her reported experience was one of humiliation and frustration, with a suggestion that the council officer treated her with a lack of cultural understanding. As the participant said, she completed what she needed to do by following the officer's prompts, but this experience was not necessarily meaningful and, thus, not conducive to learning the functional digital literacies needed in this complex space. At the same time, she did not let this upsetting experience damage her motivation to learn these complex digital literacies: she remained determined to learn them.

Using desktop computers represented a challenge for all the participants in the context of the classroom, while using mobile devices for learning was reported to be easier. In fact, they often separated these two different technologies in their narratives about learning at Langfield. On participant said:

> I can use an iPad, but I am terrible at using the computer... The computer has a mouse... When I am in the computer class, I am confused using the mouse.

Two other learners referred to the same experience:

> About the computer, I am very slow in using it. But for the iPad, I think I can handle it better.

> I feel that the iPad is more suitable for us. We are not used to manipulating the computer because using the mouse to look for a function is [more] difficult than with the iPad. And typing is more convenient [on the iPad].

To explain their challenges, the participants mainly referred to the physical attributes of a desktop computer and their difficulties with using some computer accessories such as a mouse and a keyboard. The teachers also noted this issue. For example, Nicole reflected on teaching learners to use a computer mouse:

> The double click was hard for them because they clicked too slowly. Yeah, so the double click was hard.

For these EAL learners, using mobile devices seemed to be easier and, thus, more appealing than a desktop computer because they seemed to be more adept at haptic gestures required to navigate icons and other features of touchscreen devices. This can be explained by the similarity of the swipe and tap gestures with the gestures used in the physical everyday world (e.g. turning a page, pressing a button). The materiality of mobile devices appears to be a better match with the embodied everyday experiences of these learners.

In contrast, using a mouse and keyboard was viewed as foreign to their lifeworld and, thus, deemed to be more difficult. To describe how difficult manipulating them was, one participant used a metaphor, "a tiger eating peanuts". This metaphor suggests that the fine motor control and complex eye-hand coordination required to operate a computer and associated peripherals were difficult for the participants. The interface design between the desktop computer and the user was the key issue. Whereas for many users, there is an implicit understanding of and proficiency with the design of a desktop computer, this cannot be assumed for new settlers from refugee and migrant backgrounds. Given that the materiality (the shape, "feel", and input protocols) of a computer is fundamental to the successful input from a user, it is likely to take time for learners in this context to acquire proficiency with this materiality.

Learners' strengths and resources

The participants did not seem to be anxious about their challenges with technologies in everyday life and classrooms; at the same time, they acknowledged that engaging in digital literacy practices was not easy. What was significant is how they navigated these issues and what helped them in these experiences. There were a number of strengths, assets, and resources which they actively employed in their experiences with digital technologies. They aided engagement in digital literacy practices and extended the participants' digital literacies: awareness of oneself as a learner, familiarity with mobile devices, home languages, personal networks, and teachers.

Awareness of oneself as learner

Langfield's learners appeared to be very self-aware of their feelings, motives, values, actions, and preferences related to learning. In other words, each of them had a very good awareness of oneself as a learner. Enjoyment of learning, including learning digital literacies, appeared to be the strongest theme in the participants' narratives. Many learners shared this passion during the focus groups. Here are three examples:

> I like learning and want to know more things.
>
> Learning is great. I love learning.
>
> I like to know more things.

The same passion was evident in their discussion of the *Techno-Tuesday* programme and the opportunities for learning digital literacies that it provided. Reflecting the perspective of all focus group participants, one learner said:

> I like to study this class [*Techno-Tuesday*] so that when I need to go to some council office, I know what to do. They [council officers] often point me to a computer and ask me to do this and that. If I know how to use the computer by learning it here [Langfield], I will know how to handle it, at least a little.

The participants saw digital literacies as functional and purposeful in their lives, and so there was a clear motivation to learn them for significant personal outcomes. In the quote above, as well as in the participant's description of the humiliating incident in the council office referred to earlier, it is evident that these learners were astute about the place of digital technologies in mediating their lives: for education, for information, for job seeking, for accessing services, and for many other essential components of settlement in Australia. Such awareness motivated these adult learners, even when facing multiple challenges and emotionally unpleasant experiences associated with using digital technologies. They did not appear to us to be discouraged by these difficulties, technological or communicational, but instead, were persistent in grappling with the inherent complexities of (what was for them) new technologies.

The learners also displayed a constructive attitude to challenges in using some technologies at Langfield. We mentioned earlier, they found it difficult to learn in the computer room, but, paradoxically, they also appreciated and preferred this component of *Techno-Tuesday*:

> My preference would go for the computer. Although I do not know much about it, I still like it. I do like it, so I always join the computer group on Tuesday afternoon. One of the reasons is because I have known how to use the iPad, I want to learn something new. And in the computer, there are more functions, so it is better.

Another participant noted:

> When the teacher asked us to go to the computer lab, we moved immediately, but it took me hours to get into the e-mail. I do not use it often, but

the teacher asked us to compose it. People usually spend some minutes to complete, but it took me hours but [still] unfinished. The mouse just did not move, it stuck. It was so difficult for me, like it was dead. But I tried to learn. Every Tuesday afternoon, we are here to learn.

What stands out in these quotes is that while they found the use of computers demanding, they did not avoid the computer room. Rather, they felt very motivated to embrace these difficulties. They recognised that "learning something new" and wrestling with obstacles, such as a "stuck" mouse, are part of their ongoing learning journey. For the most part, they were looking for longer term rewards as an outcome of persevering with short-term frustrations and difficulties.

The adult EAL learners appeared to be aware of their ongoing learning needs and preferences which helped them to remain committed to the encumbrances often experienced with technologies. Indeed, in our engagement with them and from the point of view of their teachers, they employed every opportunity provided at Langfield to further enhance their digital skills and knowledge. This is noteworthy because many of the learners were adults who had experienced diverse, often difficult, life circumstances which might be expected to significantly affect their attendance at adult education classes and their motivation to learn. For example, a number of the participants referred to their age and health issues. One participant openly shared her story about physical and mental health issues associated with relocation to Australia, while another referred to her frenetic family life:

> Since I came here, my life is under huge pressure… The doctor did not agree for me to participate in learning… But I told myself that if I am here and just let my life flow wherever it wants, my life will be darkened. So, I asked my doctor to participate in learning…

> The biggest challenge is I have two kids who are studying in two different schools. The one in grade 11 does not have a fixed timetable. Some days he gets home at 12.00, sometimes at 13.00. Sometimes I want to attend a class, but it is time to pick him/her up. Then I have to pick up the younger kid, so I feel distracted. When I am learning, I suddenly remember it is time to pick them up, I have to stop and go pick them up. So, this prevents me from studying effectively. But I do try my best.

These narratives bring attention to the significant difficulties that these adult learners had to deal with in their everyday lives. At the centre of these narratives is each participant's desire to learn as well as their strong commitment to ongoing education as a pathway to success in Australia. One participant reflected on her life and realised it would be "dark" without learning and this encouraged her to ask her doctor to allow class attendance. Another describes difficulties associated with managing her children's school hours and her learning timetable. She often had to sacrifice her own learning, but she always "tried [her] best" to attend the classes and remained committed to her education. These stories of enterprise and resilience in the face of complex demands characterise the experiences of these adult EAL learners, who found ways to be flexible, adaptable, and to "bounce back" from adversity and circumstances that some might find crushing.

In addition to understanding their learning needs and recognising that learning digital literacies is core to successful settlement, the participants were capable of explaining what works best for them in learning. In the data excerpts below, the participants report what they found to be effective for their learning: teacher modelling and demonstration, utilising close observation, active listening, and attention to detail in their work.

> Initially, the teacher demonstrates how to use the devices, then I imitate her. It's all [my digital skill] thanks to her.
>
> **FOCUS GROUP PARTICIPANT:** The teacher gives each of us an iPad and shows us what to do, like how to turn it on, which button to push or touch, when we search, which one should we press…
> **RESEARCHER:** Is it effective for you?
> **FOCUS GROUP PARTICIPANT:** It is. It is.

The participants also highlighted the importance of learning in manageable and sequential small chunks. They believed that this strategy can help them to "climb step by step" in their learning as evident in this focus group conversation among participants:

> In reality, students cannot acquire all things taught on the day, and the next day, more things need to be acquired, and that cycle would continue, so the students will get overwhelmed…
>
> …It is just that our capacity is limited, so if the teacher tries to give more input, we cannot actually acquire it.
>
> Well, just one statement: The teacher should consider students' learning capacity to organise their teaching. That's it.
>
> Yeah, the teachers should know our limit, and just stay within it.
>
> True, if they teach us much, we will not improve anyway.
>
> And we feel more pressure.

Several learners emphasised the importance of repetition to reinforce and consolidate learning about digital technologies:

> If the teacher teaches something important… the next day, they should check it again. I believe that will be much better that way.

The data suggests that the participants were aware of the efficacy of their learning and were capable of articulating their own strengths and preferences as learners.

The learners articulated a substantial level of self-consciousness and demonstrated metacognition through reflexivity about learning and their learning preferences. In addition, they reported the ability to be flexible, adaptable, and relatively confident about their capacity to solve problems and find solutions to the challenges they faced. To put it simply, since they had overcome other significant life challenges, including in many cases tragedy and trauma experienced in their country of origin, they were not going to be defeated by difficulties with using digital devices and navigating online digital platforms.

Familiarity with mobile devices

As discussed above, the participants reported that their personal mobile devices were their preferred technologies, and they were familiar and confident in using them. This familiarity became another important resource for dealing with difficulties when using technologies in everyday life and in the classroom learning at Langfield. In our discussion of the participants' everyday digital literacy practices earlier in this chapter, we noted how searching the meaning of the words or phrases with their mobile devices was one of their central strategies for participation in a digital literacy practice. In the context of this section, it is important to note that the participants clearly perceived their mobile devices as an expansive learning resource in everyday life:

> I use the iPad or cell phone to translate words and learn a little further. They work as translators very nicely.

> Whenever I have free time, I log in my cell phone and study further.

Likewise, the participants deployed their mobile devices in the context of the classroom. Several participants reflected on their use of phones to support formal learning:

> Sometimes we asked the teacher to write what she talked about but we did not get what she was talking on the board, then we searched it using our phone. Then we know what the teacher was teaching about.

> When I am here at school, I often take the photos of what the teacher writes on the board to help me remember what I have learned. Whatever I do not understand, I often open my phone to review, trying to put it into my head, especially when I am bored.

During our visits to Langfield, we also observed that mobile phones were actively employed by the learners, including when learning in the computer room: they became, in effect, an important complementary technology for language learning, for recording teaching content, for assisting with understanding, and for navigating other technologies such as desktop computers. Their personal mobile devices were also an integrative technology in bringing together diverse worlds and solving complex problems using online resources. This complementary and integrative use of mobile devices by the learners is shown in this excerpt from our ethnographic field notes.

> **FIELD NOTES**
>
> The main task of Polly's session was to access the email accounts created last week and compose a short email to a peer. The learners were given a list of class emails, asked to choose anyone, and send them an email. The learners enthusiastically approached the task and, as they engaged in the learning activity, several of them took their mobile phones out of their pockets. One learner used it at the stage of accessing her email account. It soon became apparent that she was retrieving her username and password with its help as she took a picture of these important details last week while setting up her account. Another learner relied on her phone at the stage of composing. As Polly later explained to us, the learner was using Google translate on her phone to navigate the digital interface of her Gmail account as well as to compose a text. The third learner attempted to access her account on the computer but, having difficulties to do so, she switched to her phone. As she explained to the teacher, she wanted to practise sending an email rather than wasting class time trying to recover her password on a classroom computer.
>
> September 3, 2019

Langfield's policy allowed learners to use their mobile phones and teachers reported that they often observed their learners using phones for learning purposes in the classroom:

> The students are really good at using their phones. If they have the internet on their phones they use it for translating. Mainly Google translate.
>
> *(Polly)*

These examples suggest that the learners meaningfully used their personal devices for learning purposes across contexts and in different ways. The data points to the important role of their familiarity and confidence with personal devices. Many of them did not have mobile phones before arriving in Australia but even in this comparatively short journey with their phones, they accumulated valuable knowledge and experiences which they were readily bringing to new learning experiences within and outside Langfield. For them, mobile devices were an important learning resource for review, confirmation, clarification, or extension of meaning and a powerful tool for building confidence and giving learners agency over their own learning.

Home language

A home language was also identified as another integral asset that the participants used to negotiate difficulties that emerged in their digital literacy practices. As discussed above, both in everyday life and in the classrooms, the participants translated the meaning of the words or phrases which they did not know with the help of translation apps on their mobile devices. Home languages were central to all digital literacy practices that they engaged in. In other words, the continuing use of home languages as a linguistic resource was a unique feature of these learners' practices. One participant described her experiences of using her home language for meaning-making in digital spaces:

> If there is anything that I do not know, I will check it on my phone to understand the meaning. Sometimes I do not understand [a digital text], truly do not understand. So I use both English and Vietnamese.

We noted in Chapter 3 that Langfield had a strong multilingual stance, acknowledging learners' linguistic repertoires and welcoming home languages. During the observation sessions, we also saw that learners frequently used home languages as part of their meaning-making literacy practices. For example, the field notes above (e.g. Polly's email class) describe the learner who was using the cross-language features of Google translate on her phone when working with a desktop computer to navigate the digital interface of her Gmail account and then create an email. Another example was observed in Nicole's class:

FIELD NOTES

Home languages are welcomed in Nicole's class. Being bilingual herself, Nicole occasionally uses Vietnamese to interact with Vietnamese-speaking learners. This helps them better understand the learning content as well as the classroom instructions. The learners also seem to be very comfortable to use their home languages when needed. In this learning session, there were a few instances when Vietnamese-speaking learners were translating Nicole's instructions to their peers who did not fully understand the instructions on how to access a video camera on the mobile phones. As learners began to record the interviews in pairs, a pair of Vietnamese-speaking learners actively discussed the task in Vietnamese before proceeding with the task. Another pair of Mandarin-speaking learners laughed and exchanged several comments in Mandarin after watching their recording together. Moving between languages seemed so fluid and natural for these learners.

August 27, 2019

This data suggests that, for these learners, home languages played a crucial role in their digital literacy practices. They regularly employed home languages as valuable linguistic resources both in everyday and institutional context to deal with meaning-making in digital spaces. Using technology in a new language requires knowing and understanding the meaning of the words, phrases, and texts, and also more nuanced contextual understandings. These language learners understood that home languages can assist with such meaning-making and, importantly, they had a range of different strategies: translation, peer tutoring, and peer assistance. All of these approaches were endorsed and operationalised within the classroom environment. Using home languages as a resource was especially helpful in understanding learning concepts in relation to digital literacies, relevant digital vocabulary, instructions, and in developing teacher-learner and learner-learner relationships.

Personal networks

The majority of the participants reported contacting their personal networks to get help when they faced obstacles in their digital literacy practices. Family members, especially the participants' children, were frequently reported as the main source of learning digital literacies. They often viewed the younger generation as more tech-savvy:

> Sometimes my child teaches me ... if I ask him/her what it means. I feel good that way.
>
> I have a kid at home. It was difficult to start [using iPad], but I asked my kid whatever I did not know.
>
> I sometimes ask my nephew if I do not know something.

For some participants, personal networks were a valuable resource. As evident in the quotes above, they were happy and comfortable to ask their children to help with technology. It is important to note that some participants' children were adults, while others had school-aged children who assisted them with technologies. Interestingly, personal networks were not only used for dealing with immediate digital problems; they were positioned by the participants as a source of learning digital literacies. One participant, referring to YouTube, said that while initially children helped to access and navigate the platform, this collaborative experience allowed her to develop relevant skills, knowledge, and understandings to be able to use it independently. She seemed to be very confident about using this digital media platform and reported that she developed this confidence with the help of her family members:

> Previously, I asked my children and they taught me to use it [YouTube]. Then I did it by myself reasonably well.

However, whilst the children were an important source of support for some learners, it was not the case for everyone in this group. One learner shared her experience:

> Sometimes my son taught me to use the laptop, so I can handle it. But sometimes I use it in the wrong way, so he yells at me. My English is not like his, because he was born here, so I cannot ask him for help. He told me not to hit this and that, but sometimes, I hit a button, and all disappears. He yells at me.

While some adult learners in this study received relevant support with digital technologies at home and developed some aspects of their digital literacies from more knowledgeable others through supportive interactions, other participants did not. For them, the opportunities for such learning at home were limited and, thus, not fully empowering. In learning to use technologies effectively and in the processes of acquiring digital literacies, it is important to recognise the agency of the learner. This is the capacity of a learner to exercise choices and engage in learning independently. For choice and independence to be available to a learner in the use of technologies, baseline competencies are imperative. The data above suggests that such competencies are not learnt effectively in an atmosphere of judgement but where there is consistency of practice with technologies and the building of motivation to learn.

In addition to family members, the participants also referred to other people in their lives who were able to assist with technology such as friends and neighbours:

> Generally, my sisters [meaning her female friends, not her siblings] showed me how to use it.

> The iPad… is small, we can take it with us to our neighbours' or friend's house.

The participants' friends and neighbours were enlisted to assist in digital literacy practices as a type of collaborative community. We observed the same approach in the context of the classroom when learners sought help and assistance from their peers. As part of peer support, we noted the important role of mobile devices in this learning community experience, whether at Langfield or in the wider community. The facility of mobile phones for supportive communicative exchanges (texting, sharing content, interacting on social media platforms) was important for establishing understanding and overcoming barriers with using technologies.

Teachers

A further key resource which played a significant role in how the participants navigated different digital literacy practices within and beyond Lingfield was their teachers. To illustrate teachers' significance in the life of learners, it is worth noting that during a 30-minute focus group discussion, the word "teacher" was used 68 times in the first group and 53 times in the second group. Beyond these quantitative details, there were learners' insightful reflections on what Langfield's teachers meant to them, with three responses given below:

> Whatever I did not understand, I would call the teacher to show me.

> The teacher knows a lot. She knows more than our friends. My friends are just like me. For example, sometimes we know a word, but my friend does not know and vice versa, but the teacher knows all, knows everything. When we ask the teacher, she not only knows the word, but also explains to us related things.

> The teacher taught us to write emails, like writing an email to the teacher to inform her that I am sick, or to book for an appointment… The teacher also taught us to use the map on our phone.

In the context of classrooms at Langfield, the teachers were seen as the main source of learning. According to the learners, all that they learnt was due to the teachers' efforts. While we noted earlier in this chapter that peers were often central to the participants' learning in the classrooms, the quote above suggests that teachers were positioned as more knowledgeable and skilful than peers, so there was a hierarchy of authority that appears to operate implicitly for learners. In the classroom context, the participants mainly relied on teachers, at least initially:

> At first, I only studied when the teacher approached. But later, I accessed the page, asked people around how to do this and that, how to read this word or how that word is written.

As this participant noted, learning with and from the teacher was important, but learning became less dependent on the teacher with time as learners were developing more confidence through collaborative and independent learning experiences. This is not to diminish the significant place of teachers in the lives of their students. Two participants stated the following about how much they appreciated teachers' work:

> I think the teacher often gives help for us to learn. Generally, all teachers are helpful. In my opinion, they are all good.

> Teachers are enthusiastic and caring for each student. When someone does not understand, they would explain until that person understands.

The recognition and appreciation for the work of teachers extended beyond learning new digital and language skills. The quote shows recognition of the "caring" environment at Langfield, an environment created and maintained by its teachers and appreciated by learners. This was significant for these often "wounded" learners. They saw their teachers as pivotal to their happiness, well-being, and adjustment to a new country:

> I feel that I am happy and comfortable in the class. I can see my friends while studying here. We can communicate and see the teacher. Whenever I am sad or in trouble, she always lends a hand.

> The teacher never makes us nervous. Sometimes I feel stressed due to life circumstances, but when I am here, she is helpful.

It is important to emphasise that successful learning of digital literacies, in the context of EAL learning and settlement in a new country such as Australia, not only requires teacher expertise but also teacher empathy and deep connection to the needs and aspirations of learners from migrant and refugee backgrounds.

Thinking about curriculum and pedagogy

The conventional view may be that Langfield adult learners from immigrant, refugee, and/or asylum-seeking backgrounds have experienced and continue to experience profound trauma, challenges, inequities, and barriers to effective resettlement and employment. In many cases this is true, but this "single story" (Adichie, 2009, n.p.) is not the whole picture – it is indeed more complex than that. This chapter aims to challenge the dominant focus on what these adults lack, what is holding them back or what they need to be given. Whilst not ignoring the evident needs of this group of learners, we want to propose a more nuanced way of positioning these learners: as active and resourceful in pursuing their language and digital learning needs. The digital literacy practices of the adult EAL learners in this study should be viewed as a resource and a foundation within adult education contexts such as Langfield, so that learning opportunities to meet their growing aspirations can be offered.

This study found that, in their everyday lives, the participants consistently engaged in digital literacy practices with the help of mobile devices such as phones and iPads and felt confident and comfortable in using these devices for a range of communicative and learning purposes. This finding echoes and contributes further evidence to the previous research which documented high levels of mobile phone penetration in refugees' households (Alencar, 2020; Epp, 2017; McCaffrey & Taha, 2019). Building on this work, our research brings attention to the importance and potential of the ubiquitous "smart phone", or digital tablet – in other words, the device-in-the-hand. The findings in this chapter suggest the important role that mobile devices play in the lives of people from refugee and migrant backgrounds as they settle in a new country. It also offers additional insights into the reasons for this technological preference – the inherent materiality of the devices in terms of design, proximity, and immediacy of usage, portability, and familiar intuitive haptics similar to routine movements from everyday life.

In contrast to previous literature that often described the role of phones in a somewhat broad way – "facilitating devices, or survival tools" (Alencar, 2020, p. 9) – this research documented more specific examples of participants' everyday uses and the integrative ways that these digital devices fitted with their lives. While the participants' repertoires of digital literacy practices were not very extensive, they did connect different domains of their lives and were central to converging a range of digital needs. Their typical practices included accessing different types and sources of information, interacting with a range of people via diverse platforms, participating in leisure activities and engaging in self-initiated English language learning. These practices reflect some findings by Alam and Imran (2015) who found that digital technologies were seen by refugee participants as bringing "improvements in the lives of refugee migrants in terms of access to information, communication with family and friends, e-services, and for education and employment opportunities" (p. 358).

The participants in this study engaged in some of these practices, but digital literacies associated with using government services, banking, billing, shopping, health, and employment were not identified by the participants as their typical digital experiences. Although these are important practices for settlement (Chapman & Williams, 2015; Kenny, 2016; Shariati et al., 2017), it seems that they were not a routine part of the participants' repertoire of practices. Thus, the participants attempted to get help in government offices or, as Langfield's teachers mentioned, these digital activities were usually completed by learners' families. In both cases, someone did this for the participants which was helpful but not always conducive to ongoing learning and autonomy. The participants were willing to extend and develop their repertoire of digital literacy practices, especially those that involve the use of computers, but outside of Langfield, there were very limited relevant learning opportunities for these learners to develop these digital literacies in a safe, scaffolded, situated, and meaningful way.

Exploring the participants' digital literacy practices from a socio-cultural perspective allowed us to highlight the unique ways in which these adult EAL learners engaged in practices with mobile devices, not previously identified in the literature. Checking meaning, whether with the help of Google Translate or any other digital resources or apps, was central to all their digital literacy practices. Thus, in their digital literacy practices, the participants were constantly moving between the digital text content and the language itself to check the meaning and extend their understanding required for a practice. Previous research has also revealed that the desire to become part of the host culture can foster refugees' use of mobile phones for language and cultural learning (Alencar, 2020; Tudsri & Hebbani, 2015). However, these earlier experiences mainly included decontextualised use of specific language-learning technologies (e.g. specific apps for language learning or Google Translate) (Epp, 2017). The participants in this research *seamlessly* integrated the use of these apps into their everyday practices to support their meaning-making and ultimately their ability to settle successfully.

The participants were intentional in pursuing language learning opportunities that emerged across the array of social and learning domains in their lives. In other words, while their everyday digital literacy practices had specific social purposes (e.g. communication, accessing relevant information, entertainment, etc.), they also saw the need to be agential and independent in their English language learning. This finding suggests that the participants were active and aware language learners with technologies, not passive recipients of second language instruction. They were keen to extend and master their digital literacies although they were not necessarily thinking about mastery of digital literacies *per se*. Such identities and the associated digital literacy practices provided tangible opportunities for learning digital literacies in a very situated and contextualised way – in authentic practices with real texts, live audiences, and genuine purposes.

While the participants acknowledged that engaging in digital literacy practices was not easy, they did not seem to be anxious about their challenges with technologies in everyday life and classrooms. In challenging situations, they mobilsed a number of strengths, assets, and resources to deal with technology and language issues. Some previous research has explored the issue of digital exclusion but the literature often focuses on frustrations or inabilities to use digital technologies due to barriers related to language, access, and skills to use the technology (Lloyd et al., 2013). Similarly, Alam and Imran (2015) focus on adult learners "attitudes towards, awareness of and skills in using the technology" (p. 346), and again the emphasis rests on challenges, inequalities, and barriers – suggesting a deficit mindset. We do not think that these barriers, inequities and challenges are insignificant. Indeed, we recognise their potency and their impact.

However, this study challenges this body of research by taking a strengths-based approach in seeing adult learners in their active roles and agency as learners, both in formal learning contexts and in other settings. They felt motivated and determined to overcome their difficulties turning these into learning opportunities and using a range of resources, including their home languages, networks, prior knowledge, and affordance of their digital devices, to aid their learning. This is consistent with Deveson's work (2003) and with some other studies which argue that although adults from refugee backgrounds may have been exposed to traumatic experiences or have limited support in settlement contexts it does not mean they are "indelibly vulnerable" (Humpage et al., 2019, p. 11). This reframing that moves the discourse beyond the construct of "victim" is a valuable contribution – it is a perspective that educators can draw on, highlighting the way a new perspective can reorient practice and open up opportunities for meaningful dialogue and innovative learning strategies.

Previous research has emphasised the importance of a strengths-based perspective for exploring experiences of people from refugee backgrounds (Ryu & Tuvilla, 2018; Shapiro & MacDonald, 2017). However, this perspective has not been used previously to explore digital literacy practices. Informing our research with a strengths-based perspective, we are able to offer new insights into the strengths, assets and resources that adult language learners drew on in their personal strategies to deal with challenges and develop their digital literacies. Strategies included awareness of oneself as a learner, familiarity with mobile devices, home languages, personal networks, and teachers. These strengths included their pragmatic and self-aware stance towards seeing learning as a necessity as well as enjoyable. Their stance also reflected resilience and an ongoing commitment to learning.

We noted the participants' metacognition about their own capabilities, learning preferences, and agency as adult learners and problem-solvers. As has been echoed throughout this chapter, they actively employed their mobile devices for independent learning. They knew they were quite adept at using their devices. This perceived self-efficacy helped to build confidence which can be extended to other devices and practices. Their multilingual capability and cross-cultural experiences can also be seen as strengths. Although the Langfield learners in this study were relatively new English speakers, they employed their home languages as a positive resource to interpret their lifeworlds, build meanings, connect in networks, and enhance their formal learning at Langfield.

Viewed through this strengths-based lens, Langfield's learners also emerge as learners with effective connections and networks. This aided in rebuilding social capital, possibly eroded by previous experiences. In this ACE setting, they were rebuilding and extending their social capital (Falk et al., 2000) through their family (in Australia and overseas), neighbours, classmates, and teachers at Langfield. In turn, this enabled greater confidence for participating in digital literacy practices in the wider community, including retail settings, community contacts, and service providers. These connections played an important role in their learning of digital literacies, which became a strength needed for resettlement processes and in the quest for employment which perhaps has as much to do with social capital, networks, and connections as it does with inherent competencies or job-seeker capabilities (Nghia et al., 2020; Pham & Soltani, 2021). Adopting a strengths-based perspective does not make the challenges, inequities, and barriers go away, or disappear, but it can help to put them in a much more positive light.

Conclusion

In this chapter, we presented the first set of findings about digital literacy practices of Langfield's learners. By exploring what the participants did with technologies and the unique ways in which they engaged in multilingual digital literacy practices, we argued that these adult EAL learners enacted strong learner identities across different domains of their lives. We also discussed the participants' challenges but noted their resilience in difficult situations. This chapter challenged a deficit discourse that tends to frame these learners as helpless victims and emphasises what learners lack and cannot do. Adapting a strengths-based perspective, we reported on how the learners mobilised a number of strengths, assets, and resources to navigate these experiences. These findings have important implications for curriculum and pedagogy which are discussed in Chapter 8.

5
TEACHING AND LEARNING DIGITAL LITERACIES AT LANGFIELD

> **FIELD NOTES**
>
> Today we had an opportunity to observe the *Techno-Tuesday* programme and its creative design in action for the first time. At around 2pm after lunch, all 20 learners and three teachers – Polly, Susan, and Nicole – gathered in the classroom. After a brief discussion among the teachers, the learners were asked to form three smaller groups. One group of seven learners stayed with Nicole in this classroom; Susan, holding a set of iPads, took a group of six students to a smaller room with a round table adjacent to the classroom; Polly asked her group to move to the computer room next door. Next, three teachers simultaneously taught 30-minute sessions each focusing on a different digital practice and different digital devices – mobile phones, iPads, and desktop computers. The learners, split into three groups, rotated from one session to another while teachers stayed in the same learning space. In other words, each teacher taught the same material three times, while learners, in 90 minutes, attended three different classes with different teachers, technologies, and practices.
>
> August 27, 2019

This opening vignette offers a number of important points. It suggests a strong commitment of the participating teachers to digital literacies and finding a place for them in their already busy English language curriculum. It also highlights the richness of the learning opportunities which the programme offers within these 90 minutes. However, the most striking, perhaps, is the teachers' professional agency and their collaborative effort to initiate, conceptualise, and develop a relevant learning programme for their learners. In this chapter, we discuss these ideas in a more detailed way by exploring the place of digital literacies within teaching and learning at Langfield.

To understand how digital literacies were taught at Langfield and why certain approaches were taken, we start by exploring how participating teachers viewed the role of technology in the lives of their learners as well as how they understood the notion of digital literacies. This discussion is followed by the analysis of Langfield's approach to the provision of digital literacies with a specific focus on their unique programme, *Techno-Tuesday*, briefly introduced in Chapter 3. We explore what made this programme effective and successful for adult language learners by identifying its key features. We also analyse examples of practices observed at Langfield in relation to digital literacies to understand the extent to which digital literacies were taught and what made certain teaching practices successful. These insights are important for understanding the professional strengths and needs of the participants.

Perspectives on digital literacies: Surviving and thriving

The CEO and teachers recognised the importance of digital literacies for their learners. The CEO explained her point of view which reflected other teachers' opinions. Referring to Langfield's learners, she noted:

> It is about survival… It's becoming more and more important because all of their Centrelink engagement is now via either the web or the app. So, they've got to get handy with the app. There is so much literacy required to be able to manoeuvre… Digital literacy has become *incredibly* important for them because if they do not report to Centrelink, they lose their payments.
>
> (CEO)

Indeed, digital literacies were central to "survival" because learners' Centrelink payments were dependent on their ability to engage with the Centrelink App or website. For example, as a part of their payment plans, many Langfield's learners were required to sign in to the online system of the JobActive Program[1] every day to record their attendance to avoid payment suspensions and financial penalties. As reported by the teachers, it was not easy for learners and they often struggled and required the help of teachers or family members to access government services online. Thus, drawing on these observations, the teaching team had a pragmatic understanding that, for their learners, having digital literacies is "not a choice" (Polly), it is a necessity.

However, beyond the practicalities of accessing government payments, there was a broader vision about the importance of digital literacies for their adult learners. For example, Polly said:

> Think how much they use technology in their everyday lives! Like appointment confirmations, myGov,[2] ringing us when they are sick… It's all online

now and even when you order take-away, it can be online. I think digital literacy would make their lives easier.

(Polly)

In this excerpt, Polly reflected on the central role of digital technologies in adult learners' everyday lives. She correctly emphasised that many daily activities in different domains of their lives are increasingly digital: making appointments, accessing relevant information, communicating for different purposes, and even getting food. Polly's reflection suggests that she viewed digital literacies as important capabilities required to organise and manage everyday life. Importantly, the teachers thought that developing a foundational repertoire of digital literacies to navigate everyday life is pivotal not only to survive but also to thrive and grow in an environment of profound change. Two teachers stated:

> It's their life, it is their activities, it is their financial situation… [but] they are tied to their children when every two weeks they have to report forever. If they could just do that themselves I think it would be quite freeing.
>
> *(Tanya)*

> Some of the students often feel intimidated by their own children because their English isn't very good and so they feel disempowered a lot at home… They've said that once they learn how to operate a computer, they feel empowered and that they can usually do things online without asking their kids.
>
> *(Andrea)*

Tanya and Andrea reported that their adult learners were often digitally dependent on their families which made them feel "disempowered" and even "intimidated" at home. Viewing this as deeply problematic, Tanya and Andrea thought that developing digital literacies will be liberating and empowering for adult learners: they will be in control of their own digital experiences, needs, and aspirations, and this will provide an avenue to new opportunities in their lives and what we consider as "successful settlement". This points to an important aspect of strengths-based practices in adult education: the learning environment itself, and the positive beliefs about the capacity to learn engendered by the educators in that environment, can strongly enable learners to reach their potential and fulfil their aspirations.

Both Tanya and Andrea also recognised the significance of digital literacies that are central to the lives of their learners and shape how they manage and understand their worlds. Such practices have existential and cultural "force" in enabling positive settlement experiences in Australia. The capacity to manage digital devices and utilise them for a range of life purposes in Australian society seems to be important for the perceived self-efficacy of these adults. In developing digital literacies they are also gaining agency to create a life for themselves and their families in Australia.

As the participants of this study talked about the importance of digital literacies for adult learners from refugee and migrant backgrounds, they also shared their understanding of this complex concept. Given the dominant policy and media discourses around digital technologies, it is not surprising that the participants usually referred to the concept in a singular form (e.g. digital literacy) or used "digital skills". No one asked or questioned why we, the research team, use the term "digital literacies". In fact, one participant, Nicole, was confused by our use of "digital literacies" (plural) during the interview and clarified if we meant "digital literacy". As discussed in Chapter 2, there is a significant conceptual difference between "digital literacy" and "digital literacies". While the former conceptualises ability to use technology as a set of discrete, purposeful skills easily transferred from one context to another, the latter conceives digital literacies as dynamic social practices, closely connected and shaped by the contexts in which they are required and enacted.

The participants were probably unaware of these conceptual differences, but their definitions reflected these two different perspectives. Two teachers conceived the idea of digital literacies in the following ways:

> So for me, digital literacy means something basic: how to use the mouse, how to use the computer to do some basic things like using Word and Excel, or just go to the Internet to search for something.
>
> *(Nicole)*

> I don't know if it's right. It [digital literacy] is your ability to be able to use technology to find information to understand, maybe evaluate or to gather information in this sort of digital world.
>
> *(Susan)*

Nicole mainly viewed digital literacies as "basic" skills required to operate technology. Her example of the internet search was somewhat broad as she did not specify what skills, knowledge, and understandings are required to find information online and in what context. Susan's definition is also reflective of a mainstream discourse conceptualising digital literacy as a generic ability associated with accessing information. As evident in this data, Susan was hesitant when defining digital literacies, reflecting other teachers' experiences when defining the concept during the interviews.

In contrast, Andrea and Tanya had a more elaborated understanding of digital literacies.

> Digital literacy to me is a way of understanding something through a medium and it might be a written form, or a visual form.
>
> *(Andrea)*

> I see digital literacies as not just the skills to use it [technology]. It's part of it, but it is having that critical element of feeling confident to communicate on

these devices and understanding how to navigate them, to use them for their own purposes and being, I think, a little bit more active as a user.

(Tanya)

In her definition, Andrea explicitly refers to meaning-making as shaped by a digital environment which reflects the notion of "digital culture" that we explained in Chapter 2. Indeed, digital spaces, devices, and software shape meaning-making processes in their own unique ways. By referring to "a visual form", Andrea seems to understand that meaning-making in digital spaces can be multimodal. While she did not elaborate on a range of modes that have become increasingly central to digital literacy practices (e.g. aural, spatial, gestural), her acknowledgement of the importance of a visual mode is still significant. Tanya's definition seemed to be the most elaborated among the participants. While not ignoring the ability to operate technology mentioned by Susan and Nicole, Tanya thought that the use of technology is closely connected to social purposes, critical literacy, and agency. Her perspective seems to be aligned with a socio-cultural perspective on digital literacies by viewing them as situated social practices closely connected to social contexts reflecting different purposes.

It is evident that the teachers' definitions of digital literacies varied in terms of the scope, depth and complexity. Their confidence in articulating what they meant by "digital literacies" varied too. This is not to criticise the participants but to illuminate that the teachers may not have had opportunities to consider this complex term. The reciprocal exchange of ideas between the researchers and the teachers provided a unique opportunity for exploration of what digital literacies mean in practice (see Tour et al., 2020).

The *Techno-Tuesday* programme

As the importance of digital literacies has been recognised at Langfield, all participating teachers attempted to address the learners' digital needs in their class time. At the same time, the teachers honestly acknowledged that they "do not have a strong focus at this organisation on digital literacy" (Andrea) and "everyone's been doing bits and pieces on digital literacy" (CEO). The CEO seemed to be concerned about this ad hoc and reactive approach. During the interview, she emphasised several times a need for a renewed approach to digital literacies:

> I think we need a more systematic approach… So I would like to have an organisation-wide approach to digital literacy provision, so that everyone's sort of doing the same thing.

As the CEO explained, all teachers at Langfield used technology to teach different aspects of digital literacies, but her words imply a somewhat fragmented and disconnected approach across the organisation. While there was no cohesive initiative in relation to the provision of digital literacies in the institution, the need for this was recognised by the CEO, which she viewed as an essential step forward.

Importantly, Langfield had a practice foundation to build on: the *Techno-Tuesday* programme, collaboratively developed and taught by three teachers, was dedicated to digital literacies for adult learners who had an experience of disrupted schooling and often had only oral home language. The programme was well known in the institution, acknowledged by other teachers, and actively supported by the CEO. From the participants' perspectives, the programme was successful and effective for the learners. For example, Tanya said that "it's been a change" in learners' digital skills with introduction of *Techno-Tuesday*. While Polly reflected on the programme's success in the following way:

> I feel really positive that we do *Techno-Tuesday*. The students really enjoy it if you ask them. We did "what did I learn this year?" and most of them said "computers".
>
> *(Polly)*

During our visits to Langfield and observations of the programme, we noted high levels of engagement and productive work during these learning sessions. The learners also spoke highly about the programme during the focus groups as we reported in Chapter 4.

Thus, our research attention was immediately attracted by this programme as we wanted to understand what makes it effective for adult learners. The data analysis identified three important features of the *Techno-Tuesday* programme as contributing to its success: (1) integratedness, (2) comprehensiveness, and (3) collegiality. Below, we examine these features of the programme design and discuss what learning opportunities such design provided.

Integratedness

One of the central features of the *Techno-Tuesday* programme was what we call "integratedness". The programme was embedded into the language curriculum used by these three teachers. The programme appeared to be very popular among the adult EAL learners due to its unique design which we illustrate in Figure 5.1:

The rotating *Techno-Tuesday* programme with three teachers simultaneously teaching 30-minute sessions, each focusing on a different digital practice, was characterised by a high degree of integratedness within the EAL curriculum. Building on EAL content, it offered learning activities with mobile phones, iPads, and desktop computers. Many activities and content in the *Techno-Tuesday* programme were "very much interwoven" (CEO) into the language content that the learners were learning at the time. For example, Nicole said that the focus of *Techno-Tuesday* classes was often guided by the question – "What did we do this morning?". She further elaborated that if there was a focus on particular vocabulary in the morning, then the activities with technology in the *Techno-Tuesday*

Teaching and learning digital literacies 89

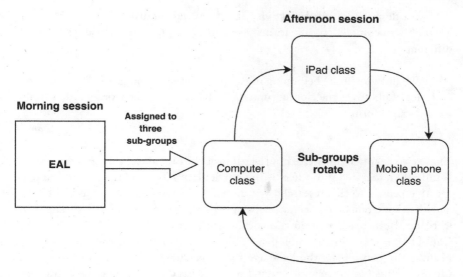

FIGURE 5.1 Design of *Techno-Tuesday*

class were also centred around this vocabulary. Indeed, these connections were evident in teaching as our field notes below suggest:

> **FIELD NOTES**
>
> To teach learners how to use a video-recording function on their mobile phones, Nicole started with a warm-up activity using the prompts on the whiteboard: (1) Your name; (2) Home country; (3) What fruit or vegetable do you like? (4) Why? Every learner had a chance to answer these questions and they seemed to be confident doing this. The learners referred to a wide range of fruit and vegetables and were using relevant vocabulary: cherry, bok choy, delicious, sweet, crisp. It was clear that the learners were well familiar with this content. Then Nicole paired the learners and asked them to interview each other, recording these short interviews using their personal smartphones. After some initial instructions about using the camera function of the smartphone, the students enthusiastically participated in the task. During the interviews and recording, there was significant student engagement, indicated by the laughter, active discussions, and the degree of focus evident. Following the turn-taking in recording interviews, Nicole gathered the whole group together and each pair showcased their recorded interviews for the whole group.
>
> August 27, 2019

Tanya described a similar activity that involved the use of Google forms to learn how to complete online forms often used for questionnaires and surveys in different contexts:

> We did a lot at the beginning of the year around clothing. So, I'd put a whole lot of photos of the clothing and they'd have to type the word in. It's basically Google forms.
>
> *(Tanya)*

These two examples illustrate how learning about digital technologies was almost seamlessly integrated into the existing curriculum reflecting the theoretical perspective central to this research: that digital literacies are new forms of literacy, and that far from being seen as separate, they should be integral to language learning. Both teachers used the vocabulary developed earlier to organise and scaffold learning with technologies. This allowed them not only to "recycle" (Tanya) and consolidate the language that was taught earlier but also to extend the use of this vocabulary into digital spaces. This created a solid foundation for developing new capabilities associated with the use of mobile phones and online forms and, as we observed in Nicole's class, made learning engaging and effective for the learners. Interestingly, Polly said:

> I think we could improve a lot more [when integrating digital literacies into the EAL curriculum] and I would like to have it more fluid in the classroom… not something separate.
>
> *(Polly)*

This quote suggests that the teachers felt that integrating digital literacies into their EAL curriculum offered many benefits to learners. However, it was not a consistent approach within the broader programmes at Langfield because they did not always know how to connect these different elements, or dimensions of their work. They felt that connections between the existing curriculum and the *Techno-Tuesday* content could be further strengthened. Still, the vision for this integratedness fits strongly with our notion in the book of seeing the learning context as a pivotal concern in understanding strengths-based learning.

Comprehensiveness

Comprehensiveness was another feature of the *Techno-Tuesday* programme. This was especially evident in how the programme was organised as captured in our field notes at the beginning of this chapter. The wide range of digital experiences available to learners in this 90-minute session, allowed by the rotating model of the programme, stood out for us in this observation session. This observation was also confirmed by the teachers during the interviews. For instance, reflecting on the main aim of the rotating model, Susan said: "Our idea was to expose them to all different types of technologies".

Tanya also reported that *Techno-Tuesday* allowed the "trialing [of] a whole lot of different activities". This was important for the learners because, for example, in Tanya's words, different digital technologies require "very different skills". Tanya's discourse is well aligned with some of the key theoretical considerations that inform this research. In particular, her language reflects the notion of "a digital literacy practice" that is situated and shaped by context, circumstances, and purposes. This data suggests that the *Techno-Tuesday* programme was designed to maximise the opportunities for students in the 90-minute learning session by including a range of digital technologies that can be typically found in people's everyday lives such as mobile phones, iPads, and desktop computers.

The materiality and presence of these devices in the lives and learning of the students should be seen as a resource that can build agency. Socio-material theory reminds us that the materiality of these devices (and the associated applications) is not peripheral to the lifeworld of people but central to meaning-making and to how people choose to act in the world. In short, digital devices not only make a difference in the lives of these learners, they, in fact, now create new life possibilities. The teachers recognised the need to engage with a range of different digital experiences technologies in the course of the programme, alongside language learning. In other words, the scope of the programme was quite comprehensive in terms of digital literacy practices that learners experienced, participated in, and learnt about.

Indeed, Langfield's learners also referred to the diversity of the learning experiences within the *Techno-Tuesday* programme as reflected in the response of the focus group participants below:

> Every Tuesday afternoon, we are here to learn about the computer, iPad and phones. The teacher taught us how to compose and send emails, use messenger, etc.

The learners recognised that *Techno-Tuesday* provided opportunities to experience and learn about diverse technologies and engage in different practices with these devices. Thus, learners' interactions with technology operated affectively and pragmatically in their lives.

Collegiality

Another feature of the programme design was the collegiality of the teachers that included a strong emphasis on team-teaching. As mentioned above, the three teachers simultaneously taught different components of the programme but their collaboration extended beyond simultaneous teaching. Tanya said that within this programme they "use each other as a resource" to deliver the programme signalling that collegiality was central to their work. Indeed, collaboration between the teachers was evident in the variety of activities related to the delivery of the *Techno-Tuesday* programme. The three teachers working in the *Techno-Tuesday* programme collaboratively planned for teaching, created a repository of teaching resources and critically reflected on their work.

For example, Polly said that they "try to get together in the holidays and plan" for the upcoming term, suggesting that they worked cooperatively to plan and set goals for the programme and lesson planning. As an example, Polly reported that, for several sessions, she focused on learners' mouse skills, which were further consolidated by Nicole in her sessions as the teachers did the rotation:

> They were just starting to get better at using their mouse skills. So, I asked Nicole if she could do another week or two just focusing on mouse skills. That was good.
>
> *(Polly)*

This collegial feature of the programme helped to achieve more flexibility and adaptability in the learning experiences of the learners and provided them with further opportunities to consolidate core skills with using input devices. The teachers also showed us what Polly called "a digital literacy folder" (Figure 5.2).

In this context, Tanya referred to another example of a teaching resource – interactive digital books. She described how these books were developed:

> So Langfield got a grant to create our own book. I've taken the photos, like the teachers wrote the stories... We recorded my voice for one and a whole lot of different teachers.
>
> *(Tanya)*

These two examples illuminate that, similarly to planning and delivery of the programme, the development of learning resources within the *Techno-Tuesday* team was also highly collaborative. This "digital literacy folder" was a collection of resources such as handouts and information sheets on different topics to which all teachers contributed. The digital multimodal interactive books were also an outcome of their team-teaching philosophy which extended beyond the programme and involved other Langfield's teachers.

Importantly, collegiality within *Techno-Tuesday* provided opportunities for collaborative reflection on the work of the programme, as noted by the participants:

> Each Tuesday we have a quick chat about what worked, what did not and what we should do next week.
>
> *(Polly)*

> [At the end of the day] then we debrief – how did you go? And it's so lovely because it's reflecting on your practice but also sharing the ups and the downs.
>
> *(Tanya)*

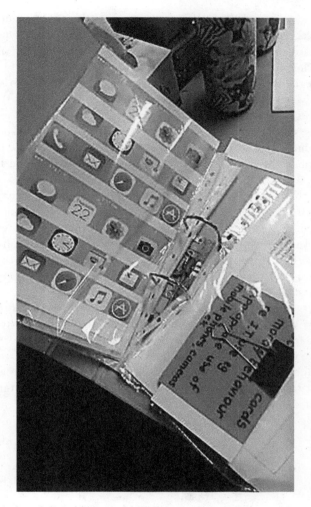

FIGURE 5.2 A shared digital literacy folder

Such collegiality was important for evaluating the effectiveness of the programme and for solving the issues that needed to be resolved collectively. Importantly, collaborative reflections were part of a discursive space for productive conversations through which these teachers supported each other. Tanya offered this reflection about this space:

> I think it's the support. I think, feeling supported is gold in this situation, and being able to also break up into three and then come back.

The delivery of the programme was not easy for many reasons, and, as noted by the teachers, sometimes the learning activities did not work as planned. While being a normal part of any educational environment, these failures and challenges can make teachers disappointed, stressed, and potentially burnt out. However, the collaborative reflections and problem-solving that collegiality allowed provided a valuable opportunity for mutual support.

The collegial dimension of the programme not only helped to increase the comprehensiveness of *Techno-Tuesday* because of the range of topics that could be covered across the team but, importantly, provided opportunities for learning in small groups, enabled greater focus on differentiated instruction and facilitated more individualised feedback on learners' progress. Because of these possibilities, Tanya described the programme as being "really beneficial", and this evaluation accords with our observations. For example, in Nicole's class with mobile phones, we observed that every student had an opportunity to engage with the teacher's questions, practise their oral language, and receive substantial help and feedback from the teacher, while also using their mobile phone to video record their responses. Every learner was also able to share their recording with the class, enabled by the small group size. This was significant given that language classrooms are often dominated by teacher's talk leaving limited opportunities for students to speak.

Our observations of Susan's class with iPads and interactive books (Figure 5.3) also supports the view that the teaching became more differentiated, student-centred, and feedback-oriented as the result of team-teaching.

The photo in Figure 5.3 captures Susan assisting an individual learner with an iPad. As we observed, Susan used iPads to engage learners in reading interactive books. Most learners were quite confident about accessing and using the app. Susan provided initial instructions for the task and, as they independently engaged in the reading activity, Susan assisted a learner who required her help. She guided

FIGURE 5.3 Susan assisting an individual learner with an iPad

the learner through the navigation process prompting the steps and, as evident in the photo, the gestures required to navigate touchscreen technology. The small group size enabled by the rotation format and the team-teaching environment within the *Techno-Tuesday* programme provided significant opportunities for differentiated learning and feedback and enabled more focus on learners' agency. The team-teaching environment also engendered a purposeful, ordered, and collegial programme that brought together the initiatives of individual teachers.

The role of digital literacies at Langfield

The participating teachers emphasised that there was no curriculum for digital literacies at Langfield to guide their teaching, including the *Techno-Tuesday* programme. In Polly's words, there was no "clear directive" to where they were going. During the focus group, the teachers used the metaphor of a "black hole" to describe the gap in the curriculum about digital literacies and their associated concern:

> It's a black hole... A black hole that we find ourselves in because we're lost and we can't go any further because of the ineffectiveness of equipment and not [being] skilled enough. We don't have a curriculum.
>
> Lack of a curriculum or like something to follow... direction maybe.
>
> We do not have a curriculum that we follow for this [digital literacies]. So, what does it look like over a term? Something like that would be really useful.

The teachers were disappointed that there was no formal documentation providing essential guidelines for teaching digital literacies, including content areas, topics, and pedagogies linked to Langfield's educational goals. As evident in the data, a long-term developmental plan for incorporating digital literacies in teaching and learning was missing at Langfield. The absence of guidelines and an institutional plan made it difficult for teachers to instantiate digital literacies into teaching on a daily basis. One teacher in the focus group explained how topics and content in relation to digital literacies were typically chosen:

> It's a bit hit and miss, like we just sort of choose whatever has inspired us.

As evident from this quote, the choice of what to teach in terms of digital literacies was somewhat *ad hoc*. Teachers in the focus group expressed their own frustration with this situation and suggested that comprehensive learning about digital literacies was not possible.

Despite the apparent lack of a systematic approach to teaching digital literacies, the data analysis identified two main focus areas in teaching at Langfield that incorporated technologies. We associated the first one with what *The EAL Framework* (2018) calls "basic digital technology language and skills" (p. 169), while the second focus area was associated with digital literacies as social practices.

Focus one: Basic digital technology language and skills

The data analysis suggests that there was a strong focus on basic digital technology language and skills at Langfield, both within the *Techno-Tuesday* programme and in other teaching programmes. Within *The EAL Framework* (State of Victoria, 2018) basic digital technology language and skills refer to (1) using correct digital terminology, (2) performing a simple task using a digital device, and (3) using digital technology for language learning (p. 169). All three focus points were evident in the participants' teaching practices.

For example, all participating teachers reported that they taught a range of terms and concepts associated with digital technology. Tanya referred to digital terminology necessary to discuss and use digital devices. This terminology for the iPad included "the front cover", "home button", "keypad", "camera", "swipe function", "volume up/down controls", and "the cursor". Kate said that she often used an activity on "different parts of the computer" asking the learners to match "a picture with the word". Polly also shared a similar example:

> Understanding the language around digital literacy which is another thing that they really struggle with... Yesterday I said "Press the spacebar to log in", and no-one knew what "the spacebar" was and we have taught it... several times.

As evident in Polly's comment, understanding and knowing digital and computer terminology was central to many classroom activities with technologies. In other words, to engage learners efficiently in activities involving digital technologies the first step was to equip them with a common technology discourse: key terms and digital terminology to be able to recognise key words and expressions in relation to digital technologies as well as to be able to talk about and use devices, programmes, and their functions. The participants reported a range of classroom practices at Langfield aiming to introduce and consolidate relevant technology vocabulary. The teachers also noted that this learning was challenging and time-consuming but it was opening up new learning opportunities afforded through shared digital language.

Further, for all the teachers, there was a significant focus on adopting terminology associated with the functions of different programmes and apps. The teachers worked with learners to help them recognise and name different icons and their user functions. Polly provided an example of teaching learners to recognise and understand the icons such as start button, saving, copying, and pasting in MS Word. Kate and Tanya said they encouraged the learners to associate the Google icon and Safari icon with its functionalities. We also observed Susan doing a re-cap activity on iPad icons.

> **FIELD NOTES**
>
> Susan started her class with iPads with a warm-up activity aiming to reactivate learners' prior knowledge about iPads. She gave learners handouts capturing an iPad home screen with a variety of icons. Asking "What can you see?", she encouraged the learners to name and show icons of the calendar, clock, map, mail, message, music, Safari, camera, YouTube. They also discussed the function of some applications. The interaction unfolded in the following way:
>
> SUSAN: What's this? (pointing to the Safari icon on the handout)
> LEARNER 1: Safari
> LEARNER 2: Safari
> SUSAN: This has 3 syllables – sa-fa-ri. Listen where the stress is: sa-FA-ri
> LEARNERS (all together): sa-FA-ri, sa-FA-ri
> SUSAN: If you tap on Safari, where does it take you?
> LEARNER 3: Download, you know… saving, you know?
> SUSAN: Good. Sometimes there can be a download there.
> LEARNER 4: Internet?
> SUSAN: Good! It can take you to the Internet. What could you look at on the Internet? What could you look at?
> LEARNER 1: Shopping (all learners smile and giggle)
> SUSAN: Shopping! Yes! A lot of people do shopping.
>
> This activity was followed by a similar task unpacking the meaning of the magnifying glass icon on Youtube that allows searching specific content.
>
> September 3, 2019

From Susan's perspective, knowing and understanding terminology around different programmes and their functions was important for their learners to "feel confident to select the right icon and then understand what that involves". Indeed, these icons are symbols for input actions that will happen when the users click or tap onto the image. They are complex semiotic entities. As these icons embody the complex functionalities afforded by their designers, they may be unclear or even confusing to the inexperienced users. This is especially true for the users from diverse cultural backgrounds who may have limited experience with technology. With this group of learners in mind, there was a need to develop knowledge of the sign systems associated with technologies, digital interfaces, and icons and their functions.

The participating teachers also focused on teaching learners how to perform simple tasks using digital devices. These tasks were mainly associated with the basics of digital navigation, such as moving and operating a mouse in order to shift the cursor on the screen, operating the keys of a keyboard, and haptic movements on touch devices. Nicole reported how she taught learners to use the mouse:

> We started with something super basic like navigating the mouse because most of the students never touched a computer before. I said "Can you go to the left side? Can you go to the right side of the screen?". We started with basic things like that. Then clicking. The double click was hard for them because they clicked too slowly. Then the right click and the left click.

Using a computer mouse and keyboard is one of the fundamental skills for operating what might now be considered more "traditional" computer technology. As evident in the data, some teaching practices aimed to familiarise learners with these computer accessories and develop essential skills and understandings required for performing basic computing tasks. These included controlling a cursor on the screen by moving a mouse, single clicking to select items or open a menu, double clicking to open items, right clicking to display context menus, and scrolling up and down pages.

The teachers also reported that significant attention was given to a range of typing activities that provided opportunities to learn about the position of letters in and familiarity with the layout of the keyboard. Several teachers shared that a typical activity was "a little text to copy" (Tanya) to understand how to use a keyboard. While a wide range of tasks can be performed with the keyboard, the teachers reported mainly focusing on "working out where the letters were" (Tanya), including capital letters and spacing between the words.

Teachers also focused on the interfaces of touch screen devices such as an iPad and smartphones. Andrea shared an example of a vocabulary game on iPads that provided opportunities to practise "moving things around on the screen". Polly mentioned her focus on "touch and hold, swiping, tapping and double tapping".

These examples from practice suggest that the main teaching focus centred on basic digital tasks with different devices and familiarity with terminology. A strong focus on these two aspects of technology competence suggests that the participating teachers deemed them essential for their learners, laying an important foundation for more advanced interactions with technologies. Tanya called this a "skills building stage" which helps learners "get ready" for reading, writing, and communication in digital spaces. This stage is often taken for granted by those who are familiar with technology but it seems to be a very important stage for EAL learners from refugee background who have had little or no exposure and experience with digital technologies due to life circumstances.

Tanya explained how ability to use a keyboard is central to many other digital practices:

> We have to hone in on typing because we wanted them to do a whole other thing that required them to be able to type.

From Tanya's perspective, engaging learners in complex digital work is challenging, even impossible, if they do not have the requisite input skills. In this sense, having relevant digital terminology and being able to perform basic digital tasks was seen by the teachers as a necessary condition for engaging learners in more sophisticated digital experiences. They also recognised that these input skills and basic computer knowledge were not easy to develop for Langfield's learners.

All participating teachers also actively used technology to practise certain English language skills. For example, Andrea referred to the websites *News in Levels* (https://www.newsinlevels.com/) and *Behind the News* (https://www.abc.net.au/btn/) that provided opportunities "to focus on a particular grammar activity" and "listening and reading skills" (Andrea). Kate named *Adele's ESL Corner* (http://www.adelescorner.org/) as her typical resource for a range of grammar or vocabulary activities. Another teaching practice typical at Langfield, as illustrated in Figure 5.4, involved the use of interactive books that were collaboratively designed by Langfield's teachers for their EAL learners.

The books were available on iOS and Android devices and they featured everyday practices and relevant language associated with life in Australia such as seeing a doctor, reporting children's absence at school, community volunteering, and others. The typical activity involved listening to the audio and reading with or after the audio, repeating as many times as desired. The interactive design of the books allowed learners to select parts of the text such as sentences, language chunks, and words and practise them separately if desired. According to the teachers, books had a significant focus on English language "to provide them [learners] with a language" (Susan) for the activities that they do in their everyday life.

FIGURE 5.4 Reading digital books

Focusing on these basic digital technology language and skills was important for Langfield's learners. After all, for many learners, using technology was a new experience. Tanya said:

> We're just at the skill building stage and boosting confidence and trying to help them to use some of the tools to learn English, but I'd love to progress to that next step where we start to, you know, decipher.

However, Tanya seemed to be aware that these basics may not be enough for adult EAL learners. The word "decipher" points to Tanya's awareness that beyond the digital basics technology use requires sophisticated socio-cultural understandings.

Focus two: digital literacies

While the dominant focus was on basic digital technology language and skills across all participating teachers, some classroom activities at Langfield engaged learners in more sophisticated practices with technology. These practices still catered for the digital basics but, importantly, they provided opportunities to use authentic language and semiotic resources in digital spaces, as well as to consider how digital culture, social contexts, social purposes, and audiences shape reading, writing, and communication mediated by digital devices. These practices included digital multimodal composing, interacting with digital texts, filling in online forms, text messaging, and emailing a friend. They provided rich opportunities for learning digital literacies although the teachers were often unaware of this.

Several participants reported examples of teaching practices that we associated with what is often called in the research literature "digital multimodal composing" – "a textual practice that involves the use of digital tools to produce texts by combining multiple semiotic modes" (Jiang, 2017, p. 413). For example, Andrea shared that she encouraged learners to use MS Word and "write a recount of what they did on the weekend and then to use the skills like in bold or different fonts". Similarly, Kate's and Tanya's learners wrote short reflections about their weekend activities experimenting with fonts and colours and using Google images to complement their writing. We also observed digital multimodal composing in Nicole's class with mobile phones that we referred to earlier in this chapter. The excerpt below describes what happened in a *Techno-Tuesday* session.

FIELD NOTES

After a quick warm-up activity aiming to activate learners' prior knowledge of the relevant vocabulary, the learners were asked to interview a peer using four questions from the warm-up activity and to video record this short dialogue to share with the class.

> Video recording was a new experience for the learners and a significant part of the session was devoted to teaching how to make a video although not ignoring the focus on pronunciation, clarity, and intelligibility of speaking. There was a significant focus on how to access the video recording function, switching between photo and video, recognising and using different media control buttons to record and play the video. When the learners were comfortable with these functions, they worked in pairs interviewing each other and recording the dialogues.
>
> Once they completed their recordings, they came together as a group and shared their work. After playing the video recorded by one pair, the group discussed that the sound was too quiet and some responses were difficult to understand for the audience. The teacher also mentioned that the phones have an option to record the voice rather than a face which can be a good tool for practising pronunciation.
>
> August 27, 2019

These field notes suggest that to engage in digital multimodal composing, Nicole started with teaching basic terminology and basic digital navigation tasks that we discussed above. This was also reflective of other teachers' experiences. Then these teaching practices moved beyond the basics to working with different modes of meaning-making and more complex writing and composing experiences. Nicole encouraged learners to use an aural mode, while Tanya, Kate, and Andrea provided opportunities for creation of multimodal texts combining linguistic and visual modes of expression. As an evaluation of her own practice, Kate reported that these activities were "quite a successful thing". This is not surprising given that all these digital texts had clear social purposes which made composing meaningful, enjoyable, and, thus, effective for learners. Tanya's practice example suggests that creating digital multimodal texts gives opportunities for using the array of Google applications, moving between different platforms, and thinking about the key words and relevant images to deploy multimodal composition.

These multimodal composing experiences extended learners' repertoires of digital literacy practices which was not always apparent to the teachers. When asked what students learn in these activities, Andrea said: "how to use the techniques on Word". It seemed that she was associating digital multimodal composing with digital basics rather than digital composing. This was reflective of other participants' teaching experiences. The teachers did not seem to have the conceptual and theoretical language to talk about multimodality and digital literacies as social practices.

The similar issue was observed in the participants' use of interactive books (Figure 5.4). The books provided opportunities for interactions with digital texts prevalent these days in different contexts. However, only Tanya recognised that these experiences help to consolidate important haptic skills such as tapping and swiping. Other teachers mainly viewed them as a tool for language learning rather than developing learners' digital literacies. They did not seem to recognise that these books help learners to become more familiar with the design of such texts and understand that interacting with some digital texts may require digital navigational skills based on gestures and direct manipulation of objects on pages. Being multimodal, the books provide opportunities for multimodal meaning-making and developing multimodal competence. Furthermore, the books featured voice-overs from speakers for whom English is an additional language, mirroring the multicultural and multilingual context of Australia and preparing the learners for a variety of accents that they may come across in virtual or face-to-face communication.

As mentioned earlier in this chapter, Tanya engaged learners in filling in a Google form. She explained how she viewed the value of this activity that focused on the topic "Clothing":

> I think [it helped with] developing their reading skills on the platform and knowing how to scroll up and down on the page… knowing where to type in the answer.

As Tanya explained, this activity provided an opportunity for learners to familiarise themselves with the design features of online forms. She recognised that this experience helped students to learn the capabilities associated with navigating and making sense of online forms. This is an important skill set because online forms are especially ubiquitous in digital platforms for the provision of government and other services. Despite the value of her grounded understandings of professional practice, she did not seem to be aware of other important opportunities offered by this experience – such as developing an awareness of the design of online forms and the associated literacy demands (e.g. reading a question, choosing or typing an answer, submitting, etc.) involved in completing such forms. The capabilities involved in completing a form have application to learners' other real-life needs (e.g. online shopping, customer surveys, application forms) but Tanya questioned the value of using the Google forms in the classroom. She said she "hesitate[ed]" to associate this activity with digital literacies.

Several teachers said that they taught learners how to send a text message to teachers for reporting an absence. Tanya explained what this involved: "We do an example and I get them in class to then send me a message". Similarly, Andrea shared a teaching resource for teaching abbreviation in text messages and talked about her approach:

> We were talking about texting. We were doing message writing and we were talking about abbreviations and synonyms and how do you use that.

And we did a couple of little activities based around that... I get the students to text me with abbreviated messages and we talked about the formation of language and all the bastardisation of language, if I can say that, and how it's changing through texting and emails.

In this instance, Langfield's teachers engaged learners in a digital literacy practice which had an authentic purpose (e.g. reporting an absence), happened in a specific context (e.g. Langfield), and targeted a real audience (e.g. their teacher). In other words, learning was focused on a social purpose that closely mirrored one in a real setting. Furthermore, as mentioned by Andrea, the teaching included a new linguistic register associated with digital communication – textspeak – and included familiarisation with digital culture and the ways in which it shapes language use. Together, these learning experiences helped to engage learners in authentic meaning making for real purposes, which in turn prompted them to recognise the pragmatics of effective language use and interactions in text messaging.

Finally, in the context of *Techno-Tuesday*, the teachers engaged students in email communication. We observed three sessions which aimed to develop the skills and knowledge required to send an email to a peer. As the learners did not have email accounts, the first session was devoted to learning about the concept of the email and setting up accounts; the second session focused on logging in and learning about the digital interface of inbox; and the third session focused on composing a short email to a peer. Like the teaching of text messaging, this learning experience was also informed by an authentic audience and purpose. However, we noted that this learning was time-consuming and difficult for the majority of learners, suggesting that this had not been part of their prior experiences. The teachers recognised that, given this low level of familiarity with this task, more targeted practice and further opportunities were needed to consolidate their learning. This practice might include engaging in email communication in other social contexts and with other audiences as well as creative experimentation with language to gauge its suitability.

Teaching from learners' strengths

We argued earlier in this chapter that there were many effective teaching practices at Langfield and, thus, we were especially interested in what made these practices effective for learners. Exploring teachers' work through a strengths-based perspective (Lopez & Louis, 2009) helped us to focus more on their successes and identify areas that need more attention. Teaching different aspects of digital literacies was effective for adult EAL learners when teachers employed strengths-based practices. Several strengths-based practices were clearly evident in teachers' work in the classrooms. These included (1) individualised learning, (2) purposeful peer-learning, (3) deliberate application of strengths, and (4) development of strengths through building on prior experiences. These practices are explored below.

Individualised learning

Individualised and differentiated learning was often observed in the participants' classrooms and reported by teachers. An example of Susan's practice captured in Figure 5.1 above illustrates her working one-on-one with a learner. In this particular example, the learner could not access interactive books on the iPad. Susan organised the work of other learners and then she spent one-on-one time with the learner who needed further assistance with navigating the multimodal text. As captured in Figure 5.1, in her work with this learner, Susan started at the learner's level – with gestures required to navigate an iPad (e.g. swiping and tapping) – and scaffolded the learner through to successful accessing of the text.

Individualised and differentiated learning was also used by Polly in her email classes that we observed:

> **FIELD NOTES**
>
> It was the second class on email communication taught by Polly and a volunteer assistant as a part of the *Techno-Tuesday* program in a small computer lab of the community house with eight desktop computers along the walls… It was a productive class for students and the majority (except for one) were able to send a message. However, the class seemed to be very laborious for the teachers who mainly worked with the learners individually assisting with the navigation process, prompting and repeating the steps, helping to use a mouse, supporting typing, managing password recovery, and troubleshooting different issues.
>
> Once the students left the classroom, Polly said that she felt "a little bit frustrated" about this class.
>
> September 3, 2019

Polly mainly worked with learners individually as some learners were more familiar with email and others had gaps in their understanding. One-on-one support worked for learners: the majority (except for one) were able to achieve the learning objectives of this class.

However, as we noted, providing individual assistance was very "laborious" for Polly and her volunteer assistant, which affected Polly's levels of job satisfaction. This sense of unease and dissatisfaction was also reflected in other teachers' experiences. For example, Andrea said:

> I have fifteen, sometimes twenty, students *all* wanting my attention and I'm the only person in the room and that is taxing and stressful.

One aspect of teaching work in an ACE setting and with EAL students is the intensity of the work and its potential effects on the wellbeing of teachers, suggesting the need for a range of support to do the role effectively.

Purposeful peer-learning

Peer-learning was also present in the participants' classrooms, although to a less extent than individualised learning. For example, Andrea said that she often got learners "to work in pairs" to help each other in different activities with technologies. In Chapter 3, we discussed that multilingualism was highly valued at Langfield and the use of learners' home languages was often central to peer-learning in the classrooms. We often observed that learners felt free (and were encouraged) to interact in their home languages in their peer-interactions to support each other in learning. In Nicole's class with mobile phones that we referred to throughout this chapter, peer-learning was central to the activities with mobile phones. Polly, whose class on writing email is described previously, started with a group discussion (Figure 5.5).

As a warm-up activity for this class, Polly asked learners to sit in a circle to discuss two questions: "What is email?" and "Why do we need email?" The learners in this class had different experiences with emails and Polly managed the limited knowledge of some learners about emails by leveraging other learners' strengths. The group collaboratively offered a range of ideas in relation to the questions posed and Polly's smile suggests that she was satisfied with the discussion. This made learning about email more meaningful for her learners.

FIGURE 5.5 Group discussion in a computer room

Interestingly, as evident in the image, a traditional layout of a computer room is not very conducive to group work: when working with technology learners were facing the walls. Nevertheless, Polly effectively re-constructed the physical space of the computer room to engage learners in a productive group discussion. However, in the debriefing interview after the class, Polly said, "I find it a challenge in that room. Like there's no teaching space really". She never referred to this activity as contributing to successful learning and did not seem to realise that despite the constraints of this physical space, she used it quite astutely.

Deliberate application of strengths

The practice of deliberate identification and application of strengths was especially evident in teachers' use of interactive books on iPads (Figure 5.2). Susan explained:

> We're seeing the students use it [the app] in their free time... They're just reading the stories using their mobile phone because they've learned the skills in class, and the stories are familiar, the language is relevant, and it gives them an opportunity to be able to practice it on their mobile phones in their free time.

Through the use of these interactive books on the learners' most favourite devices, the teachers created opportunities for successful application of strengths in the classroom so that learners could "translate" this experience to other domains of life. The learning space and the technologies in it became a source of strength for supporting learning. As evident in Susan's data, this approach worked – the learners were using the books in their free time. In the same way, learners' home languages were used by the teachers as a resource for learning with and about technology. Nicole, a Vietnamese-speaking teacher, often used Vietnamese in the classroom, while monolingual teachers also found creative ways to incorporate home languages. Susan described her approach:

> We are acknowledging people's linguistic repertoires that they have... [For example], I drew an acorn and they knew what that word was and they were looking it up on their phone in their language and then they were able to see what that word was in English... [Or] I used Google Translate and just said the word in Vietnamese and then the whole class can read it. I often play the audio and then we'll all practise saying it in Vietnamese.

Such innovative practices generated opportunities for learners to be successful in the classroom modelling experiences for everyday life. Susan's comment, "So we're seeing the students use it [the app] in their free time" is especially illustrative that deliberate application of strengths in the classrooms had positive implications for learners' practices outside Langfield. They could engage in these practices independently. In this sense, the teachers encouraged learners' autonomy, agency, and potential for continuing learning within and beyond Langfield's classes. The deliberate application of the technological and linguistic strengths was especially important for empowering learners. This theme of empowerment was very strong across all interviews. For instance, some teachers said:

> When they come here, I'd like to think that if I could give them the skill... that empowers them a little bit. They can take that skill home and they might feel a little empowered... I love to see them empowered.
>
> *(Andrea)*

> I want some support to help them engage with the digital space so that they can participate in society and live a rich life in Melbourne. That's what I want. And I think we can do that for a beginner level learner, but how do you do it?
>
> *(Tanya)*

These visionary statements illuminate the depth of the commitment of teachers at Langfield to their adult learners and point to the importance of empowerment and autonomy enabled through digital literacies. However, while all teachers wanted to empower their learners, they thought that what they were doing was not good enough. As Tanya's rhetorical question suggests, they did not recognise that what they did *was* empowering. Furthermore, Andrea's perspective suggests that she thought that empowerment is something that she has to "give" to learners rather than conceptualising it around learners' capacities for agency, voice, and decision-making.

Development of strengths through building on prior experiences

The development of strengths through building on the prior experiences of learners was another practice central to the participants' teaching. For example, in her class with mobile phones described earlier, Nicole started her class with the phrase, "Show me your phone". This phrase effectively connected new learning with the existing and, thus, familiar, material world and resources of the learners. She then drew on learners' ability to take photos with their cameras and extended this to taking videos with cameras. As we discussed earlier in this chapter, the *Techno-Tuesday* programme was designed with the idea to build on prior learning. This allowed teachers to consolidate and, importantly, extend what the learners already knew and could do with language and technology.

While there were many innovative practices involving technologies and digital literacies at Langfield, as mentioned earlier, there was no overall framework, or curriculum, to guide the teaching of digital literacies. Thus, this conscious identification and development of strengths was present in some, but not all teaching practices. Polly's class on writing email described above was followed by a brief but very reflective interaction with the researcher which we mentioned in our field notes:

> **FIELD NOTES**
>
> As a part of this insightful and deeply reflective conversation, Polly asked me what *I*, as an educator, would do next and what else can be done to extend students' email skills.
>
> September 3, 2019

In this brief conversation, Polly asked the researcher to provide professional advice on her further lesson planning. While this characterises Polly as a proactive teacher seeking informal opportunities to learn and grow professionally (Tour et al., 2020), it also illuminated to us that Polly, as well as all other teachers participating in this research, did not always know how to use the learners' existing skills, knowledge, and experiences with technology to extend understandings of digital literacies.

Teachers' perspectives on strengths

Although the teaching of participants in the study often seemed to include effective strengths-based practices, the teachers' perspectives on their learners often focussed on what they lacked. When talking about the learners, they often used the terms such as "low" and "illiterate", both in terms of print-based literacies and digital literacies. The CEO said that Langfield is "working with *very* low-level learners". Nicole described learners' digital literacies as "too low" and Polly referred to her learners as "low-level learners". Similarly, this evaluation of their learners was evident across the data set, suggesting a deficit discourse and prevailing assumptions about learners' literacies and capacities to use digital technologies. As noted above, the teachers did not seem to recognise that their learners have many substantial strengths. This stance is understandable, even normative; after all, from a policy perspective, these perceived "deficits" are the reason for the programme's existence in the first place. Nevertheless, we see this "default" position as problematic and potentially unhelpful.

Similarly, when talking about themselves and their work, the teachers often expressed a lot of uncertainty about their own ability to address learners' needs associated with digital literacies. During the focus group, several of them questioned if what they were doing was enough:

> I wouldn't say that I've been overly successful in teaching technology.

> As a teacher, I am not sure how I can help the students [to learn digital literacies].
>
> I don't think I'd be confident going into any classroom and doing it [teaching digital literacies].

These quotes convey a feeling of frustration and inadequacy shared by all the teachers and reflects teachers' uncertainty about their professional efficacy and strengths. The teachers did not think that their practices were successful, or successful enough. In fact, they often thought their teaching was deficient in various ways although they were also unclear about how their work was inadequate, what else might be done, or what might be done differently. They reflected the uncomfortable sense of not knowing what it was that they did not know. Hence, they were very uncertain about their teaching with technologies and they did not always realise that their teaching practices provided many important learning opportunities. In other words, their practices were better than they thought. They did not seem to recognise their own agential power as well as fully appreciate the power of their learners.

Exploring possibilities for digital literacies

In this chapter, we focused on the role of digital literacies at Langfield by exploring the participants' perspectives on digital literacies and their teaching practices with digital technologies to understand the professional strengths and needs of the teachers and Langfield as a community-based EAL provider. Detailed attention was given to Langfield's unique programme *Techno-Tuesday* that was specifically dedicated to learning about digital technologies and literacies central to life and settlement of adult EAL learners. We also analysed different teaching practices with technologies to understand to what extent they helped learners to develop digital literacies as well as what made some of these practices successful and productive.

Reflecting previous research (Driessen et al., 2011), this study found that all participants, including the CEO and teachers, recognised the importance of digital literacies for their learners and saw these capabilities as central not only to survival in a new country but also to thriving and strengthening their agency – being confident, successful, and independent in their practices with digital technologies. While these were important aspirations, the teachers' understandings and definitions of digital literacies varied in terms of their scope, depth, and complexity. The teachers at Langfield certainly held positive educational values and this was an important strength in their teaching. At the same time, professional knowledge about digital literacies was still developing. Research on teaching with technology suggests that what teachers do in classrooms is highly dependent on what they know and believe about technology (Taimalu & Luik, 2019). This means that while valuing digital literacies is important, high-quality teaching of digital literacies also requires an understanding of what digital literacies are.

Teaching digital literacies in a way that prepares language learners for the complexity of digital literacy practices outside of the classroom require sophisticated understanding that is often not part of teacher training or ongoing professional learning. Langfield's teachers needed additional professional learning support to move beyond just conceptualising digital literacy as a relatively simple set of generic decontextualised skills. Such a shift in thinking and practice is not easy (Tour, 2015). As evident in this research, the participants' agency in teaching digital literacies was uncertain and tentative. It reflected the lack of relevant conceptual and theoretical guidance. The teachers needed support to further enhance and deepen their professional knowledge in this area. Given the conceptual complexity of digital literacies and the dominance of relatively simplistic mainstream definitions, it was apparent to us that Langfield's teachers needed an opportunity to develop a more nuanced and critical perspective on digital literacies as closely connected to the social contexts in which they happen, including their social purposes and audiences. There is no single line to be crossed, or gate to be opened to "digital literacies". Nor is "digital literacy" a state of completion, a mythic standard where all has been mastered and there is nothing left to learn.

Both the CEO and the teachers honestly acknowledged that there was no well-developed, systematic, and organisation-wide approach to the provision of digital literacies as well as relevant curriculum at Langfield that addressed this need. The teachers felt somewhat lost. They were "left to their own devices", both literally and metaphorically. Their perspectives suggest that they critically analysed their work at the institutional and individual levels and evaluated their approach to digital literacies. This characterises the participants as reflective and critical which is an important strength of any educator. Such "reflection-on-action" (Killion & Todnem, 1991, p. 15) in which practitioners look back and learn from experience is important and central to professional growth but, as Killion and Todnem (1991) argue, there is also a need for a "reflection-for-action" (p. 15). This type of reflection is more agentic as it aims to close the gap between what happens now and what might be done. In Langfield's case, this raises two questions. First, what might a systematic and organisation-wide approach to the provision of digital literacies look like in the Langfield's setting? Second, what might a relevant curriculum for digital literacies look like? The participants did not have answers to these important questions. A systematic change, especially in relation to the teaching about digital technologies and literacies as situated practices, is a difficult task (Falloon, 2020; Hinrichsen & Coombs, 2013) and many institutions do not have the capacity, time, and resources to develop an effective organisation-wide approach and curriculum without relevant support. Substantial and effective educational leadership is required as we argue in Chapter 7.

However, in their attempts to enhance the provision of digital literacies, Langfield has developed a strong foundation from which further development is possible. The *Techno-Tuesday* programme, designed and delivered by three teachers, approached teaching digital literacies in a more systematic way and it provided many opportunities for learning different aspects of digital literacies. Previous research emphasised that integrating digital literacies in language learning is "a double learning path" (Driessen et al., 2011, p. viii) because to be able to use technology in English, learners from refugee backgrounds need both language and digital capacities (van Rensburg & Son, 2010). Our research documented a useful practical approach, consistent with contemporary literacy theories, that can be used to enhance the provision of digital literacies by integrating them more seamlessly within EAL programmes. The findings also highlight the creativity and agency of this group of teachers who, in an attempt to address their learners' digital needs and preferences, came up with an original and workable way of sequencing a programme.

Another important finding is about the content choices of what to teach in relation to digital literacies both within *Techno-Tuesday* and in the broader work of teachers at Langfield. These choices were mostly not based on a systematic approach and on clear documented guidance. This lack of a systematic approach has been noted by previous research (Traxler, 2018). Across all participating teachers, there was a strong focus on basic digital technology language and skills. These capabilities are, of course, important prerequisites for digital literacy practices for adult EAL learners with limited exposure and experience with digital technologies and English. However, privileging these capabilities may not allow teachers to move beyond this focus to more complex dimensions of digital literacies (Peromingo & Pieterson, 2018; van Rensburg & Son, 2010).

At the same time, we also note several promising examples of teaching practices which successfully moved beyond just pushing buttons to important aspects of digital literacy practices including the nature of digital texts, the role of shifting contexts, audiences, and power relationships. This is noteworthy given that the need for these important dimensions has been widely acknowledged in the literature (Lankshear et al., 2000; Peromingo & Pieterson, 2018; Traxler, 2018). Certainly, there is scope for Langfield not only to deepen the scope of their existing teaching repertoires but also to include more digital literacies required for settlement, participation, and engagement with social and cultural life in Australia.

This research offers valuable insights by documenting how adult EAL learners with limited exposure to technologies and language still can be engaged in digital literacies in a much more sophisticated way – beyond the digital basics. While examples of digital literacies were not very extensive at Langfield, this study found that some classroom experiences with technology were effective for adult EAL learners. They were successful when teaching included strengths-based practices proposed by Lopez and Louis (2009) such as individualised learning, peer-learning, deliberate application of strengths, and intentional development of strengths. Strengths-based education has been conceptualised and advocated for literacy and language learning (Lopez & Louis, 2009; Roy & Roxas, 2011; Shapiro & MacDonald, 2017; Waterhouse & Virgona, 2008). We believe that such practices are also useful for teaching digital literacies in the adult EAL context, and our study offers new insights to the field of digital literacies which is searching currently for suitable approaches to teaching digital literacies in language learning contexts (Hafner, 2019; Hafner et al., 2015; Lotherington & Jenson, 2011; Murray, 2008).

However, the participating teachers did not always realise that their own practices were effective; they did not always recognise what made their teaching practices successful. They tended to think they were deficient and inadequate, as evidenced by the "black hole" metaphor noted earlier. They expressed anxiety about what they were doing, even though the analysis in Chapter 4 suggests that the learners really enjoyed the programme and found it useful both in terms of its content and pedagogies used. This finding is significant because as McClanahan (2014) argues, the quality provision of digital literacies within adult language learning programmes can be negatively affected if educators have deficit assumptions and concerns. Similarly, Lopez and Louis (2009) emphasise the need for educators to discover and be aware of their own strengths as part of strengths-based education.

Langfield's teachers have the capacity to move beyond a deficit perspective and uncertainty about their own work with technologies because they already drew on the learners' resourcefulness and developed a number of suitable approaches for teaching digital literacies. There is a need to empower Langfield's teachers because they often neither realised that they were teaching important aspects of digital literacies nor recognised what made them effective for learners. Their approaches were intuitive rather than well-informed and theorised. This finding reflects previous research reporting that teachers often do not know how to teach with technologies and how to use them to their fullest potential in adult language classrooms (Driessen et al., 2011). This is not to criticise the teachers but to suggest that having such knowledge was not something that was naturally apparent. Teachers need opportunities for developing these understandings and, importantly, agency.

Conclusion

In this chapter, we explored the place of digital literacies at Langfield. This research found that while all teachers and the CEO recognised the importance of digital literacies for their learners, there was no well-developed, systematic, and organisation-wide approach to the provision of digital literacies and the teachers often felt lost. However, in their attempts to enhance the provision of digital literacies, Langfield had something to build on. The *Techno-Tuesday* programme, designed and delivered by three teachers, approached teaching digital literacies in a more systematic way. This programme provided many opportunities for learning different aspects of digital literacies but, generally, the choice of what to teach was random and accidental. Across all participating teachers, there was a strong focus on basic digital technology language and skills. While examples of digital literacies were not very extensive at Langfield, this study found that teaching was were effective for adult EAL learner when informed by a number of strengths-based practices such as individualised learning, peer-learning, deliberate application of strengths, and development of strengths through. As this approach was intuitive rather than a well-informed and theorised professional decision, the teachers felt very unconfident and even anxious about what they were doing.

Notes

1 JobActive is an Australian Government program and the main employment services program for those who receive income support payments (https://jobsearch.gov.au).
2 myGov is an online platform for accessing key government services in Australia (https://my.gov.au/).

6
ESCAPING THE BLACK HOLE THROUGH PROFESSIONAL LEARNING

FIELD NOTES

Late one afternoon at the end of a teaching day, five teachers assembled with the researchers to participate in a focus group. Rather than being just a talk-reflection time, this focus group was designed as an active and embodied creative research activity. The teacher-participants were asked to create a visual collage of their experiences using paper, scissors, and a variety of materials supplied by the researchers. They visually constructed what they believed to be "a picture of their needs" in terms of professional learning about digital literacies and institutional practices that are needed to support this learning. The creation of the collage was characterised by laughter, much negotiation between participants, and reflections about practice. At the end of the focus group, the participants said:

TANYA: Well, I think opening up this discussion is great. It's huge and it's more than we've ever had.
POLLY: Yeah...
TANYA: And to just talk openly about the challenges and where we're at and how we're feeling is such an important start. We haven't done this before.
SUSAN: No.
ANDREA: I think it's great. It's the first time we've had an opportunity to do this and thank you because I really feel that it's opening up something that we've needed to talk about for quite some time.

July 15, 2019

DOI: 10.4324/9781003132684-6

This vignette describes the focus group that we conducted in this study to gain insights into the teachers' perspectives on their professional learning needs in relation to teaching digital literacies. The focus group was designed as a data generating activity and, while it achieved this aim, it also unexpectedly transformed into a highly engaging professional learning activity for the participating teachers. Initially, we mainly hoped that this focus group would encourage sharing of teaching experiences and concerns in a safe space, but, to our surprise, this activity was transformed into a unique learning event. The teachers reframed this research activity as reflexive professional learning. It became very apparent to us that Langfield's teachers wanted to learn and grow professionally; they were passionate about teaching and hoped to further enhance their practices with digital technologies. It was also very clear to us that there was strong collegiality and rapport, and a consequent willingness to learn with and from each other. It gave us a strong feeling that this form of professional learning is central to Langfield's culture.

This chapter builds on the previous chapter in which we discussed the participants' frustrations and dismay about their own perceived professional inadequacies to the extent that some felt they were in a "black hole" and unable to progress and reach their aspirations. Nevertheless, there was also a strong interest across all the participants in incorporating technologies and digital literacies into their practice as they saw their importance for Langfield's learners. Thus, they all expressed a desire to be better equipped to meet the challenges of teaching and learning for a "digital age". This chapter draws attention to the opportunities for professional learning about digital literacies at Langfield and also explores additional needs.

We also seek to explore in this chapter the forms of professional learning about technologies and digital literacies in which the teachers engaged, including the quality of the provisions, both within and beyond their institutional context. We elaborate on what the participants believed they needed in their unique and complex teaching context to be able to teach digital literacies effectively. In broader terms, these insights are important for understanding how professional learning initiatives and programmes may be designed for community-based institutions such as Langfield.

Teachers' experiences of professional learning

The analysis of the data identified three main forms of professional learning about technologies and digital literacies at Langfield: in-house professional learning, external professional learning, and peer-learning. The data suggests that there was a range of experiences with these forms. Teachers' views on the quality of these learning opportunities also varied, and there were certainly strengths and limitations in each form of professional learning as reported by the participants.

In-house professional learning

There was a clear institutional focus on professional learning at Langfield. The CEO and the participating teachers noted there were multiple opportunities for learning offered by what the participants called "in-house professional learning". The CEO explained her perspective on professional learning and her approach to the provision of learning opportunities for teachers:

> I consider professional learning so important! We do a lot in professional development here at Langfield. We probably do more than many adult centres do. In our monthly meetings we always have PD [professional development] and we have to make room for it. We have to include a lot of things in our PD that are important to include.

The participating teachers' views echoed those of the CEO:

> So, we've had lots of PD because we have a really strong focus on professional development.
>
> *(Susan)*

> I think there is a focus on professional learning. We learn… every time we meet we have a particular focus.
>
> *(Andrea)*

Professional learning was regarded as essential for effective teaching at Langfield. Thus, opportunities for teachers' learning were deliberately and consistently created: different professional learning activities happened once a month during the staff meetings. These in-house professional learning sessions were usually delivered by Langfield's teachers and were informal, drawing mainly on professional sharing, exchanges of ideas, and peer discussions. Embedding professional learning into staff meetings helped to ensure that almost *all* teachers attended and participated. This, in turn, helped to achieve what the CEO called "an organisation-wide approach" to professional learning.

These in-house professional learning activities had different foci, as noted by the CEO, in an attempt to cover a range of pertinent topics that the leadership deemed as important for the learners and teachers. However, when asked if this professional learning included topics about technology and digital literacies, the participants, including the CEO, conceded that this knowledge area has not been a priority and the issue had not been addressed systematically. The CEO said:

> What we've done with digital literacy has been sporadic and not systematic. We haven't done a lot of professional learning [about digital literacies], we haven't taken an organisation-wide approach to the professional learning for teachers in this space, but I've been very aware of it.

Andrea and Polly also noted:

> I just think the culture [of Langfield] is not digital literacy. We really do a lot of work on pronunciation. That's our focus.
>
> *(Andrea)*

> We don't really talk about digital technologies. It always surprises me, especially at the beginning of the year. Like this year technology wasn't mentioned at all. There was nothing. So, I was quite surprised and, I guess, disappointed because I don't think it's something we can ignore. The technology PDs are never mentioned.
>
> *(Polly)*

It was evident in the data that digital literacies were not prioritised in Langfield's professional learning programme to the same extent as some more traditional language learning topics (e.g. teaching pronunciation). However, what is also clear from the interview data is that the participants had a high level of awareness about this issue and this extended to their recognition of the importance of relevant professional learning.

Among the various examples of in-house professional learning cited, the participants only remembered two events related to technology and digital literacies. Polly mentioned that they were "a long time ago — a year and a half ago" and "pretty short". One session was about the "tricks with Google Translate" (Susan), delivered by another Langfield's teacher who attended an external professional development workshop and shared her knowledge with other colleagues. Another session focused on how basic operational skills associated with iPads can be taught and it was delivered by Tanya. Being one of the founders and a leader of *Techno-Tuesday*, Tanya was often seen by her colleagues and the CEO as "au fait with the whole digital world" (Kate). In-house professional learning sessions about digital technologies and digital literacies was mainly facilitated by her:

> She [Tanya] led the charge with digital literacy and technology skills. She has run some professional development sessions at work.
>
> *(Susan)*

> Tanya is the main one down there talking about digital literacy. I talk with her quite a lot because I'm encouraging her to be pushing the growth of digital literacy use here. I can support and encourage her to have a go [with technology in the classrooms] and then to share this occasionally with the staff.
>
> *(The CEO)*

The data suggests that occasional in-house professional learning at Langfield about technologies engaged all teachers and provided them with some opportunities to extend their professional knowledge in this area. These opportunities were seen by the participating teachers as important but insufficient. In particular, the teachers did not seem to be satisfied with what was offered both in terms of quantity and frequency of professional learning about digital literacies. However, they made positive comments about Tanya's sessions:

> I know that if Tanya does something here it will be good and I know it will be appropriate. She's taken the information and been able to modify it so that it's going to be appropriate for *our* learners.
>
> (Susan)

Echoing other teachers' opinions, Susan highlighted the value and relevance of Tanya's in-house sessions for her. Tanya's personal classroom experience with technologies made them relevant. In particular, the teachers found it challenging to teach with and about technology at the beginner level. Tanya's collegial sharing of practice helped them think more carefully about the complexity of digital literacy practices for adult EAL learners and, importantly, suitable pedagogical approaches to address their needs.

While "relevance" was seen as an important characteristic of professional learning, Tanya was the only source of professional learning about digital technologies at Langfield. Furthermore, as Tanya went on an extended leave in the middle of this research project, even these occasional opportunities disappeared. Everyone recognised that Tanya was a passionate, knowledgeable, and generous educator, driving significant change at Langfield. At the same time, these sessions were mainly based on her own classroom practices, which had limitations, given the complexity of the field of digital literacies in intersection with EAL and adult learning and the lack of systematic professional learning. While Langfield's teachers had some opportunities to learn from and with Tanya, this teacher said that she did not herself experience any in-house professional learning about digital literacies to enrich her own knowledge and practices. Given this fact, it is remarkable what Tanya offered in terms of leadership for her colleagues.

External professional learning

External professional learning was defined by the participants as different professional learning activities outside of Langfield and included professional conferences or short courses. A very limited number of the participants reported attending external professional learning events. Only two out of six participating teachers said they attended "a couple" of external sessions related to digital technologies:

> I have attended a couple of PDs. I've been to a couple of different things.
>
> (Susan)

> I went to a couple of PD sessions [but] I haven't been to many.
>
> (Tanya)

By contrast, other participants said that they had not attended any external professional learning activities on digital technologies:

> I haven't been to any professional technology learning as such.
>
> *(Kate)*

> Nothing at all.
>
> *(Nicole)*

> I don't attend any external professional development, no. Well, it's not available to me. I haven't seen any and I've never been to any. I haven't done it for ages.
>
> *(Andrea)*

External forms of professional learning were not typical for everyone at Langfield. It seemed that only the CEO and Susan, who was a teacher-mentor, attended such events on a more or less regular basis. Other teachers did not have opportunities to attend professional conferences or courses to develop and extend their knowledge about digital literacies. Reflecting on the lack of these opportunities, Andrea noted that Langfield does not have "a hell of a lot of money" suggesting that costs and limited resources probably compromised the organisation's ability to promote these sorts of opportunities. Yet, at the same time, the participating teachers thought that their wish to attend such events would be supported by the leadership if appropriate opportunities could be identified:

> They're (the leadership team) very good. If I went and resourced some course that I wanted to do, and they thought it was suitable, there'd be no problems.
>
> *(Kate)*

It is important to emphasise that for this government-funded and not-for-profit organisation, costs mitigated against leadership being able to offer external professional learning to all teachers on a regular basis. This limitation also explains why the leadership actively encouraged the teachers to pursue in-house professional learning opportunities. With limited budgets and the high cost of external professional learning, Langfield's leadership appeared to have been pragmatic in finding new cost-effective ways for teachers to continue their professional learning. Fortunately, the agency of some teachers in being proactive in professional learning provision has served the organisation well.

While this approach helped the institution to stay within the budget allocated for professional learning, it was obvious that limited funding for external professional learning created an unequal distribution of opportunities at Langfield. Although the teachers knew that there were some opportunities for external professional learning about digital literacies, this form of professional learning seemed to be an exception rather than openly and routinely available. Some teachers seemed to be empowered to ask for it while there was some uncertainty among others in terms of how they could justify their interest in a particular professional event outside of the institution. For example, Andrea did not feel confident doing this:

> I don't know, I'm not sure whether that's a strength here, I don't know whether that's a focus.
>
> *(Andrea)*

This uncertainty, perhaps, could have been further complicated by the terms and conditions of these teachers' employment contracts. As noted in Chapter 3, most of the participants were working part-time. Andrea only worked one day per week at Langfield and her use of "I don't know" and "I'm not sure" illustrates her uncertainty about the legitimacy of her request to attend expensive external professional learning.

Those teachers who had a chance to attend the external professional learning related to digital technologies generally found them "disappointing". For example, Tanya reflected on a professional learning session that she attended several years ago:

> To be honest, it was not what I was looking for because it was just about "Oh, we use these different tools!", and it was just talking about different websites that are available. And a lot of them are about the students just using it on their own. So that was a bit disappointing.
>
> *(Tanya)*

Susan who attended such events more other than other participants had a similar opinion:

> You know the problem is, if you go outside, it can be quite disappointing. It can be hit and miss, and sometimes you can learn something and you think it's great, but then you don't actually implement it.
>
> *(Susan)*

The participants' comments suggest that the quality of external professional learning activities that they attended was not fully supporting their needs as educators. The main problem was the lack of pedagogical focus on how to teach digital literacies. Teachers also pointed out that sessions often focused on digital practices suitable for students with more advanced levels of language proficiency and, thus, they did not fully address their specific needs. There was a perceived lack of focus on digital literacies pedagogy for adult language learners who are at the beginning of the learning journey.

While the participants thought that external professional learning was not always relevant to their teaching contexts, they still thought that it had many benefits. Susan recalled a "fantastic" cybersafety conference workshop where she "learned a lot". Andrea also reflected on the learning session that she attended several years ago:

> I remember the last PD I went to. We did a great big brainstorm on various sites to help the students learn. And it was fantastic, and I still use it today.
>
> *(Andrea)*

These two examples suggest that external professional learning sessions provided Andrea and Susan with useful teaching resources. Andrea's reflection illuminated that attending this PD session was useful because she had a chance to collaborate with other EAL educators and collectively co-construct a helpful teaching resource which she has been able to use in teaching for several years. Similarly, as Susan reported, the workshop also provided her with some useful resources for teaching about cybersafety.

In addition to useful learning resources, the participants said that attending professional conferences was beneficial as they allowed them "to see different things" (Susan). Andrea explained the value of external professional learning events in a similar way:

> I think it's really good to go out because you get to meet other teachers and to discuss what they're doing, and you learn quite a lot… So, I think it's great to have in-house stuff but it's also really important to go out because you really need to be exposed to what's going on out there individually because everyone's going to interpret things differently and come back with something different.
>
> *(Andrea)*

In this example, Andrea notes the value of having a greater range of perspectives to draw on in her teaching and the value of being "exposed" to what teachers and leaders in other organisations are doing. This is important for building a knowledge base and practice understanding across the adult education sector. Emphatically, the participants believed that attending external professional conferences and PD sessions was useful because attending big professional events and meeting peers was an opportunity to "get out of the bubble" and discover new ideas, resources, and approaches used in the field.

Simply by being exposed to something new encourages people to consider the unknown. The teachers acknowledged that this experience may not have immediate implications for classrooms. Teachers often need time to process new information and consider if and how it can be applied in their classrooms. At the same time, being exposed to new ideas is central to challenging teachers' thinking, extending their professional knowledge and developing new teaching practices. As Andrea emphasised, this learning experience is unique for individuals as every teacher constructs this knowledge differently. This clearly points to professional development being as much about the ongoing transformation of teachers as professionals with agency as it is about acquiring a set of discrete teaching skills.

A team of three: Peer-learning

Our work with Langfield identified the significance of peer-learning for three teachers involved in this research – Tanya, Polly, and Nicole. As we discussed in previous chapters, these three teachers had a strong professional interest in digital literacies which encouraged them to initiate *Techno-Tuesday*. The CEO noted that these three teachers worked "very much as a team" and, indeed, collegiality was identified as central to the programme design allowing for collaborative planning, creation of a repository of teaching resources, team-teaching, and critical reflections. Tanya, Polly, and Nicole reported that these different collaborative activities provided many opportunities for informal peer-learning fostering their professional growth.

Tanya reflected on how the idea to teach email writing emerged in their team discussion. From her memory, it was Polly who said that this is a valuable skill for learners and this made Tanya think about the inclusion of the learning unit on email in the *Techno-Tuesday* programme. For Polly, their discussions of "what worked and what didn't" provided many learning opportunities as they often resulted in collaborative problem-solving of the issues and challenges that they faced in teaching with technologies. Nicole's observations reflect her experience of being involved, although not necessarily at the core of these developments:

> Sometimes I feel like I have fewer ideas than my colleagues. My colleagues are more proactive than I am. So, I learn a lot from their ideas... If it is only me, I don't think I can have that many ideas.
>
> *(Nicole)*

As emphasised by Nicole, she developed new ideas about teaching through this collaboration. This was significant for her given that she was an early career teacher. This collaboration provided these three teachers with rich opportunities for peer-learning about technologies and digital literacies. In Tanya's words, they were "using each other as a resource" which helped them develop new ideas, gain fresh insights, be more willing to take on difficult tasks typical in the everyday reality of teaching with technology, and be risk-takers in their teaching practices. This collaboration was a positive practice within the institution noted by the CEO:

> They're doing team-teaching which has been made possible by the set-up where they are. But it's also their personalities and how they work together. And I think that that has really enabled a lot of collaboration and peer-sharing. They can achieve more when they're working together and learning from each other and I feel that it's really important.
>
> *(The CEO)*

In addition to personal relationships between these teachers and their shared professional interests that fostered such learning, the CEO also noted the importance of the disparate physical teaching spaces in which these three teachers worked. Teaching spaces, like all elements of materiality in teaching and learning, can shape and determine what is and is not possible. As we described in Chapter 3, Langfield's classrooms were located across several sites in their attempt to reach their learners. While the sprawling structure of classroom spaces was important for learners, in being where the learners lived and felt most comfortable, it had significant implications for relationships between the teachers. These three teachers happened to work in one location and, thus, had opportunities not only for team-teaching but also for quick catch-ups, corridor conversations, and lunches together which, perhaps, helped to establish and maintain their collegial bonds and enable peer-learning. In contrast, other participants did not report collegial professional learning about technologies through interactions and collaborations as noted by Susan:

> [Teachers] they're not having those incidental moments where they bump into someone and say "Oh, I just did this and it was great!"
>
> *(Susan)*

Ongoing sharing, exchange, collaboration, and, thus, informal collegial professional learning were typical for this team of three teachers, but not necessarily true for all teachers at Langfield, suggesting that the multi-site structure of the institution constrained such opportunities and affordances.

Teachers' preferences about professional learning

The participants felt that their professional learning needs about technologies and digital literacies had not been addressed in a satisfactory manner within and beyond Langfield, both in terms of quality and quality. First, they all expressed their desire to have more professional learning about digital literacies. Second, they thought that the quality needed to be improved. In their reflections on how the quality can be improved to make professional learning useful and relevant, they referred to (1) "the what" of professional learning – what would be helpful in terms of the content – and (2) "the how" of professional learning – what approach would work well for them.

Content: Digital literacies, learners' needs, and pedagogy

As noted in Chapter 5, the participants' definitions of digital literacies varied in sophistication. While all of them named relevant aspects of digital literacies, they did not seem to know fully about this concept and they were well aware of this fact. Building on this awareness, the participants wanted to know more about digital literacies. Tanya said:

> I think I'd love clarity around it all, like what do we mean by digital literacies? I can Google that and find it out, but what do we mean about it for these learners?

The same concern was raised during the focus group. As the participants collaboratively constructed a collage to capture their ideas about "preferred professional learning" (Figure 6.1), they represented their uncertainty about the notion of digital literacies with a big question mark in the centre of the collage. To explain what this question mark represented, one teacher said:

> [I'd like] clarity over what digital literacy is and what as a language teacher I should be doing.
>
> *(Focus group)*

The participants believed that clarifying how digital literacies are defined should be central to professional learning. Given the variety of existing definitions which we explored in Chapter 2, this is a very critical point. Importantly, the data above suggests, they thought it was their responsibility as language teachers to teach digital literacies. Indeed, from a socio-cultural perspective of literacy which informs this research, digital literacies are new forms of literacy that are just as significant as traditional print-based literacies. Thus, language and literacy teachers have been actively encouraged by the research literature and policies to include digital literacies in their teaching practices. In this research, there was no need to convince these participants to include digital literacies in their

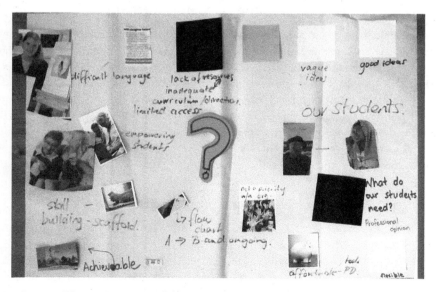

FIGURE 6.1 The participants' collaborative collage

curriculum and practices. They wanted to integrate digital literacies in language learning. But, as evident in their comments, their concerns were about having enough theoretical knowledge to teach digital literacies in EAL contexts.

The participants believed that such knowledge would help them to understand what should be taught. In the upper right corner of their collage, they added two squares with labels "good ideas" and "vague ideas". These elements refer to the content of their teaching in relation to digital literacies, and are juxtaposed to the "black hole" metaphor that we discussed in Chapter 5. While they recognised that there were some successful topics in their programme, many were more or less "hit and miss" and reflected a lack of understanding of how to teach digital literacies in a comprehensive way. The same concern was raised by Polly during the interview:

> I'm always a bit confused. Should we mainly focus on *Word*? Should we be focusing more on the internet and doing pronunciation games on the websites? Or is it better to do what we're doing where they practice typing and copying and pasting pictures? What exactly to teach? So, it's hard to know. We need to get more direction.
>
> *(Polly)*

Polly's words are especially illustrative of a very close connection between understanding of digital literacies and identifying what capabilities should be taught in the classroom. As she did not know much about the notion of digital literacies, she felt uncertain about which of these practices are digital literacies and which are not. This is a very relevant concern because technology use in language classrooms often focuses on improving language skills (such as pronunciation games in Polly's example) rather than preparing learners for the demands of reading, writing, and communication in complex and demanding digital spaces. Her rhetorical questions, however, illustrate her criticality and awareness about her professional knowledge around digital literacies as well as clearly articulate the need for professional learning to address this issue.

Another aspect of their professional knowledge that the teachers believed should be addressed in professional learning is adult EAL learners' needs in relation to digital literacies. Although the participants were experienced EAL teachers, they were very uncertain about what the learners needed. Tanya explained:

> So, what do they [learners] need? I can think about what they need, but that's from my angle. I'd like to know from them. And we try and ask them but when they don't have the language and we don't have interpreters. You don't get those rich answers.

The collaborative collage produced as part of the focus group also has a number of elements which signal the need for this focus in professional learning. The right part of the collage has a heading "our students" and a question "what do our students need/professional opinion". There are also several images of culturally diverse people in the collage as well as a reference to "difficult language" and "skill building" on the left side. Reflecting Tanya's words, the focus group participants explained these elements in the following way:

> We would like a professional opinion on what our students – low literacy level – need because we've done many surveys with them and we've asked them, but we still are not really sure…

A similar comment was made by Susan during the interview:

> For me, being able to go to a professional development that is geared towards beginner level learners would be great.
>
> *(Susan)*

The participants believed that teaching digital literacies should be driven by learners' needs, but they felt that they needed to know more about the specificities of these needs. They were aware that their learners were just at the beginning of their English language learning journey, had many complex needs, and required relevant support and scaffolding to engage with digital literacies within and beyond classrooms. As evident in Tanya's data, she enthusiastically wanted to address these needs but was uncertain what exactly should be addressed. As their comments suggest, eliciting these responses from learners was difficult due to the language barriers. The participants believed that professional learning should equip them with such knowledge. Their emphasis on "professional opinion" may also signal their interest in research evidence rather than anecdotal observations or speculations, including their own. While the desires of these teachers to understand learners' digital needs are not surprising, there was less emphasis given to the consideration of the learners' resources, which we identified in Chapter 4.

Finally, as captured in their collage, the teachers wanted assistance to be able to teach digital literacies. In other words, they wanted professional learning about the pedagogical foundations for successful teaching of digital literacies. During the focus group discussion, one teacher said:

> We have an office full of books about how to teach reading phonics and we don't have one book about how to teach digital technology… [We need] some ideas, activities, resources that we can just take and go.

The same need was referred to during the individual interviews:

> For our students, the phone is the most important; it's what they use every day. So, how to scaffold their learning so that they become more proficient using their phone?
>
> *(Polly)*

> I would want to be taught about computer resources that were available for teaching students ... I think learning how to teach the students to use specific sites like the MyGov app or website.
>
> *(Kate)*

The participants wanted their professional learning to have a strong focus on pedagogies suitable for digital literacies. Reflecting on their past professional learning experiences, they thought that just offering a list of websites or apps is insufficient. There should be more guidance on how to teach digital literacies and what can be done in the classroom to scaffold learning with and about technologies. They believed that professional learning about digital literacies should be very "practical" (Polly) and oriented towards pedagogies. Furthermore, the teachers wanted more guidance on pedagogies associated with the very specific digital literacy practices required for successful settlement in Australia, especially those involving smartphones and computers for engaging online and accessing services.

Approach: Organisation-wide/in-house, expert-delivered, ongoing

Langfield's participants also had a number of preferences in terms of how the provision of professional learning about digital literacies should be organised to be effective for their teaching context and needs. These preferences were influenced by the prevailing approach to professional learning at Langfield. The CEO clearly articulated the preference for an organisation-wide in-house professional learning:

> We like to have organisation-wide approaches to things. So that everyone's doing the same thing. It's better if we've got an in-house thing where everyone is on the same page and then we can build as a team... It's not that one person can do it and the other person doesn't know anything about it. It's everyone's learning and you bring everybody along. This is what we expect at Langfield.
>
> *(The CEO)*

This perspective was also supported by Susan who further explained why such an approach to professional learning is beneficial for Langfield:

> [We need] something that [spreads] across the organisation: so that everybody was onboard with it. An organisation-wide approach. I think that [the structure of Langfield] probably makes it even more important that we do pursue an organisation-wide approach. A lot of people are at different sites all at once, and the students move from different sites.
>
> *(Susan)*

All teacher-participants said that they preferred in-house professional learning. Polly's comment was representative of this opinion:

> In-house is probably the most realistic and most useful.

The participants believed that organisation-wide in-house professional learning about digital literacies would be the most suitable for them. From the leadership perspective, successful teaching of digital literacies across the institution was dependent on consistency. Achieving such consistency across an institutional setting with a quite distributed geographical structure and with multiple locations is not easy. An organisation-wide approach was seen as having the best potential for consistency while also providing opportunities to maintain regular professional interactions and relationships. We mentioned earlier that the majority of teachers at Langfield did not see each other on a regular basis. The leadership team strategically thought that an organisation-wide in-house approach to professional learning can enhance these opportunities for professional connection. This preference was also reflected in the focus group collage. The focus group participants uniformly thought in-house learning was the "most useful" for their learning needs within the constitution of the workforce at Langfield. In addition, their use of an image of a pig money bank with a caption "affordable" suggests that they also understood that in the current financial climate, in-house learning is "the most realistic" for Langfield's budget.

Another preference in terms of approach to professional learning shared across all participants is the involvement of external experts. Earlier, we mentioned that the majority of in-house professional learning sessions at Langfield were delivered by their own teachers. This approach had a number of benefits but it appeared to be a necessity rather than a preference, as illustrated in the data below:

RESEARCHER: If money wasn't a consideration, what sort of professional support or professional learning provision would you like for your staff?
THE CEO: If we could have people come in and help us. Build our knowledge, skills and passion in the area of what's possible.

Sharing the CEO's preference, the teachers had a similar sentiment during the focus group and in individual interviews. Two excerpts from the interviews reveal this shared concern.

> I think it would be really good to get somebody to come in and maybe deliver particular sessions on effective ways of teaching students with digital literacy, but it's been tried and tested. I'm not interested in anyone just coming in and winging something. I want to know that you know they've done it before, and it has been tried and tested and it works really well.
>
> *(Andrea)*

> I would love to know from someone professional how important they feel computer skills are when students don't have computers. Is this something we should be focusing on? Is there a lot of research happening in this field about low level literacy adult learners using technology?
>
> *(Polly)*

These comments reflect the participants' beliefs that their professional learning should be delivered by, or, at the very least, include input from experts. This might include practitioners from other institutions who have developed a substantial repertoire of successful teaching practices and resources as noted by Andrea. Polly's comment suggests her confidence in academics/researchers having the capacity to bridge theory and practice in the teaching of digital literacies. In other words, they wanted professional learning that draws on research and evidence-based practice. Indeed, such partnerships can provide useful learning opportunities. However, as mentioned by the CEO, additional funding is required to address such requests.

Finally, while the CEO said she was still trying to "figure out what [their] organisation-wide approach" to professional learning about digital literacies could be, the teacher-participants believed that professional learning needs to be ongoing rather than "one off" (Tanya). Given their preference for an organisation-wide in-house approach, include a series of ongoing collaborative and individual activities: (1) sharing experiences to identify professional needs; (2) learning something new; (3) implementing new ideas in the classroom; (4) reporting to the community; and (5) reflecting and problem-solving with colleagues.

The teachers thought that professional learning about digital literacies should begin with sharing their teaching experiences to identify their own concerns and needs. Their voices and agency as practitioners were critical as a starting point for professional learning. This idea of open professional dialogue was likely inspired by the focus group activity described in the vignette to this chapter. They thought that professional learning should be "starting here and then building on" (Focus group) such conversations. Though the focus group was intended as a research data gathering activity to ascertain teacher attitudes, opinions, and experiences, it also became a time for professional exchanges and solidarity about their shared concerns as educators. During the interviews, the teachers also referred to the importance of such dialogues in professional learning. Tanya mentioned that it needs to be "conversation-based" and "dialogic". Similarly, Andrea said:

> [What I'd like to know is] how are people looking at things and what problems are they encountering. I'd like to know – are they similar to the problems that I encounter?

This data suggests that the participants wanted an opportunity for a professional dialogue to voice their needs, challenges and uncertainties. From their perspective, such a dialogue can help to understand and crystallise their professional learning needs. They thought this should be a starting point in their learning journey about digital literacies leading to the next sequence of the following professional learning activities: learning something new through readings, presentations, or classroom observations; implementing these ideas in their own classrooms; reporting to the community and reflecting and problem-solving with colleagues. These ideas were reflected in the majority of the interviews:

> I think it's quite good if you have an ongoing professional development. Maybe it's a series of four: you actually learn something, you're required to practise it, come back and report on it, learn something else. Like that sort of model where it's a series of PDs that requires you to actually implement something. That's probably quite a good model.
>
> *(Susan)*

> I basically learn by doing. I'm happy for someone to show me something and then I'll do it. I love to read too, but I'm more a hands-on person really. That's how I learn best.
>
> *(Andrea)*

> I would prefer to learn by doing it because it's more helpful. Sometimes if I've read about it only I cannot really imagine how to do it. It would be ideal if the presenter has something like the lesson plan or the model lesson plan and they would get us to do it.
>
> *(Nicole)*

During the focus group poster activity, the participants used "a flow chart" image to illustrate this idea. They explained why they thought ongoing learning, comprising of several professional learning activities is important:

> We want to support it [ongoing professional learning] within the organisation. So, the flowchart would be here: we start at A and we go to B and then from there something else. [So it is] ongoing.
>
> *(Focus group)*

The participants believed that teaching digital literacies requires not only a profound understanding of the concept but also a repertoire of sophisticated pedagogies and teaching practices. It is difficult for teachers to develop these without relevant support. From their perspectives, such support can be provided by ongoing professional learning consisting of a number of conceptual, practical, and reflective activities, both collaborative and individual. They thought that only this type of professional learning could support their professional growth in relation to digital literacies.

Deliberations about professional learning

This chapter explored the participants' experiences with professional learning in relation to digital literacies. This dimension of teachers' work is very important to us because, being concerned with effective provision of digital literacies in adult EAL settings, we know that successful incorporation of digital literacies largely depends on teacher knowledge, skills, and ways of thinking about technologies (Tour, 2015). The integration of digital literacies in language learning contexts is not always easy because it may require a significant "paradigm shift" (Friedrich & Trainin, 2016, p. 1457) about the role of technologies in the practices of language classrooms and the underlying pedagogy. Such thinking and relevant teaching skills are usually built through appropriate professional learning (Chik, 2011; Dooly, 2009; Lotherington & Jenson, 2011). Thus, there is a continuing necessity to explore the quality of professional learning about digital literacies in this sector because high-quality professional learning makes a difference to the outcomes for students (Bubb & Earley, 2007).

In response to these calls, we found that our research participants, both the CEO and teachers, recognised the importance of professional learning. There was a strong interest by all participants in incorporating digital literacies into their teaching and all participants expressed a desire to be better equipped for teaching in the "digital age". At the same time, while Langfield had a strong focus on professional learning as a broad policy position, participants concluded that professional learning about digital literacies was insufficient. There were three main forms of professional learning about technologies and digital literacies in which the participants engaged: in-house professional learning, external professional learning, and peer-learning. The teaching staff at Langfield had different access to and varied experiences with these forms, indicating insufficient quantity and quality of professional learning available to the participants.

These findings mean that the opportunities for professional learning about digital literacies within and beyond Langfield were very limited. The empirical research about EAL teachers' professional learning about digital literacies in Australia and elsewhere is relatively scarce. Even less is known about professional learning experiences in the adult EAL sector which, as we have explored in previous chapters, has its own specific needs. Hanson-Smith (2016) argues that as digital technologies continue to develop, "without further training or education, any teachers five years out of college will find themselves hopelessly behind the times" (p. 287). Langfield's teachers already felt they were falling into "a black hole". If relevant professional learning opportunities are not offered in the sector, their professional readiness for the "digital age" is likely to be at risk.

In this research, we also documented teachers' needs and preferences for professional learning about digital literacies both in terms of its form (the "how" of professional learning) and content (the "what" of professional learning). This is important research knowledge given that very little is known about professional learning in this educational context. Such knowledge, rather than assumptions about teachers' needs, should be used to re-orientate existing professional learning initiatives and programmes (Jacobson, 2016). Our research findings provide a strong evidence base for innovation in the sector.

The findings of our research help us to understand the "how" of professional learning about digital literacies as envisioned by the participants (Figure 6.2). The research participants preferred an ongoing, organisation-wide approach, articulating directions that are being explored (and evaluated) across the organisation. They wanted it to be in-house learning but open to external influences and expertise, consisting of conceptual, practical, and reflective activities completed collaboratively with their colleagues, but still leaving space for individual teachers. They thought it should be collegiate and immediate, linked to continuous processes of practice and critical reflection. All these aspects are connected, linked, and inter-dependent. They cannot be separated, as none of these aspects alone is sufficient. They need to be tightly interwoven because one part supports and fits with all the others.

FIGURE 6.2 Towards a model of professional learning about digital literacies

The approach to professional learning which we conceptualise here is not simple, neat, or linear. It is generative, cyclic, and involves iterations that can be messy. The "glue" that holds it all together is a continuing genuine dialogue, teamwork, trust, and collaboration within the institution. While teaching is often individual and somewhat isolated, the *Techno-Tuesday* programme illustrates that teaching can be profoundly collaborative and intuitive. When learning programmes are designed and managed to promote and facilitate sharing, and the relationships are positive, teaching provides important professional learning opportunities for practitioners. As evident in this research, the participants wanted to learn with each other and from each other. In their professional learning, they valued and wanted genuine dialogue enabling authentic conversations about needs, aspirations, pedagogy, and professional practice relating to their learners. They thought such an approach to professional learning would suit Langfield given its community-based governance, multi-site structure, and the complexity of the learning contexts.

Previous research on professional learning has emphasised the importance and value of teacher interactions, collaboration, and cooperation focussed on practice. Mockler (2015) argues for ongoing teacher inquiry as a generative developmental stance for teachers:

> Inquiry as stance, then, is an orientation on the part of teachers toward generation of, and engagement with, their own curiosities about their work, ongoing grappling with critical questions they confront in their classrooms, and a willingness to engage in debates about practice both within and beyond the school.
>
> *(p. 123)*

This is precisely the kind of orientation being demonstrated by the *Techno-Tuesday* teachers. This collaborative approach resonates with a broader body of research and scholarship on learning organisations (Robinson, 2001; Senge, 1990), and it also highlights the importance of the internal culture of the enterprise, especially about interpersonal relationships. All communications within an organisation, including messaging related to values, purposes, priorities, and professional learning, are mediated through relationships. One of the purposes of this institutional ethnography was to highlight the capacity of such relationships to build an organisational culture. Figgis et al. (2001) report that a key finding of their study was,

> that the kind of culture an enterprise has, and particularly the tenor of interpersonal relations throughout the enterprise, shapes the value of the investment in training and learning.
>
> *(p. 8)*

Another important characteristic of professional learning as envisioned by the participants is learning and growing through acting in the classroom. Having collegial conversations about the issues, no matter how honest and authentic, was not seen as enough if it is not followed with action. This suggests that Langfield's teachers had a strong interest in a practice-based approach to continuous improvement and development which requires the implementation of new ideas, trialling, experimenting, and innovating, and observing what happens when new approaches or strategies are tried out. There was interest in recording, documenting, and gathering evidence, not necessarily in a formal way – but noticing of "what works" or "what does not" – and considering why. In short, the approach they advocated for is one which enables action and considered practice. Such an approach reflects the classic action-learning method described by Kolb (1984) and more recent researchers (Marquardt & Waddill, 2004).

We found that all participants were committed to professional learning and expressed their desire to have more frequent and more targeted professional learning; but while there was some clarity around the "how" of professional learning, there was less clarity about the "what" among the research participants. The "black hole" metaphor suggests that there were unknowns, and a growing awareness of knowledge gaps. This study has thrown light into those shadows. The findings suggest that there are several interrelated domains, or areas of focus, of the professional knowledge that Langfield's teachers needed to enhance the provision of digital literacies. However, identifying professional learning needs is neither simple nor straightforward. Our findings resonate with the work of Noguerón-Liu (2017) who stresses the importance of adopting multi-layered models to appreciate the complexity and the situated, encultured, and ecological nature of digital literacies.

The first area of focus involves appreciating learners' strengths. As we could see in this research, for Langfield's teachers, adopting strengths-based thinking about learners requires a significant shift in thinking and awareness that may need support through relevant professional learning. It is important for teachers to learn to appreciate the resources that learners already have and bring to their learning. This includes what they have achieved and what they are already doing in relation to digital technologies. Strengths-based practices entail an attitude and a philosophical orientation to the work which enables teachers to see their learners through the lens of what learners have, not what they do not have. Strengths-based practice is a disposition which both shapes and colours the work of educators shifting perceptions and practices, and highlighting opportunities and affordances, while not ignoring needs and problems.

A second and related dimension involves valuing learners' existing digital worlds and their literacy practices in those worlds: what they do with various apps, programmes, platforms, systems, and devices at play in their lives. We have consistently pointed out in this book that globally there is an increasingly digitisation of governance, economy, business, health systems, transport and logistics, agriculture, education, tourism, and leisure (Broadband Commission for Sustainable Development, 2017; Morrison, 2021; Shariati et al., 2017; Smythe, 2018). It is important to appreciate the diverse digital expectations and requirements of institutions, agencies, and service providers with whom adult EAL learners need to engage, as well as to develop awareness of learners' socio-material agency. For instance, it may make a difference whether one has or prefers to use (or has access to) a smartphone, or a laptop, or a desktop computer; or a digital "kiosk" in a shopping centre, or a government office; whether one is comfortable with accessing a voice file or a PDF; or whether one chooses to send an email or ask a chatbot. It also involves teachers appreciating the affective dimensions of their learners' and their complex identities (which may or may not include experience of trauma and dislocation). Professional learning about effective pedagogies for digital literacies in adult EAL contexts needs to be built on rich understandings of the complex interplay of multiple factors shaping adult learners' lives, including their digital lifeworlds.

Finally, but importantly, a third set of understandings, involves teachers moving their thinking about "digital literacy" away from a singular, generic, and readily transferable skill to a complex, culturally situated set of critical thinking practices that are mediated and shaped by evolving technologies as well as shifting social norms and expectations. This is the socio-cultural view of digital literacies that we have articulated throughout this study. Furthermore, as the findings of this research illuminated, the teachers had a strong interest in relevant pedagogies for digital literacies, especially for learners who are at the beginning of their EAL journey.

Despite their self-declared anxieties and perceptions of being in a "black hole", Langfield's teaching team appear to be adapting to the challenges they face in a digital world. These teachers recognised that in many respects they are at the beginning of a professional revolution that is global. They need to know more, they need to do more; but they are already in dialogue, they are already doing, and reflecting critically on their actions. They are building their own multilayered understandings of digital literacies, in concert with their learners and their learners' digital lifeworlds that are so pivotal to successful settlement in Australia. Their professional challenges, and the challenge for all who may wish to follow them, is to find ways of identifying, articulating, and building upon the strengths inherent in their practice. Professional learning informed by evidence is a critically important way to build this strength.

Conclusion

Drawing on the discussion of the teachers' sense of inadequacy about their pedagogy and practice in the previous chapter, here we focused on professional learning. The study found that Langfield had a strong focus on professional learning as an aspirational policy position, but, from the participants' perspectives, professional learning about digital literacies was insufficient. There were three main forms of professional learning about technologies and digital literacies in which the participants engaged: in-house professional learning, external professional learning, and peer-learning. However, different teachers had different access to and different experiences with these forms of learning, illuminating insufficient quantity and quality of learning overall. All participants were committed to professional learning and expressed their desire to have more frequent and more targeted learning. They also had a particular vision on professional learning about digital literacies that would suit their needs. The chapter concludes by outlining the "how" and the "what" of professional learning that may suit Langfield given their community-based governance, multi-site structure, and complexity of the learning contexts.

7
ENABLING LEADERSHIP FOR EFFECTIVE PRACTICE

> **FIELD NOTES**
>
> We have only just met the Langfield CEO, and she is walking us around the Centre's main base, one of several locations from which services are offered and in which classes are conducted. She is describing her complex and multifaceted role. She describes Langfield providing a broad range of "wrap around" services for learners because "they come to us really for everything… for anything that they need help with" from help with finance, to counselling, to childcare, to housing. The CEO stresses the importance of offering programmes and services locally:
>
>> We're small, we're nimble, we just go, we'll find another room down there and we'll run a class out of it. You know, we can be quite responsive.
>
> Indeed, being friendly, accessible, and responsive is core business. It is about building relationships and trust. When the trust is developed, she explains "they'll come and ask us". Of course, Langfield cannot provide all the answers, nor all the services; but it is ambitious in striving to provide a one-stop shop, staffed by people who care and are willing to help; no matter what their role is, or where they are located within the organisation. Developing this culture of care and professionalism is important to the CEO and she strives to cultivate it across the organisation with all of her staff:
>
>> Everybody has their own way of doing things, [but] we don't want people to be just off doing their own thing… In terms of good professional

DOI: 10.4324/9781003132684-7

> learning, I think so much of it is around the peer-to-peer stuff, and that it's a culture... It's a culture of professional learning where you've never finished learning. It's just that it's an ongoing process and we're doing it all the time and we only want people working with us who are interested in that.
>
> June 18, 2019

It is clear across all sectors of education that progressive and sustainable change has to be led. This is especially true in the context of the extensive digitisation of society and education. In our opening vignette, we have a glimpse of the CEO's leadership style. From our first engagement in the introductory tour, we noted that her focus is on effective responses to learners' needs and on building a culture of care, professionalism, and professional learning within the organisation. What is noticeable from the outset is the way she positions herself *with* her people as she says "they come to *us* [emphasis added]" and "*we* [emphasis added] can be quite responsive". It is not "I", or "me", being showcased here; it is the collective "we" that makes things possible. We further see here that the CEO's leadership approach is founded upon the importance of learning – not just for students but for everyone. She wants to employ and work with teachers who see themselves as learners, as she states "we only want people working with us who are interested in that". The CEO's language here is also important. She says "we want "people *working with us* [emphasis added]", not working *for* us or *for* me. Effective leadership for change should be inclusive and grounded, democratic, and informed by research evidence. In this chapter, we explore these themes and consider how the CEO of Langfield orchestrates challenging work in difficult circumstances.

The CEO of Langfield sits in that uneasy space of leading for change and managing her staff and resources so that the organisation can deliver effective programmes for learning English, digital literacies as well as other skills for work and connection in the community. Interviews and several informal conversations with the CEO in the context of this study have revealed the extent to which she wishes to prioritise digital literacies as part of Langfield language programme. Earlier, in Chapter 2, we conceptualised the qualities of effective leadership as including strength-based principles and being democratic. In this chapter, we focus on leadership and vision for change at Langfield, looking at leadership on the ground – situated and using organisational thinking that is adaptive to specific needs. We also focus on the importance of strengths-based and evidence-driven ideas to manage digital change in the institutional setting of Langfield, though we are also aware of the barriers and limitations that all leaders face in encountering organisational change. We start by exploring Langfield leadership and organisational structure. This is followed by the discussion of the CEO's vision for change and digital literacies as well as her leadership values and style. This chapter also provides insights into the situated difficulties of enacting change in a community-based EAL provider and the urgent need for adequate material provision required for the changes.

Distributed and connected understandings of leadership

Leaders operate within organisational boundaries, economic constraints, and legal frameworks, and, in the not-for-profit ACE sector, this includes governance according to rules of incorporation and quality assurance related to maintaining status as a registered training organisation (RTO). In the interview conducted with the CEO, the organisation structure and governance of Langfield were outlined in the following way:

> We're governed by a Board of Governors. I'm the CEO and then we have an education manager who looks after the education programmes and the teachers. We have a community development manager who looks after the community development programmes that we do. A volunteer manager because we have volunteers involved in a lot of our programmes. We can do more things and that requires management. And a finance manager who looks after our finance and our data. And then we have staff sitting under that. Principally teachers sitting under the education manager and a couple of community development people sitting under the community development manager.

This quote indicates that there is a middle management and distributed leadership structure within Langfield charged with overseeing both its operational and educational needs. It also illuminates the CEO's clear awareness of the connection with various stakeholders in the organisation such as community connection and volunteers, for instance. The CEO's words also point out that there is an evident hierarchy that operates from the CEO and Board of Management down to the middle managers and then the practitioners. Langfield is an independent, not-for-profit entity that exists to meet community educational needs in the context of the wider ACE environment in Victoria under the auspices of the Department of Education and Training and the Minister for Training and Skills.

The CEO then moves to the complexity of the funding that supports the existence of Langfield:

> So, we are pretty reliant on government funding. We have a number of programmes. We've got the Skills for Education and Employment programme funded federally – that's for Centrelink registered participants. We have the AMEP which is the 510 free hours for new migrants, and they're federally funded. And then we're a training organisation in terms of what we're offering in Victoria under Victorian Government funding accredited courses in EAL, and also pre-accredited courses, which is another of the Victorian Government funding. We also get philanthropic funding for a lot

of our community development projects. We get assistance with a couple of those too from the local municipality. We have assistance with some of our rent; they charge us low rent for being a not-for-profit and they're quite interested to support us with our community development.

This funding is derived from four discrete sources, including the Federal and State Governments, local council, and charitable endeavours for their community outreach work. Some of this funding is related to their status as an RTO. This means that there are layers of compliance and quality assurance necessary for funding to be approved, as explained by the CEO:

> There's been a lot of compliance requirements for us in our sector. I know it's in every sector, but we've had a new AMEP contract… We are just audited 'til the cows come home… Yes, you look after the compliance. We must do that otherwise we'll go under.

The EAL courses related directly to the research reported in this book are subject to that compliance and auditing regime. This means that any change and reform, including the overt introduction of digital literacies, must maintain compliance with the mandated frameworks. The data suggests that the CEO functions as a liaison person between the Board of Management, funding providers, compliance bodies, community organisations, and the educational work of the organisation and its teachers. From this perspective, she is more than an educational leader in negotiating the complex intricacies of running a community-based adult education organisation in what might be characterised as a fragile funding landscape.

It was clear from the interview with the CEO and the wider data set that, despite the complexity of her role (which includes much more than educational concerns), there is a high priority given to the work of the teachers at Langfield. She emphasised her continuous desire "to upskill teachers". As an example, focussing on language learning, she described the recent approach taken to teaching pronunciation

> We've done a lot of work in teaching pronunciation, working on the skills of teachers in teaching pronunciation, which teachers don't get taught in teacher education very much. They get a little bit of phonology but they don't learn how to teach it. And there's a real need for students to be able to speak and be understood. They've identified it, teachers have identified it, so we've done a lot of work there.

Across the hierarchical but distributed leadership structure, there are also opportunities to hear and value the views and concerns of the teachers on the ground who are working with the adult learners. Importantly, her use of "they've identified it" refers to Langfield's learners, suggesting her listening not only to the teachers but also to the learners. The CEO seemed to be well aware that the progress and wellbeing of these learners is the reason for the organisation's existence. The hierarchical leadership structure appears not to negate broader democratic processes of listening to those on the ground who are best able to articulate success and identify issues of concern. The fact that a group of teachers were given freedom to design, introduce, and deliver *Techno-Tuesday* extending Langfield's programmes is another example of democratic leadership practices. The tacit connection between the teachers and the CEO was also evident in teachers' data as well as in a range of exchanges we observed between educators and the CEO in situations outside the interviews:

> I think the management is really open to us giving feedback. They're so supportive.
>
> *(Tanya)*

Envisioning change through teachers' strengths

As discussed in Chapter 5, all Langfield's participants recognised the importance of digital literacies but were uncertain about teaching them. Reflecting this issue, the CEO described their current approach to digital literacies as "sporadic and not systematic" but articulated her wish for this situation to change. She believed there is a need for a change: the institution needs to develop "a more systematic approach" (The CEO) to digital literacies. The CEO had a particular vision for Langfield which is pivotal to the organisation's immediate and future success as she explained:

> I've been keen to make a difference with what's happening with quality in the classroom…[and] upskill teachers to really meet the needs of their students. We're also working with low level, beginner level adults, especially those with low literacy because they are quite difficult. It's a difficult cohort to teach … So, really incorporated in all of that is digital literacy. We've got some teachers there who are doing some interesting things with digital literacy. It's quite an amazing thing – the importance of digital literacy – and it's becoming more and more important with each day really rather than less important. Because all of their Centrelink engagement is now via either the web or the app.

This quote strongly suggests that the quality of the learning is central to the CEO's vision. Consequently, support for the professional learning of the teachers, including professional learning on digital literacies as core settlement capabilities, is pivotal to the provision of high-quality learning for the learners. She was also aware of the specific needs of learners in relation to the key government services and believed that the organisational vision needed to be about meeting those needs. The CEO's awareness, recognition, and appreciation of the teachers who are "doing some interesting things with digital literacy" shows her willingness to embrace a strengths-based approach as part of the vision and lead the change building on what these teachers are already doing.

The CEO also had a clear perspective on how this vision for organisational change in relation to teaching digital literacies can happen:

> We have to have people with passion in the organisation driving the organisation-wide approach. So, it has to really come from me because if I'm not interested, well, it's probably not going to get driven. But I don't need to be the one who's the expert really. I need to support some people and allow them to drive it and support them to drive it. What are they doing about such and such, where they bring their problems and they discuss the challenges that they've had and how they might have overcome them and they get ideas from their peers. So, to set up that professional learning culture.

As evident, the CEO believed that organisational change does not necessarily have to sit only with her. In this quote, the CEO is also articulating the idea that this vision for change around digital literacies has to be supported by the organisational leader but also needs to be a vision shared by all and understood as a concern grounded in practice as part of what Mant (1999) calls "intelligent leadership" (p. 8). Such leadership requires what he calls "broadband" intelligence (p. 39) which is inclusive, socially and emotionally intelligent, and based on a shared vision and goals. In her study of female headteachers in the UK, Coleman (1996) noted that female leaders will often take the best qualities from male leaders and add qualities that come from being a woman, including more collaborative interpersonal approaches and shared decision-making. This stance might be also conceived as what Greenleaf (2002) calls servant leadership, where the leader adopts the positions of advocate, resource, or support person in order to serve the needs of people in the organisation. Echoing her democratic style and distributed approach to leadership, the CEO also appears to embrace a more democratic model of engaging peer support and developing the expertise of staff so that they can support each other.

During the interview, the CEO referred to different strategies for professional learning and change that reflect this democratic leadership style. For example, she identifies "peer observations", "teachers then meet afterwards and feedback", and "reflection" as important strategies that she believes have a "really important place for [the] learning" of teachers and, thus, a change in the institution. In this sense, the CEO continued looking through a strengths-based lens to see what staff can do to support each other and to develop their pedagogies for digital literacies. Clearly, the CEO was open for change to be led by others, indicating her vision of change led from the grassroots and across the consistency of the organisation. Many of the characteristics of democratic leadership were embodied in her looking to her teachers for ideas about change and building from what is already in motion in their classroom practices. The aim is to "leverage", expand, or amplify what works.

Collaboration as the core leadership value

As suggested above, the CEO worked in the complex territory involving funding bodies, compliance organisations, community connections, and the particular needs of learners and staff. What appeared to drive her in the role, however, was her essential values as they were related to the core business of the organisation. When asked to articulate her values, she responded this way:

> To get better outcomes for our students and to really try to meet their needs. They're aspirational and sometimes that's really tough. We don't want them coming to English [classes] forever. If they've got goals to work to improve their lives, we want to support them in that. So that's where the wrap-around services that we provide are important to the teaching. It's not just what you're doing in the class. It's some other things that need to happen to support people to progress.

In this excerpt from the interview, the CEO is voicing her value of comprehensive care: providing a strongly holistic approach to the learners at Langfield, which includes not only English learning but what she describes as "wrap-around services" that deliver support for learners from migrant and refugee backgrounds. Her use of "we" in this excerpt suggests the collaborative basis for this value of comprehensive care. Using teachers' collaboration within *Techno-Tuesday* as an example, she then spoke about her values in terms of the intersubjectivity of her teaching staff:

> It's their personalities and how they work together. And I think that that has really enabled a lot of collaboration; it's really back to that peer sharing model. So, they're problem solving it together. Teachers actually, when they can get on that, they can achieve more when they're working together and learning from each other and I feel that's really important.

This reference to "collaboration" and the "peer sharing model" points to the importance of teachers' agency and cooperation as a central value and goal at Langfield to resolve issues and move forward. This is, again, an example of a grounded and democratic approach to education in which there is a distributed notion of how teachers can do professional learning and develop ideas together through peer-to-peer collaboration and mentoring – the theme evident throughout our previous chapters. There is implicit permission evident from the CEO for this level of independent operationalising of curriculum, pedagogical and practical decision-making for the teachers, rather than a top-down approach in which the ability to act has to be sanctioned, or controlled, in an onerous bureaucratic sense. Of course, this level of trust to operate agentially was built on leadership knowledge of the team as well as individual teachers' work and strengths within the team. In relation to this, the CEO pointed to the value of grass-roots leadership:

> I'm not in the classroom anymore, [so] I need someone who is and who I can support and say "You know – try this, go for that" and so to encourage her to have a go and then to share occasionally with the staff.

Instead of a more hierarchical control of teaching and learning, the CEO appeared to prefer provision for a more open approach to decision-making in which a considerable allowance for risk-taking and experimentation was evident. This may be due, in part, because she still carried her teacher identity as part of her manager-leader role, and this played out in the everyday connections that she had with her staff. In reference to grounded leadership for more systematic inclusion of digital literacies and deploying supporting pedagogies, the CEO again referred to teachers within *Techno-Tuesday*:

> They're quite learners, quite keen professional learners. And the other teachers are just a little bit different. Some of them are quite keen, some of them are just... they've got plenty to do. They've got so much to do that they're just not doing that [digital literacies] but they're doing other good things. So it's just a matter of bringing them in, I think, and bringing them along more than we've done with this.

Here the CEO is pointing to the collaborative experience of three teachers as exemplars of practice that she would like to extend beyond *Techno-Tuesday*. There is again an embracing of change and risk as part of the new learning and the "figuring out" of how this can be achieved in relation to digital literacies and expanded into other aspects of the organisation's work. She also recognised and valued the work of teachers who were not necessarily that digitally focused and innovative *per se* but were still doing vital teaching work that supports the vision of Langfield. This example points again to the implicit democratic approach to leadership and change as well as the recognition of strengths-based practice and collegiality where the innovative work of colleagues is utilised to realise the institutional vision and the core values. It also highlights her differentiated recognition that her staff are not clones of one another; they each bring particular strengths, sensibilities, and needs into the work.

Situated difficulties of enacting change

There appeared to be a more or less progressive approach to leadership at Langfield that was characterised as distributed and democratic with strong valuing of student learning and the development of teachers to support that learning. Drawing on a strengths-based approach, we have looked for what was effective and exemplary in Langfield leadership practice. However, we would not want to give the impression that Langfield was without its challenges and capacities for growth. As a point of disclosure about their circumstances, the CEO was erudite in describing the barriers and issues that the institution faces, not only with teachers and learners embracing digital technologies but also learners' language skills, general educational backgrounds, and prior learning experiences. She stated:

> It's language; it's navigating the technologies and it's also literacy. So those particular students do literacy as well as the language because they might have not had much schooling themselves. So they're not particularly literate. For instance, the Sudanese and Somali, Ethiopian, Horn of African women really have had interrupted schooling. You know, they've got really serious barriers.

The CEO refers to the diverse educational backgrounds of Langfield's adult learners which makes it difficult to integrate digital literacies more consistently in teaching and learning. While this may be true, the CEO conceives these as "barriers" rather than as possibilities that can be built from the existing linguistic and cultural resources of the learners. As we mentioned in Chapter 5, such thinking was evident across all participants of this research. While teachers and the CEO had good intentions, such perspectives on learners sometimes prevented them from seeing, recognising, and using a wider range of learners' strengths in a more systematic way. Importantly, such thinking may be problematic for how institutional change in relation to digital literacies is conceptualised and enacted.

The CEO also identified another situated difficulty in promoting change to bring digital literacies into teaching and learning in her organisation. The logistic and economic difficulties of enacting "organisation-wide" strategies for change were clearly articulated by the CEO. Interestingly, the provision of digital technologies did not seem to be a substantial problem from the CEO's perspective. She said that they "have got a provision of devices". However, she thought that "just" getting the devices for the institution is not enough for effective change. The devices need to be centralised in teaching which requires additional investment:

> It takes a bit of energy to have an organisation-wide approach [laugh] because you've got to keep at it and you've got to make sure you make time for it… And it's making room for it. If we're asking teachers to do extra things, there might need to be some budget for that. We haven't got a great big budget; we're a not-for-profit, but we do try to make a budget where we can.

While the provision of digital technologies did not seem to be a problem from the CEO's perspective, she understood that additional budgets are required for supporting teachers in such a change. As a not-for-profit community-based learning organisation, Langfield was limited by budgets and, thus, had limited material support to engage teachers in additional professional learning required for teaching digital literacies. Most of Langfield's teachers were working part-time. Thus, asking them to invest their time and effort in professional learning or development of a new programme required substantial budgets which the institution did not have. From this perspective, a vision for the instantiation of digital literacies into teaching and learning was closely related to a holistic vision about material provisions required for this change. It was not just technologies that were required but shifts in curriculum, pedagogies, programmes, and, perhaps, teacher attitudes and capabilities as well. Hence, we were witnessing a period of transition where there was tension between the *vision* for full implementation of technologies in teaching and learning and the limited resources for implementation, including strategic professional learning in regard to digital literacies.

The CEO's perspective on additional material support echoed teachers' opinions although it had a different focus point. As we discussed in Chapters 3 and 5, the access to digital devices seemed to be reasonable at Langfield. There were sets of iPads and computer rooms. The teachers also actively incorporated learners' personal mobile phones in teaching and learning. However, Andrea said:

> The logistics of doing that [using digital technologies] is often quite difficult because the machines often don't work, the internet often breaks down, the equipment is outdated. The programmes that I work on at home and that I bring into here are very different, so there's no compatibility and I find that extremely frustrating.

Andrea suggested that while Langfield's teachers had access to technologies, they did not always work smoothly. Thus, it became teachers' responsibility to troubleshoot and deal with technical issues which were often beyond teachers' existing knowledge and skills. Indeed, many teachers do not necessarily have relevant technical skills to deal with hardware and the internet connectivity. Andrea's quote suggests that to teach digital literacies, she needed relevant on-demand technical support. Having a technician on the site during teaching hours, of course, requires a budget.

However, the CEO questioned if investments should be made into computer rooms given that their learners mainly rely on personal mobile phones and there were successful examples of classroom practices with mobile devices at Langfield – some of which were described in Chapter 5. The CEO said:

> I feel that desktops are less relevant to many of the students' lives because they rely on their personal devices I think… Everyone's got a phone now. A few years ago, some of those women wouldn't have had a phone, but

now they've got a phone... They're not going to get a desktop and really work with it.

Langfield had some devices at the disposal of learners, which indicates there was impetus in terms of the use of technologies in classes. At the same time, the material provisioning of staff for teaching is not a simple matter. There is the complexity of what the students themselves have access to at home, especially in terms of what "students get out of their phones" (the CEO) but, importantly, what skills they want to develop. We reported in Chapter 4 that many learners wanted to learn how to use a computer because mobile phones can be less convenient (or even unsuitable) for certain practices (e.g. composing a CV). The CEO saw the use of learners' own devices as an opportunity for pursuing change in terms of digital literacies at Langfield but this, as evident, may not necessarily meet the learners' needs and aspirations.

Supporting change through strategic provisioning

The discussion above links to the final theme that was evident in the CEO's interview data. The study found that there was a need to support substantial change through provisions for both learners and staff at Langfield. One of these areas of provisioning was to evaluate the third space practices of the learners and see what they can bring out of these spaces in terms of technologies and existing digital literacies. The CEO stated:

> Let's really harness that [learners' use of mobile phones] and they [teachers] are having this conversation about perhaps moving away from using desktops for some of these people... They've got their phone. So, what are the things we can do with the phone?

In this statement, the CEO is intimating that instead of resourcing for what students do not have technologically (a deficit perspective), it is better to build on what they already have. She thinks that it is important to ask questions about what devices are central to the current lives and needs of learners in order to extend their digital literacies. This suggests the importance of grounded local knowledge in order to build effective leadership for digital change. This grounded local knowledge is based on an assessment of needs and possibilities and an evaluation of what is there already and what can be added, or enhanced, to address learners' needs. She states:

> I think it's probably really doing proper needs analysis and devising an approach to incorporating digital literacy that is really meaningful to the students. I think it has to be relevant – getting them to do things and job searching. What are the skills required to do that? Let's unpack that and build the skills in a meaningful way for the students... The needs of the

students. Principally, it's the needs of the students. We want better outcomes for the students.

The CEO focuses on the needs of the learners as the driving force for change for both her and the teachers she leads. She believed that a "systematic approach" to the provision of digital literacies needs to come from the basis of learner needs. This is a version of classic approach, commonly referred to as a training needs analysis (TNA). Traditionally, the TNA identifies, through formal assessment processes, what the learners already know and then targets what they still need to know as the focus of training. At times this can be a narrow and reductionist process, often justified in the interests of efficiency.

However, the question is whether developing change from this needs base and from the insider distributed leadership approach at Langfield is enough. She explained:

> We've done a lot of work ourselves. A couple of us have done a lot of work and we do a bit of in-house stuff just because there's not much else out there. But where we can, we bring in external experts to help out and to give an injection of ideas and strategies. Again, what we've done with digital literacy has been sporadic and not systematic.

This perspective suggests that there was a focus here on facilitating internal leadership and collegial initiatives for change in relation to digital literacies, motivated by the perceived lack of worthwhile professional learning to support digital change. The CEO's comments about bringing in "external experts" are perhaps a reflection of her intuitive recognition that the lens sometimes needs to be set wider, rather than narrower. Sefton et al. (1995) discussed the value of a learning environment analysis (LEA) seeing the traditional TNA as only part of a more comprehensive process that considered the diverse opportunities, or affordances for learning (Billett, 2001) that may be presented by the environment.

This broader perspective, including the possible use of "external experts", offers potential to take Langfield to new ideas and inspire more than "sporadic" innovation. This perspective echoes our findings reported in Chapter 6: the teachers wanted to learn more about digital literacies and were interested in research and practical ideas delivered by external experts. In this sense, leadership for change was positioned by the CEO as a larger picture awareness of what an organisation needs and can sponsor.

This macro view of the needs in terms of digital change at Langfield was also positioned by the CEO in terms of the pedagogical capacities and agency of teachers. She stated:

> Not so long ago we didn't have iPads. So, they [teachers] have had to learn. Of course, some teachers are right on it and are all across quickly and others are less so. They have less natural tendency to have a go [in the classroom]

because they're a bit scared themselves. So, where teachers don't feel in control, they tend to leave it.

The grounded awareness of the uneven capacities and "readiness" of teachers is clear in this statement and points to the need for a systematic, organisation-wide approach to professional learning. Given her position as CEO, it is indicative of her grounded and connected approach to show awareness of the differentiated levels of apprehension ("they're a bit sacred") among some teachers about a greater focus on technology and digital literacies. This greater focus on technologies also brings necessary attention to the agency of the material itself: to the technologies and devices that will mediate how digital literacies are inculcated.

Considering transformational leadership

The data set examined in this chapter represents the views, practices, and outlook of one educational leader in the community-based adult EAL sector – the CEO of Langfield. Her views are certainly not taken as representative of the sector, nor are they positioned as being necessarily model leadership practice in a time of digital change across all educational sectors. What the data does illuminate is the reflexivity of one leader grappling with change in her organisation and using clearly democratic processes and feminist sensibilities to instantiate that change, even in the face of difficulties and limitations (Biesta, 2015; Glover, 2017).

This research found that the CEO was candid about the issues facing Langfield and the need for strategic change, pointing to what she saw as a lack of a consistently systemic approach to the inclusion of digital literacies in the EAL programme and bringing technologies from the margins into the centre of practice. There was a vision for change in which practices, curriculum, and the frameworks that support effective pedagogy come under scrutiny (Sarros et al., 2011). She insisted that such change must come from understanding the learning and developmental needs and opportunities of both learners and teachers in terms of digital literacies. Importantly, her understanding of these needs was taken from her awareness of the views of the teachers and their existing practices that showed promise for further elaboration, extension, or dissemination within and across the organisation. For change to be systematic and substantive, leadership at Langfield was primarily about awareness and making connections to what was happening on the ground (MacGillivray, 2018).

As part of a democratic approach involving grounded awareness of need, consultation, and accounting for the views of all stakeholders in decision-making, the CEO looked to best practice and appeared to adopt a strengths-based approach in moving forward. She opened pathways for distributed leadership and supported staff who became exemplars of effective practice (Spillane et al., 2001). However, she was also aware that change needs conceptual and research grounding and that enlisting the help of outside organisations to support the internal leadership at Langfield was vital. Emphatically, the findings here suggest that the leadership

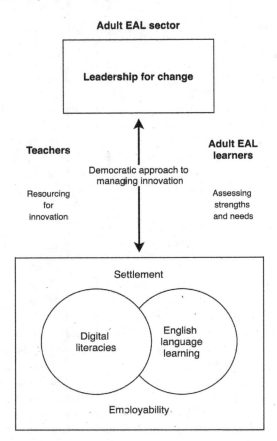

FIGURE 7.1 A framework for leadership towards digital literacies

work undertaken by the CEO was complex and multifaceted, full of clear tensions, and sometimes fraught. The sector contained within it challenging funding and regulatory/compliance pressures (Brown, 2020; Hodge et al., 2020). Thus, there were difficulties in providing the sort of resources needed to support learners and teachers. This includes the professional learning needs of teachers, which can be problematic in the sector given the cost and efficacy of what is currently available for teaching about digital literacies.

These findings offer important insights based in this illustrative example of leadership practice in the challenging space of implementing change for digital literacies in teaching and learning in adult education; and allow us to conceptualise a framework (Figure 7.1) for leading change, specifically in terms of digital literacies in EAL programmes for adult learners. Such a framework is an important contribution. While a significant body of research advocates for stronger inclusion of digital literacies in language programmes (Godwin-Jones, 2015; Hafner et al., 2015), there was no conceptual guidance for doing this. This model offers conceptual scaffolding, and it is of relevance for leaders, practitioners, and researchers working in the field. This leadership framework should be viewed as expansive and generative (not definitive): as a way of opening discussion and further considerations about policy and practice.

As illuminated throughout this chapter, leadership for change in this sector is complex because it involves the intersection of funding, compliance requirements, and the demands of a range of stakeholders, not to mention the needs of learners and their teachers, often part-time (sometimes volunteers), and the provision of appropriate resources. The framework centres on the core business of adult EAL providers – English language learning that includes digital literacies as integral capacities for settlement in Australia, being employable and feeling included.

This framework, emerging from the findings of our engagement with Langfield, reflects the need to bring digital literacies to centre stage, making them integral to English language and literacy learning as well as to the totality of settlement, inclusion in the community and employability. This positioning is well aligned with calls in research literature (Alam & Imran, 2015; Kenny, 2016; van Rensburg & Son, 2010). Through this centrality, we challenge the notion that digital literacies are important but peripheral. In line with the focus on materiality in this book, consideration should also be given to designing for and with the agency of diverse digital technologies in the learning of students.

Therefore, we contend that leadership for change in the adult EAL sector should be about the totality of the digital and linguistic context for learning. It needs to be a direct, designed, and deliberative approach that drives change not only in pedagogies and practices about English language learning but also in the pivotal place of digital literacies as part of language and literacy learning and as key aspects of settlement, social inclusion, and employability. The word "approach" is meant to evoke the idea of democratic leadership in as much as effecting change necessitates a whole-organisation approach (Beycioglu & Kondakci, 2020). As illustrated in the framework, this approach needs to include dialogue and be inclusive of many perspectives and experiences. It needs to consider the perspectives of teachers in the classrooms as well as the needs and strengths of learners. This will facilitate a more distributed multi-level and engaged form of change which will be more nuanced than the one led just by the person at the top. The CEO of Langfield explicitly indicated that examples of excellent practice and ongoing purposeful communication with staff were foremost in her approach to instigating such change.

The framework also directs attention to two important qualities of the approach that are required to ensure the ongoing and sustained success of change leadership for integrating digital literacies in adult EAL programmes. The first is resourcing change to support teachers. This might include technological provisions and support, but it would also need to include professional learning that addresses the pedagogical approaches that facilitate digital change. The findings of this project suggest the value of both internal reflections, evaluation, and trials, as well as stimulus and input from outside the organisation. The second key quality is continuing close attention to the needs and, importantly, the strengths of the adult learners, which are fluid, changeable, and related to individual circumstances, personalities, and aspirations. Strategies for understanding these needs and strengths and responding to them effectively are clearly needed if digital literacies are to be fully incorporated into the curriculum and day-to-day classroom activities.

Conclusion

In this chapter, we have engaged with three important ideas that are strongly connected to the concepts explored in other chapters of this book. The first is to point to the important place of leadership in driving change, and this is especially the case for change in terms of digital literacies. The findings and the literature suggest that a workplace culture of collegiality, inclusion, and distributed leadership (built on democratic principles) is best placed to promote the possibilities for productive change. This view of organisational change seems essential in order to fully embrace digital literacies and to authorise and support the necessary pedagogical innovations to enable adult EAL learners not merely to settle in Australia but to thrive in an increasingly digitised society.

Second, educational leaders, such as Langfield's CEO, are people of vision who both nurture and drive change, and this is especially important in the wake of the technological revolution that has swept society in the last 20 years, with increasing impact in the last five years. The findings in this chapter suggest that the CEO was well aware of the broader and constantly shifting societal landscape, the internal and external support networks for change, and the need to account for the multiple stakeholders who are pivotal to effective and sustainable change. Our findings showcase the importance of the CEO's commitment to the organisation and its vision as well as the articulation and sharing of this vision – both within and beyond the organisation's walls.

Finally, on the back of the literature and in concert with this leadership case study, we developed a leadership framework of change for digital literacies in the adult EAL sector, and also for future research in the field. This framework might be used to understand and evaluate factors that are essential for change in the context of introducing digital literacies in a cohesive manner within an adult community education organisation.

8
LEFT TO THEIR OWN DEVICES
Implications for change

This book and the research which it reports were informed by our strong belief in the importance of digital literacies for adults from migrant and refugee backgrounds as they settle in Australia and the need for relevant learning opportunities within EAL programmes. It was also driven by the need for relevant theoretical and practical insights that would help the sector to enhance the provision of digital literacies and better prepare adult EAL learners for highly digitised everyday life, work, and education in Australia. We believed that if progress is to be made to enhance the provision of digital literacies in such a complex sector in meaningful and relevant ways, we need a holistic and multidimensional understanding of institutional practices with digital literacies which can be only achieved by hearing multiple voices – the voices of the learners, teachers, and the CEO. This is how a story of Langfield and its community, reported in this book, emerged.

This final chapter synthesises multiple issues which have been discussed throughout this book related to teaching and learning digital literacies as well as associated professional learning and leadership practices at Langfield. One of our central arguments is that Langfield attempted to do its best to provide opportunities for learning digital literacies and equip its adult EAL learners with relevant capabilities; however, inclusion of digital literacies in EAL programmes was a day-to-day battle, often characterised by a range of challenges and complexities. Langfield's teachers tried new things with digital technologies and wanted to do more for their learners, but they did not have enough centralised support and resources to develop deeper knowledge about digital literacies. In other words, both metaphorically and literally, Langfield was generally left to its own devices in terms of its overall institutional approach to digital literacies, classroom practices around digital literacies, and relevant professional learning. While we identified a strong sense of uncertainty among the participating teachers about whether they were providing what was needed, pockets of innovative practice as well as their

DOI: 10.4324/9781003132684-8

strong desire to learn, grow, and improve were evident. In addition, the institutional culture, supporting "in-house" collaboration and experimentation, helped navigate some of the challenges. Nevertheless, significant constraints remained, especially regarding theorising practice and developing consistent pedagogies to support the integration of digital literacies into English language learning.

Drawing on the findings of this research, this concluding chapter outlines an extensive set of implications for different stakeholders concerned about the provision of digital literacies within adult EAL programmes. It starts with the discussion of implications for curriculum and pedagogy by exploring what educators in the community-based adult EAL sector might utilise from this detailed examination of Langfield learners' everyday digital literacy practices as well as teaching and learning practices at Langfield explored in Chapters 4 and 5. We then present implications for EAL teachers' professional learning drawing on our findings reported in Chapters 5 and 6, followed by the discussion of the implications for leadership in the sector prompted by the findings in Chapter 7. Next, this chapter suggests implications for policy highlighting the need for reasonable funding and multifaceted support so that, in the light of the current reforms in the sector, institutions like Langfield feel they are supported, well-resourced, and, importantly, appreciated for their important work. Finally, we refer to implications for research. From a methodological perspective, we point to the possibilities for further research on digital literacies, especially in a sector where published research is not extensive. Considering the very limited research in the field, we call for more research and propose possible new directions in this seemingly neglected field. From an ethical perspective, we reflect on the relationships that we, as researchers, developed with Langfield over the course of this research and explore the opportunities and responsibilities which such relationships entail. In this context, to conclude this book, we offer a short reflective narrative about Langfield's move to fully online delivery of its programmes during the Covid-19 pandemic – which continues, with Melbourne still in lockdown at the time of writing.

Re-thinking curriculum and pedagogy

The findings of this research have important implications for curriculum and pedagogy in the adult EAL sector. In all sectors of education, the content of the curriculum within an educational organisation and the pedagogical practices that are used by teachers to implement this content are pivotal to educational outcomes and successful learning. By curriculum we mean the formal and informal texts that are created within and outside an organisation that mediate and regulate content delivery and determine the sequences and structures of teaching and learning. This might include government level frameworks, organisational documentation of teaching content, and the planning documents created by educators, individually or in teams.

Centralisation of digital literacies in the EAL curriculum

If progress is to be made to enhance digital literacies within EAL programmes, greater consideration can be given to the centralisation of digital literacies in the EAL curriculum. It would be useful to shift overtly the content and emphasis in the curriculum (both central and teacher-specific) from the use of technologies for skill-and-drill language activities, teaching digital terminology and teaching how to perform simple digital tasks towards the explicit teaching of digital literacies. Certainly, skill-and-drill activities, teaching digital terminology and basic operational skills, can be still important and desirable. However, only having such a focus is not enough. Rich repertoires of digital literacies, as part of socio-cultural and socio-material practices, are essential for the settlement of adult EAL learners in Australia. From this perspective, there is a need to frame digital literacies as practices or, in other words, meaning-making activities in digital spaces and include a wider range of digital literacy practices central to different domains of life and settlement. Those digital literacy practices associated with the settlement, such as the use of the central government services, banking, billing, shopping, health, and employment are of particular importance and they should be given more attention in the curriculum.

Importantly, as it was evident in this research, it is important (and possible) to integrate digital literacies into the existing English language curriculum seamlessly. Digital literacies should not be positioned in the curriculum as an "add-on" or something optional to teach. Digital literacies are as important for adult EAL learners as print-based literacies. Consistent with a socio-cultural theory of literacy, *The EAL Framework* encourages teachers to consider social contexts and purposes when engaging with print-based and digital texts. This can be a useful starting point for educators developing their curriculum. When focusing on print-based literacies, it might be useful to consider how these practices now happen in digital contexts and what learners need to know, understand, and be able to do to engage in them. For instance, in many cases, (traditional) letters have become SMS texts; postcards have become *WhatsApp* or *Facebook* postings; a traditional workplace memo is now likely to be in an email; networking may be conducted via *LinkedIn* or *Instagram;* booking a medical appointment can be now done not only over the phone but on an online platform. What it means to be literate continues, as it always has, to shape-shift, including shifts into digital forms. Identifying and discussing explicitly such changes will help to connect English language learning and digital literacies, make learning richer and more meaningful, and, importantly, significantly extend the learners' repertoires of literacies in a seamless manner.

Consideration of the curriculum in the milieu of digital change

Another important implication prompted by this research is related to consideration of the curriculum in the milieu of digital change. The global movement to the ubiquitous use of digital modalities and platforms for teaching and learning in the last five years has proceeded at an astonishing pace. The development and spread of mobile devices as well as the mobile internet have been significant too. While, of course, we are aware that the uptake of smartphones and tablets is not even, the participants in this study could afford mobile phones or tablets and felt very comfortable when using them. Curriculum documentation needs to be responsive to such change and reflect not only the centrality of digital literacies but also learners' preferred devices, modes of content delivery, and types of online interactions.

However, at the same time, exposure to other technologies that are less familiar to learners is also important. As it was illustrated in this research, mobile phones are not always the best devices to engage in certain practices and people also need to use public devices such as self-service technologies, automatic teller machines (ATMs), bar-code scanners, interactive screens, and many other digital devices. It would be useful for the curriculum to take these sorts of technologies, their agency, and affordances into account. The focus, however, should be on digital literacy practices (rather than the devices themselves) and how literacy and meaning-making changes as reading, writing, and communication are practised with the help of such devices.

An organisation-wide approach to digital literacies

If EAL providers are committed to the quality provision of digital literacies programmes, it might be useful to consider an organisation-wide approach to digital literacies. The *Techno-Tuesday* programme that we illustrated in this book is an excellent example of how teaching digital literacies can be organised across the institution. The rotating model of the *Techno-Tuesday* programme illustrated in Figure 5.1 and its principles can be used to guide the development of an organisation-wide approach to digital literacies. While, reflecting the findings of our research, the model is based on the collaboration of three teachers; it can be expanded to include more practitioners or duplicated to involve different groups of practitioners in different courses, timetable slots, or locations. Given that Langfield's model was based on very close and collegial relationships between the three teachers (which, perhaps, contributed to its effectiveness), it might be useful for institutions to let teachers form their own teaching groups rather than impose the model that is mainly driven by the logistics of teaching.

Development of suitable pedagogies for digital literacies

The discussion in this book as well as our implications for curriculum also prompt important implications for pedagogy in EAL settings. Our choice of the word "pedagogy" here is deliberate. While we recognise that the term "andragogy" is used in some contexts to refer to teaching and learning processes with adult learners, it is not universally accepted. It also implies a distinction between the ways in which children and adults develop digital literacies which we found problematic. Thus, we adopt the more commonly used language of pedagogy and critical pedagogy which is consistent with a socio-cultural theory of literacy used in this research.

By pedagogy, we mean the conceptual understandings and approaches that underlie and inform teaching and learning as seen in practice settings. These understandings and approaches might be deliberative and overt. Alternatively, they could be implicit, not especially theorised in practice. In other words, they might be what is often called folk pedagogies – ways of teaching that have evolved from practices on the ground and reflected what has always worked for teachers. From this perspective, there is a need for educators in the sector to conceptualise and employ suitable pedagogies for digital literacies. Our findings about the effective practices around digital literacies at Langfield as well as strong language learner identities enacted by Lanfield's learners across different domains of their lives offer important insights into how effective pedagogies for digital literacies might look. Digital literacies are best taught through authentic practices with real digital platforms, digital texts, audiences, and social purposes. It has been widely recognised in the field literature (Hafner, 2014; Milton & Vozzo, 2013) and illustrated in our research. To be effective, pedagogy for digital literacies needs to be informed by a constructivist view of learning and use a situated learning approach in which learning is "embedded in real or simulated social contexts" (Hafner, 2014, p. 657).

This approach allows learners to engage with digital literacies in authentic and situated ways. They engage in authentic meaning-making which provides multiple opportunities for learning both a new language and digital literacies. For example, instead of teaching learners how to type by copying a short text or typing a hand-written text, it would be more productive to engage them in a genuine, authentic social practice that requires typing and focus on typing within the practice (e.g. sending an email/text message to a friend) while attending to other skills, knowledge, and understandings required. Such an approach offers richer learning opportunities to learners than typing as a decontextualised set of skills.

Another important aspect of effective pedagogies for digital literacies, especially in the adult EAL context, is an opportunity for learners to exercise their agency and draw on their strengths. Earlier we identified the considerable strengths that Langfield's learners brought to their EAL learning. Not least significant were their identity resources as consciously committed English language learners, and as continuing lifelong learners. We also noted how they were already accessing information, connecting with friends and family, utilising home languages (sometimes more than one) alongside and with their developing English language skills. We admired their resilience and their capacity for problem-solving, a capacity honed in many cases through challenging life circumstances. These adult learners have capacities to turn problems inside-out, revealing the learning they may contain.

From this perspective, problem-based learning may be especially generative for adult EAL learners. Informed by a situated learning approach, it positions knowledge as "problematic rather than as fixed" (Milton & Vozzo, 2013, p. 76) in learning which shifts the focus from superficially remembering content to gaining a deeper understanding through participation in social practices. Thus, one way to organise such learning in EAL classrooms is to engage learners, particularly adult learners, in realistic problem-centred tasks with digital technologies, allowing them to use their existing knowledge, experiences, and assets but, when needed, scaffold them in solving the problem. Let us elaborate on the typing example used above to illustrate how problem-based learning of digital literacies might look. For example, learners can be engaged in real authentic communication with peers, teachers, or communities. They can be asked (and scaffolded) to text their peers to organise a catch up, or text their teacher to notify them about their absence, or contact someone for an inquiry they need. In doing so, they can be encouraged *to figure out* certain aspects of digital literacy practice by drawing on what they already know and can do, while the development of new skills and knowledge can be scaffolded with relevant activities. This experience will not only provide opportunities for developing typing skills but also knowledge and understandings required for composing and reading digital texts in different contexts and for different purposes.

We also argued that consideration of the power and impact of technologies and the material should be factored into the development of pedagogical understandings. This was emphasised in the use of socio-material theory, in which, alongside the institutional, the social and the personal, materials, and technologies also have agency. They affect how learning happens and shape the meanings that are formed in using the technologies and the materials. The example of using mobile phones in working with the students illustrates that the affordance and limitations of the devices is pivotal to what is learned.

Such overt, active, and deliberative pedagogies need to be supported by leadership. In other words, pedagogies for digital literacies are not an afterthought but need to be centralised and integral in the decision-making of adult EAL organisations.

Enhancing professional learning

This research suggests a number of implications for EAL teachers' professional learning both in terms of what could be included in the professional learning and how the provision of professional learning in the sector might be organised. This research found that while there were examples of sustained practices around digital literacies at Langfield, there was a need for supporting the theorisation and deeper pedagogical understandings to ground these practices and to deepen links to the notion of digital literacies as part of the EAL work with learners. Clearly relevant professional learning was needed to foster such development.

Across all sectors in education professional learning is pivotal to the capacity for positive change and innovation. Teachers who receive targeted and regular professional learning are more likely to be adaptive in teaching and learning, open to new thinking and practices, and responsive to shifts in local and global conditions. We understand professional learning to be about the in-service learning activities that teachers engage in to extend their skills, capacities, and understandings, and this includes, importantly, pedagogies appropriate for the circumstances of the teaching and learning. From this perspective, to enhance the provision of digital literacies in EAL settings, teachers need opportunities for relevant professional learning, both in terms of content and forms of delivery.

Three conceptual areas of focus in professional learning

To address EAL teachers' professional needs, professional learning opportunities about digital literacies can be developed around three inter-related conceptual areas of focus identified in this research: (1) learners' strengths, (2) learners' digital landscapes, and (3) digital literacies.

Within the first area of focus, professional learning needs to introduce teachers to a strengths-based approach to education to help them move away from deficit discourses. It would be useful not only to increase EAL practitioners' awareness about such discourses and their implications but also to help them learn how to recognise and employ their learners' material, cultural, and social assets. Connected to this focus area, professional learning needs to encourage and support teachers to explore, discover, understand, and utilise the digital worlds, digital literacy practices, and associated identities of their language learners which are not always easy to see but crucial for developing effective learning environments. Professional learning needs to equip teachers with relevant strategies and resources for such identity work. Within the third focus area, teachers need opportunities to understand what the notion of "digital literacies" means, given the complexity of the concept and multiplicity of definitions. Language teachers will especially benefit from a socio-cultural perspective of literacy used in this book. Professional learning needs to help teachers to move from "digital literacy" as a singular, fixed, and readily transferable set of skills to "digital literacies" – a more complex, culturally situated critical thinking practices that are mediated and shaped by socio-cultural contexts.

Pedagogies for digital literacies

As has been emphasised throughout this book, instantiating digital literacies into practice and into the day-to-day life of a language classroom cannot be achieved without consideration of pedagogy. Alongside understandings of digital literacies, strengths-based approaches, and learners' digital lives, professional learning needs to address pedagogical understandings that are at the core of effecting teaching and learning. A useful starting point can be the consideration of the importance of technologies and modalities. Any consideration of appropriate pedagogies for teaching digital literacies should be seen in juncture with the technologies that embody the literacies. Professional learning needs to incorporate the notion that context, technologies, and literacies are co-extensive. In other words, effective professional learning needs to make explicit connections between conceptual ideas/theories, learning contexts, and practice to provide teachers with opportunities to develop relevant pedagogies for digital literacies.

In the section above, we provided a detailed discussion of suitable pedagogies for digital literacies drawing on the ideas of situated problem-based learning which allows learners to engage in authentic digital literacy practices and learn through this experience. Professional learning should familiarise teachers with these pedagogical approaches, their principles, and relevant examples. Furthermore, pedagogical ideas that need to be addressed in professional learning include designing a sequence of learning activities to integrate digital literacies meaningfully, examples of scaffolding activities that can be used to teach digital literacies in an EAL class, considerations about the agency and strengths of learners, and developing relevant assessments. Some of these were documented in this research and reported in Chapter 5. They can serve as a model for developing tasks and activities in relation to other digital literacy practices.

As demonstrated in this research, for EAL learners, learning digital literacies is no longer only a matter of what happens during class time, face to face. Learning digital literacies happens everywhere – at home, at a friend's place, in the Centrelink office, at the supermarket self-serve checkout, and at many other places. Part of this reorientation of the place of technologies in learning, as well as consideration of learners' digital lives and strengths, is to understand and apply the idea of the hybridity of teaching and learning environments that span across face-to-face, offline, and online interactions. Thus, professional learning that brings attention to emerging hybrid learning environments and the multiple opportunities (and challenges) for learning outside of classrooms appears to be significant for the future work of teachers in the EAL adult learning sector.

New forms of professional learning

This book points out the need for relevant professional learning about digital literacies, both in terms of quantity and quality, and the discussion above can be considered by external providers of professional learning to fine-tune their courses and workshops on digital literacies. However, our book also calls for new forms of professional learning in the sector by illuminating that external professional learning can be too expensive or too structured by fixed dates, times, and venues. For community-based EAL settings, such as Langfield, where resources are limited, the institutional structure is distributed across multiple physical locations, and teachers work part-time, external professional learning is not always possible or desirable. Drawing on the participants' experiences with professional learning at Langfield and their perspectives on a workable and meaningful form of professional learning for them, our research conceptualised a new form of professional learning which might be suitable for such contexts (Figure 6.2).

Implementation of organisation-based or in-house professional learning, central to the model, can be a useful approach for the sector. The main advantage of this approach is that it can contextualise understanding of what teachers and learners within a particular setting need and what is most workable, or feasible. Thus, professional learning can be better oriented to grounded practice in classrooms. From this perspective, teachers' professional needs are considered more carefully which can make learning more relevant and meaningful. Such an approach can help to overcome some logistical challenges associated with different locations and timetables of teachers. As it was evident in Langfield's case, professional learning can be situated with formal gatherings (e.g. extensions to staff meetings) but it can also be enabled by co-locating teachers, promoting team teaching, and collaboration. In this environment, even coffee conversations can turn into professional dialogue and valuable sharing.

Furthermore, professional learning needs to introduce teachers to new theories, concepts, and teaching ideas in relation to their needs. In other words, there are times when teachers' learning from and with external expertise can be very useful. In the case of Langfield, professional learning was in championing ideas and practices at the classroom level that came from some of the teachers themselves and then leveraging these to enact change. From this perspective, in this form of professional learning, peers can act as "experts". Teachers and leaders within an organisation who develop expertise can provide nuanced understandings that are more easily implemented in situ. The championing of targeted practice ideas, such as the inclusion of digital literacies in teaching and learning, provides a situated and strengths-based approach to professional learning that is more likely to be taken up and implemented by teaching staff who can see how it works in classrooms. Part of this peer-based professional learning is collegial sharing of practices that are effective, and the integral role of peer mentoring. Such collegial, contextualised, and democratic professional learning can be especially useful and applicable in ACE settings because it both reflects and extends the distinctive strengths in the "pedagogy of plACE" which our own study and previous investigations (Dymock, 2007; Sanguinetti et al., 2004; Walstab et al., 2006) have identified as key characteristics of the ACE sector. It may be also useful to centralise this approach in the discourses and practices organisation wide. Using an individual's strengths as a resource, every teacher can be encouraged to act as "an expert"; and every teacher can exercise agency through their own practice, with their own learners. Building individual teacher's agency not only develops a more systematic approach to peer-learning but, importantly, builds capacity within the institution to develop a self-sustaining model of professional learning. Through effective collaboration and sharing such individual professional agency can be both fed and tempered by collegial conversations and collective reflection on practice.

Clearly, an in-house approach can offer targeted, meaningful, and relevant professional learning. The question remains, however, whether it is enough to sustain the growth of teachers in the face of the emerging digital futures in education and evolving research knowledge. Is such an approach sufficient to move teachers and leaders confidently to new understandings of digital literacies with supporting pedagogies? Our research suggests that it may not be sufficient and some connections to outside expertise are probably necessary. Furthermore, in some contexts, new knowledge and pedagogical practices may not be available within the skills set of employees in an organisation. Thus, there is a strong case for external input into the professional learning of teachers about digital literacies. Teachers need opportunities to attend professional conferences, short courses, and other professional learning initiatives outside the institutions which are important not only for developing new knowledge but also for developing professional networks. Thus, other possibilities need to be brought to the table and our model of professional learning has opportunities for this. For example, one of these possibilities is practitioner-researcher relationships that we shall explore in a more detailed way later in this chapter. Resourcing organisations and staff through connections to university researchers can be a useful and low-cost approach for the organisations in the sector.

Finally, professional learning about digital literacies needs to go beyond theorisation. Teachers need opportunities to plan for, teach, and assess digital literacies. They need opportunities to try things they have not tried before. In this sense, professional learning needs a strong link between theory and practice. Importantly, the learning settings (which may be physical and/or virtual environments) need to provide spaces, opportunities, and a culture to both challenge and support teachers in their risk-taking, innovative classroom practice, professional learning, collaborations, post-teaching reflection, and problem-solving. We concluded Chapter 6 by suggesting a model, based on action-research and action learning principles, that could connect professional learning about digital literacies with the strengths, needs, and digital life worlds of adult learners. We see the rich potential in such a model. However, realising such an approach systemically has significant implications for leadership and for policy and resourcing, particularly within such a distinctive field as the adult community-based education sector in Australia. In the following sections, we turn to a consideration of these implications.

Developing democratic leadership practices

The findings of this research have important implications for leaders working within adult EAL settings although we are well aware of the limitations of this research. While our findings are mainly based on the data from one leader, they illuminate that leadership is pivotal to change and to futures. It needs to be responsive to shifts in global communication systems because of the digital age and the demands of a globalised world. Leaders are change agents, but they are also part of organisations that have stakeholders who are invested in the success of the organisation. Leaders set directions and embody a vision that is central to this success. The direction and vision, though, are not arbitrary decisions: they come from the best available data and from an understanding of context. Educational organisations set this vision within the entanglements of three factors: the learning of students and successful outcomes for students, the effectiveness of staff to sustain student learning in the circumstances of change, and the viability and sustainability of the organisation. In sum, leadership in education is complex and is enacted in times of profound change, including changes brought by the digitisation of society. Thus, there is a need for effective leadership practices in this space.

Contextual knowledge, situated understandings, and an organisational vision

To bring effective inclusion of digital literacies into teaching and learning, educational leaders, especially in adult community-based settings, require an ear to the ground and intimate and situated knowledge to understand and affect change. It is important for leaders to be overt in their support of this integration. It needs to be a high priority in terms of the current and ongoing needs of students as well as the subsequent needs of teachers. Such understanding should be based on the grounded knowledge of the setting. To be attuned to need, it is important for leadership to know their staff, learners, and the happenings in classrooms. It is crucial to be sensitive to what is happening within the teams in the organisation and especially regarding any innovative practices. Such knowledge of the setting and of the individual work of teachers, including innovative practices about the uses of technology in teaching and learning, is absolutely vital.

This groundedness can enable leaders to be aware of the practices, beliefs, strengths, and requirements of staff and learners about digital literacies and constitute the primary information upon which critical leadership decisions are made. Leadership vision is pivotal to the health and future viability of an organisation, but a vision that is not informed by practitioner and learner understandings may not reflect the needs of an organisation in terms of adapting to change.

Democratic leadership practices

In bringing about a shift to the inclusion of digital literacies in the teaching practices across the institution, democratic leadership may be a useful approach. This would entail working closely with and seeking the input of the teachers working in the classrooms. Democratic leadership in education is one in which the views of all stakeholders in an organisation are accounted for in constructing an organisational vision and that the basis for implementing change is from a substantial understanding of the experiences and needs of students and teachers. It includes, especially, the active involvement of teachers in decision-making and their ability to speak about what they need to make the teaching effective. Teachers, who will have to live with any substantial change such as introducing digital literacies into the centre of teaching and learning, need an opportunity to exercise their agency in the processes of affecting change.

The most important data available to educational leaders to inform the change is the data from the teachers themselves. Thus, instances of innovative practice with technologies need to be highlighted and championed, so that change appears to be less driven from hierarchies and more from the coalface of practitioners in their work with learners. Collegial sharing of ideas about the use of digital technologies in teaching needs to be also encouraged by senior leadership. In this case, leading change and innovations becomes an embraced collaborative process. In effect, all teachers are viewed as leaders.

Challenging policy positions

There are several implications for a policy which we define as regulations, procedures, content recommendations, funding requirements, documented authorised practices, and administrative formations as constructed by governments at all levels, across sectors, and within individual institutions. In education, private or community education providers might be autonomous and governed by an independent administrative board, but they are also subject to the policies and regulatory frameworks of local, state, and federal governments. Policy is, thus, at a macro level and distanced from the work of an individual organisation and micro in reflecting the policy positions, procedures, and practices within an organisation. But macro and micro policies are intertwined and contingent on one another.

This book is grounded in a study of one organisation within the EAL adult community education sector. Of course, we are aware that Langfield may not be representative of the range of needs and experiences in the sector. Thus, it is difficult to make generalisations about digital literacies in other organisations because each organisation has its own unique dispositions based on the history of the organisation, how it is led, and the needs of learners. However, at the same time, it seemed that Langfield used all possible internal resources to organise and sustain the provision of digital literacies but, wanting more, struggled to get additional help and guidance. For example, as discussed in Chapter 5, they used *The EAL Framework*, but they needed more guidance which did not exist. Similarly, as illustrated in Chapter 6, they were "hungry" for more professional learning but there were very limited opportunities for this. We have noted that learners, teachers and their leader alike were to a large extent, "left to their own devices". This illuminates a need for a number of sector-wide initiatives.

Digital literacies framework

There is an urgent need for a relevant framework to support educational leaders to plan a comprehensive institution-wide approach to digital literacies as well as to guide teachers' planning, teaching, and assessment. While *The EAL Framework* includes some aspects of digital literacies, there is a need for a companion resource that specifically sets out what digital literacy capabilities (e.g. skills, knowledge and understandings) adult EAL learners should develop for successful settlement in Australia and, importantly, how these can be taught in the context of English language programmes. Given the importance of digital literacies, it is also crucial that the quality assurance guidelines and procedures that are part of policy and frameworks in the sector reflect and legitimise teaching the content and skill sets associated with digital literacies.

A further important point with significant policy implications needs to be highlighted here. There is, we suggest, a conundrum, or at the very least, a tension to be managed here. The problem relates to the way digital literacy is often (mis)conceptualised, as a readily generic and transferable skill. It is as if "digital literacy" has been added to employers' shopping lists alongside problem solving, teamwork, communication and enterprise-initiative as another essential skill expected of job-ready job seekers. These so-called "generic skills" (sometimes also referred to as "key", "soft", "core", "employability", or "professional" skills) are presumed to be like soft plastic, or plasticine, generic by nature, and readily transferable to different contexts.

The presumption is that digital literacy (we break our convention and use the singular form here quite deliberately) can also be taught as a pre-requisite skill and then applied, or transferred, by learners, in relatively simple and straightforward ways, to realise employment and settlement goals. We acknowledge that from a distance, this idea looks sensible, and is attractive – particularly for system administrators, bureaucrats, and policy makers who want to keep things simple, upscale strategies, and drive systemic change. However, we see significant problems with this conception. Indeed, we see it as a (mis)conception. On the other hand, teachers are engaged with learners and the development of these skills up-close, in a much more grounded, situated, and contextualised way. At the risk of over-simplification, we suggest that the overlapping discourses of policy and practice on these issues may carry quite different meanings and expectations, even with the same words and labels. It is important to be mindful of these differences.

Our study has shown how emergent digital literacies (like other ways of making and expressing meaning) are deeply embedded, or situated, in the lives of Langfield's learners. They are enculturated and contingent on context and circumstances in multiple ways. The strengthening, consolidation, and continuing development of these digital literacies are best facilitated by grounded and contextualised pedagogies which identify current strengths, needs, and challenges and then scaffold learners to help them move on from their current practices to new, more sophisticated practices and/or to the same or similar sorts of practices but in different, more diverse, or challenging contexts.

The framework we envision needs to help learners and teachers to do this important work. It must provide in effect, a both-ways bridge between these different discourses. It should be a tool of both policy and practice. It should not be prescriptive, but it should support practitioners to plan, structure, and demonstrate the rationale for their pedagogy. This understanding can also enable policy makers, funding authorities and perhaps even auditors to appreciate the legitimacy and value of the important developmental work being done.

Relevant teaching resources

EAL educators in the sector need a relevant "resource bank" for planning and teaching digital literacies. It should be specifically tailored to the adult learners' needs and focus on digital literacies for settlement in Australia. Furthermore, EAL educators would benefit from seeing examples of sequenced learning activities that can be used in classrooms, samples of lesson plans, samples of learners' work, and illustrations of practice. To be effective, this resource bank needs to be research-informed and reflect "the best practices" in the field of digital literacies for adult language learners. Examples of practice should be authentic and capture real classrooms.

As illustrated in this research, there were some excellent "pockets of practice" at Langfield. These need to be shared with the wider professional community. Thus, there is a pressing need, intra-organisationally and cross-organisationally, to share pedagogical approaches and practices to build the practice knowledge in the sector. Together these resources can be a valuable contribution to the sector. However, it is worth reiterating here a point made earlier, that teachers' employment within this sector is often contingent, part-time, sometimes voluntary. There is little or no systemic resourcing or support for teachers to be documenting and publishing their "best practice" even when it is recognised as such at the local level. At Langfield such work is neither routine nor funded and we suspect this is likely to be the case in many other ACE providers. This begs important questions about how effective practice may best be captured and disseminated more widely. Strategic interventions and resources are needed to support this essential work.

Sector-wide professional learning about digital literacies

EAL practitioners in the sector need more opportunities for suitable high-quality professional learning about digital literacies. Teaching digital literacies requires sophisticated professional knowledge, understanding and skills. For many practitioners, it may also require a significant shift in thinking about the role of technologies in EAL education from "technologies as tools for language learning" to "technologies as social practices". To be able to help their learners develop digital literacies, teachers need opportunities to learn how to do this. Additional funding for external professional learning opportunities would be useful.

Furthermore, a more cohesive approach to teacher development within the sector is required. As the sector has its own unique features, professional learning should be context-sensitive to be effective and engaging. Currently, there is no sector-wide approach to professional learning provision about digital literacies. Thus, the learning that educators choose to engage in might often be hit-or-miss. The model of professional learning that we offered in this book can be a useful starting point to conceptualise such an approach. However, consultation across organisations within the sector is vital so that common needs in terms of professional learning about digital literacy can be ascertained. In this regard, industry associations, consultancy bodies, and universities can play a role.

Considering methodological and ethical issues in research

Future research directions

We argued in Chapter 1 that there is very limited research in the field. While our research provided many important insights, we are well aware of the limitations: it was a study of one organisation in the sector and, of course, there were time, capacity, and funding constraints. Thus, we call for more research on digital literacies in these unique but challenging settings which might unfold in a number of directions.

While we collected some data on the experiences of the adult learners from migrant and refugee backgrounds, this was not sufficient to provide a detailed account of their understanding of learning and a full picture of their needs in terms of digital literacies. Future research should include a stronger focus on the learners and on their existing digital literacy practices. There is a need to move beyond deficit discourses in research and conduct a comprehensive analysis of adult EAL learners' strengths as well as needs but articulated by the participants themselves. Such insights are required for curriculum design and development.

This research, while generative of possibilities and implications for the wider sector, is limited by only examining one provider. We envision future research that engages with several providers and, thus, offers evidence that is wider and more inclusive of the range of organisations in the sector. Such research may need to include both quantitative and qualitative approaches as well as large-scale and comparative studies exploring perspectives and practices with digital literacies across several institutions to get a broader sweep of what is needed in the field.

To advance the provision of digital literacies in the sector, research exploring "pockets" of innovative teaching practices with digital literacies would be especially useful. Such research needs to document, analyse, organise, and share these examples with the professional community.

Ethics of researcher-participant relationships

From an ethical perspective, adopting the Institutional Ethnography approach of Dorothy Smith (2005) required close contact with the people at the research site and ongoing connection over several months, with both in-person and online correspondence. As researchers, we had privileged access to generate data. However, the teachers were aware that, like them, we are also educators and former teachers (although not at Langfield) with a strong interest in digital literacies, EAL, and adult education. This inspired a lot of conversations and discussions which often extended beyond research activities. There was genuine and reciprocal interest in these interactions and, over the time, we felt we were able to establish strong professional relationships with Langfield's CEO and teachers.

These relationships were mutually beneficial. We, as researchers, were gaining more in-depth and nuanced understandings of Langfield, crucial for our qualitative research. The teachers saw opportunities for engaging in dialogue about their practices and drawing out information from us that they could utilise in their professional worlds (Tour et al., 2020). The CEO invited us to facilitate a professional learning course on digital literacies at Langfield in the upcoming year which we accepted with great enthusiasm. While these were significant benefits for all parties, such relationships encouraged us to think about some ethical considerations.

Being ethical in the conduct of research is more than just ethical approval from a university and the usual regard for protection of identities and the like. We consider, in line with the underlying principle of reciprocity, that ethical conduct is about openness and honesty in terms of negotiating the researcher-participant relationship (Fine, 1993; Watts, 2008). Being ethical, from our perspective, has to include an appraisal of what is needed in terms of the unit of analysis and focus of the research, but also needs to account for the capacities of the institution to support research. This includes a clear understanding of the limitations about what could be achieved, given time, resources, and other constraints as well as consideration of how researchers' agendas align with what an organisation can provide.

This is the issue of synchronicity between the research methods employed by researchers and the efficacy of data collection in terms of the internal machinations of an organisation. It is important that research methods are consistent with organisational ways of working and the values and vision of the organisation (see Tour et al., 2020). Developing this alignment can only come from open and honest discussion about what each of the stakeholders in the research wants and what can be delivered. At the core of doing institutional ethnography, there is the assumption of mutual respect and reciprocity so that both the researchers and the organisation benefit. However, the primary responsibility for ethical conduct remains with the researchers. It is, thus, essential that participants never feel unduly challenged by researchers' presence and demands.

Importantly, being ethical in research means to give back to the organisation. This can take multiple forms such as professional learning, research reports, teaching/learning materials, or any other concrete assistance. An ethical relationship, as we see it, is, thus, one in which reciprocity is not a theoretical label but a practical reality that is operationalised.

Engendering trust between researchers and organisation

Developing trust is a core methodological issue in ethnography (O'Reilly, 2009). Of course, trust between researchers and an organisation is not automatic and cannot be assumed at the beginning of a research relationship. Indeed, there is evidence that many organisations find trusting researchers difficult. This might be a lack of "giving back" or the tendency to withdraw from research due to time or financial constraints. Shifting the parameters of negotiated research conditions, among a range of other factors that complicate the conduct of qualitative research, can play into perceptions of trust. We argue that to "get inside" an organisation and to assume both emic and etic positionalities as researchers means being deliberative in developing trust. So, it is important for researchers to be circumspect in terms of research conditions, outcomes, and expectations. To engender trust, it is important to fulfil what is promised to institutions. This includes tangible support and feedback wherever possible, and connecting personally with participants, entering their life worlds in authentic and situated ways, including visiting teachers' classrooms, and chatting with them in their staffroom spaces.

Postscript: The pandemic, lockdowns, and beyond

We conducted this research in 2019, and we were interested in maintaining (and, in fact, were able to maintain) the relationship with Langfield beyond the project. At that stage, we were primarily concerned with the provision of digital literacies in the community-based adult EAL programme at Langfield. It seemed to be a significant topic given the increasing digitisation of Australian society in different domains of life and we wanted to support the institution in its important work. At that time, we even could not imagine that the digitalisation of life would be taken to a whole new level just within the next few months due to the Covid-19 pandemic.

In response to the growing numbers of Covid-19 cases and deaths, Victoria developed a number of regulations to prevent the spread of infection. One of them was the closure of all non-essential services, including schools, universities, and other educational institutions. At the end of March 2020, the Victorian Government made an announcement that face-to-face classes were longer possible and all non-essential organisations were asked to work and study from home. This announcement and a series of lockdowns in Melbourne during 2020 and 2021 have dramatically changed the landscape for the EAL programme delivery at Langfield.

The desire of the CEO to centralise the digital in English language learning at Langfield has been given greater impetus by the pandemic. During 2020, at the outset of the pandemic, especially in the second half of 2020, the teachers at Langfield were scrambling to cope with maintaining contacts with learners, teaching online and coping with the learners' needs in this challenging environment. It would be true to say that there was significant anxiety among the teaching staff. The teachers tried a range of strategies and apps to connect with learners in lockdown, including *WhatsApp*. Whilst helpful for maintaining social connections, *WhatsApp* proved to be inadequate for the teaching and learning.

Having maintained our connection and having engendered trust, the organisation looked to us for answers. One of the staff, Tanya, initiated a series of conversations about teaching online in lockdown. She was open to new modalities for teaching and learning. We discussed possibilities and shared resources (including academic literature) that detailed what could be done in their situation. One of such possibilities that Langfield's professional community found relevant was what they called "hybrid" delivery. Such an approach entails the ability to move between three modes of delivery: synchronous online environments for connection with students (using a platform such as *Zoom*), an asynchronous online learning management system which acts as an online repository for resources and teaching materials (e.g. *Moodle*) as well as continuing face-to-face teaching when lockdowns were lifted and re-engagement in-person was possible.

Another area of interest, as part of hybrid delivery adopted by Langfield, was associated with the "flipped" pedagogical approach to learning. Flipped learning is an approach to teaching and learning where learning is seen to occur across a wider scope of time, synchronously and asynchronously. Students do work outside of the formal class time and come to the class (be it face-to-face or online) to workshop ideas, ask questions and deepen their understandings. They are also given more agency and responsibility for their own learning. The approach was welcomed by Langfield's teachers who actively engaged in recording of short instructional, or demonstration, videos using their own devices. These digital resources were distributed to learners to stimulate pre-class (or between class) learning, engagement and language practice.

As of 2021, with Tanya championing it and assisting other staff with its implementation, these two new approaches have been substantially and successfully implemented at Langfield, utilising *Zoom* as the key tool for synchronous online engagement and *Moodle* as the online platform or repository for teaching and learning materials and resources. The distributed leadership style at Langfield has also afforded teachers such as Tanya the ability to take the lead and advocate for change. This has enabled much more flexibility considering the uncertain environment occasioned by the pandemic. Such a rapid shift to online learning was very challenging for learners as the teachers reported in our informal meetings. While it certainly provided learners with more opportunities to practise their digital literacies, it further reinforced the teachers' belief that, for EAL learners from migrant and refugee backgrounds, digital literacies are not necessarily acquired easily or naturally. Digital literacies require teaching and scaffolding and ongoing practice.

Concluding thoughts

When we began this research relationship with Langfield in early 2019, we had no idea that our initial research objectives would contribute to significant organisational change at Langfield. This was especially exciting to see in the light of our research findings. While there was very limited centralised guidance and support in the sector, Langfield was able to develop pockets of practice that had considerable promise and on which innovative practices could be developed. In this book, we have emphasised the importance of a strength-based perspective – looking for what is working and successful and using that to build confidence and develop effective practices.

Within this consideration of pedagogy, we centralised the importance of the material (including the technological) as powerfully agential. Technologies and the personal devices of learners, as well as the materials used in learning spaces, shape the learning and especially learning that is orientated to digital literacies. It is important to bring awareness of the material and the influence of the material to practitioners and to leaders.

In the spirit of Dorothy Smith, we built an ethnographic study that depended on our "deep" knowledge of the organisational context and the people in it. Trust and reciprocity were key values in our enterprise and these values have led to an ongoing and mutually fruitful relationship. We have established several important connections with the CEO and several teachers who have taken the research relationship and used it to support staff at Langfield. This has culminated in our productive collaborative work around the development of a hybrid approach for teaching and learning during the pandemic and lockdowns, an approach that integrates regular classroom contact with online modalities. The imperative of developing digital literacies has become more urgent because of Covid-19.

Throughout this chapter, the focus has been on the experiences, practices, and leadership initiatives at Langfield. But we are also cognisant of the wider implications of this study for adult community education and especially the EAL sector, where the focus is not only on language learning but critical settlement skills, which surely must include digital literacies as a core element. We, thus, offer, with awareness of the fact that this is a study of one organisation, a range of implications that might be taken up by other providers in the adult EAL sector.

REFERENCES

Aden, A., & Hillman, R. (2015). *Shining: The story of a lucky man*. Harper Collins.

Adichie, C. N. (2009, July). The danger of a single story. https://www.ted.com/talks/chimamanda_adichie_the_danger_of_a_single_story?language=en

Adult Community & Further Education Board. (2019). *ACFE guidelines and criteria for registration with the adult, community and further education board*.

Adult Learning Australia. (2015). Adult and community education in Australia. A snapshot of the status and role of the not for profit Adult and Community Education sector in 2015. *Adult learning Australia*. https://ala.asn.au/wp-content/uploads/2011/02/State-of-Ace__Final.pdf

Agar, M., & MacDonald, J. (1995). Focus groups and ethnography. *Human Organisation*, 54(1), 78–86. https://doi.org/10.17730/humo.54.1.x102372362631282

Alam, K., & Imran, S. (2015). The digital divide and social inclusion among refugee migrants. *Information Technology & People*, 28(2), 344–365. https://doi.org/10.1108/itp-04-2014-0083

Alencar, A. (2020). Mobile communication and refugees: An analytical review of academic literature. *Sociology Compass*, 14(8), 1–13. https://doi.org/10.1111/soc4.12802

AMES. (2020). *Learning English, career development & digital literacy*. https://www.ames.net.au/find-a-course/career-development-skills

Antonakis, J., Clanciolo, A., & Sternberg, R. (2004). Leadership: Past, present, future. In D. Day & J. Antonakis (Eds.), *The nature of leadership* (pp. 3–28). Sage.

Australian Bureau of Statistics. (2016). *Census*. https://www.abs.gov.au/census

Australian Council of TESOL Associations. (2019). Review of vocational education and training. https://tesol.org.au/wp-content/uploads/2019/01/598_ACTA_submission_to_the_VET_Review_-_January_2019.pdf

Australian Government. (2020). *SEE: Skills for education and employment*. https://www.dese.gov.au/skills-education-and-employment

Barton, D. (2012). Participation, deliberate learning and discourses of learning online. *Language and Education*, 26(2), 139–150. https://doi.org/10.1080/09500782.2011.642880

Barton, D. (2013). Ethnographic approaches to literacy research. In C. A. Chapelle (Ed.), *The encyclopedia of applied linguistics* (pp. 1–7). Wiley Blackwell.

Barton, D., & Hamilton, M. (1998). *Local literacies: Reading and writing in one community*. Routledge.

Batalova, J., & Fix, M. (2015). Through an immigrant lens: PIAAC assessment of the competencies of adults in the United States. *MPI National Centre on Immigrant Integration Policy*.

Baynham, M., & Prinsloo, M. (2009). *The future of literacy studies*. Palgrave Macmillan.

Beals, F., Kidman, J., & Funaki, H. (2020). Insider and outsider research: Negotiating self at the edge of the emic/etic divide. *Qualitative Inquiry, 26*(6), 593–601. https://doi.org/10.1177/1077800419843950

Beaudoin, M. (2015). Distance education leadership in the context of digital change. *The Quarterly Review of Distance Education, 16*(2), 33–44.

Benseman, J. (2014). Adult refugee learners with limited literacy: Needs and effective responses. *Refuge, 30*(1), 93–103. https://doi.org/10.25071/1920-7336.38606

Berson, Y., Shamir, B., Avolio, B. J., & Popper, M. (2001). The relationship between vision strength, leadership style, and context. *The Leadership Quarterly, 12*, 53073. https://doi.org/10.1016/S1048-9843(01)00064-9

Beycioglu, K., & Kondakci, Y. (2020). Organizational change in schools. *ECNU Review of Education*. https://doi.org/10.1177/2096531120932177

Biesta, G. (2015). What is education for? On good education, teacher judgement, and educational professionalism. *European Journal of Education, 50*(1), 75–87. https://doi.org/10.1111/ejed.12109

Billett, S. (2001). Learning through work: Workplace affordances and individual engagement. *Journal of Workplace Learning, 13*(5), 209–214. https://doi.org/10.1108/EUM0000000005548

Blomberg, J., & Karasti, H. (2012). Ethnography: Positioning ethnography within participatory design. In S. Jesper & T. Robertson (Eds.), *Routledge international handbook of participatory design* (pp. 86–116). Routledge.

Bowman, K. (2016). *Australian ACE environmental scan research project 2016: Final report*. Routledge.

Bracken, S. J. (2010). Understanding program planning theory and practice in a feminist community-based organization. *Adult Education Quarterly, 61*(2), 121–138. https://doi.org/10.1177/0741713610380446

Braun, V., & Clarke, V. (2006). Using thematic analysis in psychology. *Qualitative Research in Psychology, 3*(2), 77–101. https://doi.org/10.1191/1478088706qp063oa

Brierley, S., & Buttrose, L. (2013). *A long way home*. Penguin Books.

Broadband Commission for Sustainable Development. (2017). *Working Group on Education: Digital skills for life and work*. https://www.broadbandcommission.org/Documents/publications/WG-Education-Report2017.pdf

Brooks, M. C. (2015). School principals in Southern Thailand: Exploring trust with community leaders during conflict. *Educational Management Administration & Leadership, 43*(2), 232–252. https://doi.org/10.1177/1741143213513191

Brown, T. (2020, April). An age of endarkenment? Can adult education still make a difference? *Australian Journal of Adult Learning, 60*(1), 8–21. https://doi.org/10.3316/aeipt.226238

Bstieler, L., Hemmert, M., & Barczak, G. (2017). The changing bases of mutual trust formation in inter-organizational relationships: A dyadic study of university-industry research collaborations. *Journal of Business Research, 74*, 47–54. https://doi.org/10.1016/j.jbusres.2017.01.006

Bubb, S., & Earley, P. (2007). *Leading and managing continuing professional development* (2nd ed.). Sage Publications.

Campbell, B. (2009). *Reading the fine print; a history of the Victorian Adult Literacy and Basic Education Council (VALBRC) 1978–2008*. Victorian Adult Literacy and Basic Education Council (VALBEC).

Campbell, M., & Gregor, F. (2002). *Mapping social relations: A primer in doing institutional ethnography*. AltaMira Press

Carter, S., & Little, M. (2007). Justifying knowledge, justifying method, taking action: Epistemologies, methodologies and methods in qualitative research. *Qualitative Health Research, 17*(10), 1316–1328. https://doi.org/10.1177/1049732307306927

Centre for Creative Leadership. (2021). What are the characteristics of a good leader? https://www.ccl.org/articles/leading-effectively-articles/characteristics-good-leader//

Centre for Policy Development. (2020). *Putting language in place: Improving the adult migrant English program*. https://cpd.org.au/wp-content/uploads/2020/08/Putting-Language-In-Place-Improving-the-Adult-Migrant-English.pdf

Chapman, L., & Williams, A. (2015). Connecting with community: Helping immigrant low literacy ESL learners in local contexts. In J. Simpson & A. Whiteside (Eds.), *Adult language education and migration: Challenging agendas in policy and practice* (1st ed., pp. 35–48). Routledge. https://doi.org/10.4324/9781315718361

Chik, A. (2011). Digital gaming and social networking: English teachers' perceptions, attitudes and experiences. *Pedagogies: An International Journal, 6*(2), 154–166. https://doi.org/10.1080/1554480X.2011.554625

Choi, S. (2007). Democratic leadership: The lessons of exemplary models for democratic governance. *International Journal of Leadership Studies, 2*(3), 243–262. https://www.regent.edu/wp-content/uploads/2020/12/Choi_Vol2Iss3.pdf

Ciulla, J. B. (2002). *The ethics of leadership*. Wadsworth/Thomson Learning.

Clemans, A. (2016). Stuck at home: A portrayal of educational work in community spaces. *Studies in the Education of Adults, 42*(2), 156–169. https://doi.org/10.1080/02660830.2010.11661595

Clemans, A., Hartley, R., & Macrae, H. (2003). *ACE outcomes*. National Centre for Vocational Education Research. http://hdl.voced.edu.au/10707/144706

Coleman, M. (1996). The management style of female headteachers. *Educational Management & Administration, 24*(2), 163–174. https://doi.org/10.1177/0263211X96242005

Colucci, E., Smidt, H., Devaux, A., Vrasidas, C., Safarjalani, M., & Castaño Muñoz, J. (2017). Free digital learning opportunities for migrants and refugees. An Analysis of current initiatives and recommendations for their further use. JRC Science for Policy Report. Publications Office of the European Union. http://dx.doi.org/10.2760/684414.

Crang, M., & Cook, I. (2007). *Doing ethnographies*. SAGE.

Department of Home Affairs. (2019a). *Australia's offshore humanitarian program: 2018–19*. https://www.homeaffairs.gov.au/research-and-stats/files/australia-offshore-humanitarian-program-2018-19.pdf

Department of Home Affairs. (2019b). *Onshore humanitarian program 2018–19*. https://www.homeaffairs.gov.au/research-and-stats/files/ohp-june-19.pdf

Department of Home Affairs. (2021a). *Adult Migrant English Program (AMEP)*. https://immi.homeaffairs.gov.au/settling-in-australia/amep/about-the-program

Department of Home Affairs. (2021b). *Reform of the adult migrant English program: Discussion paper*. https://www.homeaffairs.gov.au/reports-and-pubs/PDFs/amep-reform-discussion-paper.pdf

Desmond, M. (2014). Relational ethnography. *Theory and Society, 43*, 547–579. https://doi.org/10.1007/s11186-014-9232-5

DeVault, M., & McCoy, L. (2006). Institutional ethnography: Using interviews to investigate ruling relations. In D. Smith (Ed.), *Institutional ethnography as practice* (pp. 15–43). Rowman & Littlefield.

Deveson, A. (2003). *Resilience.* Allen & Unwin.
Diamond, T. (2006). "Where did you get the fur coat, Fern?" Participant observation in Institutional Ethnography. In D. Smith (Ed.), *Institutional ethnography as practice* (pp. 45–64). Rowman & Littlefield.
Do, A. (2010). *The happiest refugee.* Allen & Unwin.
Dooly, M. (2009). New competencies in a new era? Examining the impact of a teacher training project. *ReCALL, 21*(3), 352–369. https://doi.org/10.1017/s0958344009990085
Driessen, M., van Emmerik, J., Fuhri, K., Nygren-Junkin, L., & Spotti, M. (2011). ICT use in L2 education for adult migrants. *A qualitative study in the Netherlands and Sweden.* https://ec.europa.eu/migrant-integration/library-document/ict-use-l2-education-adult-migrants-qualitative-study-netherlands-and-sweden_en?lang=de
Duckworth, V., & Smith, R. (2018, July). Women, adult literacy education and transformative bonds of care. *Australian Journal of Adult Learning, 58*(2), 157–183. https://doi.org/10.3316/ielapa.862028539859166
Dymock, D. (2007). *Engaging adult learners: The role of non-accredited learning in language, literacy and numeracy.* Adult Learning Australia. http://www.ala.asn.au/public/docs/report/ALA_Report_Dymock_FINAL_18_June.pdf
English, L. M. (2005). Foucault, feminists and funders: A study of power and policy in feminist organisations. *Studies in the Education of Adults, 37*(2), 137–150. https://doi.org/10.1080/02660830.2005.11661513
English, L. M., & Irving, C. J. (2015). *Feminism in community: Adult education for transformation.* Sense Publishers.
Epp, C. D. (2017). Migrants and mobile technology use: Gaps in the support provided by current tools. *Journal of Interactive Media in Education, 1*(2), 1–13. https://doi.org/10.5334/jime.432
Falk, I., Golding, B., & Balatti, J. (2000). *Building communities: ACE, lifelong learning and social capital: An anthology of word portraits reporting research conducted for the adult, community and further education board.* Adult, Community and Further Education Board.
Falloon, G. (2020). From digital literacy to digital competence: The teacher digital competency (TDC) framework. *Education Technology Research and Development, 68*, 2449–2472. https://doi.org/10.1007/s11423-020-09767-4
Figgis, J., Blackwell, A., Alderson, A., Mitchell, K., Zubrick, A., & Butorac, A. (2001). *What convinces enterprises to value training and learning and what does not?* National Centre for Vocational Education Research. https://ncver.edu.au/research-and-statistics/publications/all-publications/what-convinces-enterprises-to-value-training-and-learning-and-what-does-not
Fine, G. (1993). Ten lies of ethnography: Moral dilemmas in field research. *Journal of Contemporary Ethnography, 22*, 267–294. http://www.floppybunny.org/robin/web/virtualclassroom/chap5/s5/requirements_qual/fine_ten_lies_of_ethnography.pdf
Foley, A. (2005). *Searching for the 'C' in ACE.* Paper presented to Australian Vocational Education and Training Research Association conference, Nowra, NSW. https://www.avetra.org.au/pages/conference-archives-2005.html
Foley, A. (2007). ACE working within/outside VET, paper presented at Australian Vocational Education and Training Research Association Conference, Crow's Nest. https://www.avetra.org.au/pages/conference-archives-2007.html
Foroughi, B., & English, L. M. (2013). ICTs and adult education. In P. Mayo (Ed.), *Learning with adults: A reader* (pp. 153–160). Sense Publishers.
Frank, T. H. J., & Castek, J. (2017, Summer). From digital literacies to digital problem solving: Expanding technology-rich learning opportunities for adults. *Journal of Research & Practice for Adult Literacy, Secondary & Basic Education, 6*(2), 66–70.

Friedrich, L., & Trainin, G. (2016). Paving the way for new literacies integration in elementary teacher education. *Creative Education, 7*, 1456–1474. https://doi.org/10.4236/ce.2016.710151.

Fu, P., & Fox, M. M. (2012). *Bend, not break: A life in two worlds*. Portfolio Penguin.

García, O. (2009). *Bilingual education in the 21st century: A global perspective*. Wiley/Blackwell.

García, O., Batlett, L., & Kleifgen, J. (2007). From biliteracy to pluriliteracies. In P. Auer, & L. Wei (Eds.), *Handbook of multilingualism and multilingual communication* (Vol. 5, pp. 207–228). Mouton de Gruyter.

García, O., & Kleifgen, J. A. (2020). Translanguaging and literacies. *Reading Research Quarterly, 55*(4), 553–571. https://doi.org/10.1002/rrq.286

Gee, J. (2015). The new literacy studies. In J. Rowsell & K. Pahl (Eds.), *The Routledge handbook of literacy studies* (pp. 35–48). Routledge.

Glover, D. (2017). Emotional intelligence, transformational leadership, & leader efficacy of nonprofit leaders. [Doctor of Education Dissertation, Revecca Nazarene University]. ProQuest Dissertations Publishing, 2017. 10269728. https://www.proquest.com/openview/4e91533124148b586e17ca1407dc1e6c/1?pq-origsite=gscholar&cbl=18750

Godwin-Jones, R. (2015). Contributing, creating, curating: Digital literacies for language learners. *Language Learning & Technology, 19*(3), 8–20.

Golding, B., & Foley, A. (2017). Constructing narratives in later life. *Australian Journal of Adult Learning, 57*(3), 384–400.

Government of Victoria. (2008). *The economic benefit of investment in adult community education in Victoria*. https://www.education.vic.gov.au/Documents/about/research/acfe-publications/economicbenef.pdf

Greenleaf, R. K. (2002). *Servant leadership: A journey into the nature of legitimate power and greatness* (25th anniversary ed.). Paulist Press.

Hafner, C. (2019). Digital literacies for English language learners. In X. Gao (Ed.), *Second handbook of English language teaching* (pp. 899–918). Springer.

Hafner, C. A. (2014). Embedding digital literacies in English language teaching: Students' digital video projects as multimodal ensembles. *TESOL Quarterly, 48*, 655–685. https://doi.org/10.1002/tesq.138

Hafner, C. A., Chik, A., & Jones, R. (2015). Digital literacies and language learning. *Language Learning & Technology, 19*(3), 1–7.

Hammersley, M., & Atkinson, P. (2019). *Ethnography: Principles in practice* (4th ed.). Routledge.

Hanson-Smith, E. (2016). Teacher education and technology. In F. Farr & L. Murray (Eds.), *The Routledge handbook of language learning and technology* (pp. 210–222). Routledge

Hargreaves, A., & Fink, D. (2006, September). Redistributed leadership for sustainable professional learning communities. *Journal of School Leadership, 16*, 550–565. https://doi.org/10.1177/105268460601600507

Harrison, J., MacGibbon, L., & Morton, M. (2001). Regimes of trustworthiness in qualitative research: The rigors of reciprocity. *Qualitative Inquiry, 7*(3), 323–345. https://doi.org/10.1177/107780040100700305

Hayes, E. (1992). The impact of feminism on adult education publications: An analysis of British and American journals. *International Journal of Lifelong Education, 11*(2), 125–138. https://doi.org/10.1080/0260137920110205

Hayles, N. (2009). RFID: Human agency and meaning in information-intensive environments. *Theory, Culture & Society, 26*(2–3), 47–72. https://doi.org/10.1177/0263276409103107

Hayward, M. (2017). Teaching as a primary therapeutic intervention for learners from refugee backgrounds. *Intercultural Education (London, England), 28*(2), 165–181. https://doi.org/10.1080/14675986.2017.1294391

Henare, A., Holbraad, M., & Wastell, S. (Eds.). (2006). *Thinking through things: Theorising artefacts ethnographically*. Routledge.

Hersey, P., & Blanchard, K. H. (1982, May). Leadership style: Attitudes and behaviours. *Training and Development Journal, 36*, 50–52.

Hinrichsen, J., & Coombs, A. (2013). The five resources of critical digital literacy: A framework for curriculum integration. *Research in Learning Technology, 21*, 1–16. https://doi.org/10.3402/rlt.v21.21334

Hodge, S., Holford, J., Milana, M., Waller, R., & Webb, S. (2020). Adult education, vocational education and economic policy: Theory illuminates understanding. *International Journal of Lifelong Education, 39*(2), 133–138. https://doi.org/10.1080/02601370.2020.1747791

Hollander, E. P. (2009). *Inclusive leadership: The essential leader-follower relationship*. Routledge.

Humpage, L., Fozdar, F., Marlowe, J., & Hartley, L. (2019). Photovoice and refugee research: The case for a 'layers' versus 'labels' approach to vulnerability. *Research Ethics, 15*(3–4), 1–16.

Jacobson, E. (2016). Expanding notions of professional development in adults' basic education. In M. Knobel & J. Kalman (Eds.), *New literacies and teacher learning: Professional development and the digital turn* (pp. 173–194). Peter Lang.

Jiang, L. (2017). The affordances of digital multimodal composing for EFL learning. *ELT Journal, 71*(4), 413–422. https://doi.org/10.1093/elt/ccw098

Jones, R. H., & Hafner, C. A. (2012). *Understanding digital literacies: A practical introduction*. Routledge. https://doi.org/10.4324/9780203095317

Kalantzis, M., Cope, B., Chan, E., & Dalley-Trim, L. (2016). *Literacies*. Cambridge University Press.

Kaur-Gill, S., & Dutta, M. (2017). Digital ethnography. In J. Matthes (Ed.), *The international encyclopaedia of communication research methods*. Online. https://doi.org/10.1002/9781118901731.iecrm0271

Kearney, G., Corman, M., Hart, N., Johnston, J., & Gormley, G. (2019). Why institutional ethnography? Why now? Institutional ethnography in health professions education. *Perspectives on Medical Education, 8*(17), 17–24. https://doi.org/10.1007/s40037-019-0499-0

Kenny, E. (2016). *Settlement in the digital age: Digital inclusion and newly arrived young people from refugee and migrant backgrounds*. Centre for Migrant Youth. (CMY).

Killion, J. P., & Todnem, G. R. (1991, March). A process for personal theory building. *Educational Leadership, 48*(6), 14–16.

King, A. C., & Woodroffe, J. (2017). Walking interviews. In P. Liamputtong (Eds.), *Handbook of research methods in health social sciences* (pp. 1269–1290). Springer. https://doi.org/10.1007/978-981-10-2779-6_28-1

Klenk, H. (2017). An alternative understanding of education and empowerment: Local-level perspectives of refugee social integration in the United Kingdom. *European Education, 49*(2–3), 166–183. https://doi.org/10.1080/10564934.2017.1341290

Klinker, J. (2006). Qualities of democracy: Links to democratic leadership. *Journal of Thought, 41*(2), 51–63.

Knobel, M., & Kalman, J. (2016). *New literacies and teacher learning: Professional development and the digital turn* (Vol. 74). Peter Lang.

Knobel, M., & Lankshear, C. (2006). Digital literacy and digital literacies: Policy, pedagogy and research considerations for education. *Nordic Journal of Digital Literacy*, *1*(1), 12–24.

Knobel, M., & Lankshear, C. (2007). *A new literacies sampler*. Peter Lang.

Kolb, D. (1984). *Experiential learning*. Prentice-Hall.

LaFrance, M. (2018). Institutional ethnography. In P. Liamputtong (Ed.), *Handbook of research methods in health social sciences* (pp. 1–14). Springer. https://doi.org/10.1007/978-981-10-2779-6_82-1

Lakoff, G. (2010). Why it matters how we frame the environment. *Environmental Communication*, *4*(1), 70–81. https://doi.org/10.1080/17524030903529749

Lankshear, C., & Knobel, M. (2006). *New literacies: Everyday practices and classroom learning* (2nd ed.). Open University Press.

Lankshear, C., Snyder, I., & Green, B. (2000). *Teachers and technoliteracy*. Allen & Unwin.

Lassiter, L. (2001). From "reading over the shoulders of natives" to "reading alongside natives," literally: Toward a collaborative and reciprocal ethnography. *Journal of Anthropological Research*, *57*(2), 137–149. http://www.jstor.org/stable/3631564

Law, N., Woo, D., de la Torre, J., & Wong, G. (2018). *A global framework of reference on digital literacy skills for indicator 4.4.2*. http://uis.unesco.org/sites/default/files/documents/ip51-global-framework-reference-digital-literacy-skills-2018-en.pdf

Lee, N., & Tan, S. (2013). Traversing the design-language divide in the design and evaluation of physical learning environments: A trial of visual methods in focus groups. *Journal of Learning Spaces*, *2*(2). http://libjournal.uncg.edu/jls/article/view/503/383

Lee, R., & Kim, J. (2018, July). Womem and/or immigrants: A feminist reading on the marginalised adult learners in Korean lifelong learning policy and practice. *Australian Journal of Adult Learning*, *58*(2), 184–208. https://doi.org/10.3316/ielapa.862047172830424

Lees, C. (2019). 'Do you speak English?' 'Are you working me?!' Translanguaging practices online and their place in the EFL classroom: The case of Facebook. *Revue Internationale Méthodal. Méthodologie de l'enseignement et de l'apprentissage des langues*(3). https://methodal.net/?article236

Leung, L., Lamb, C. F., & Emrys, L. (2009). *Technology's refuge: The use of technology by asylum seekers and refugees*. http://library.bsl.org.au/jspui/bitstream/1/2932/1/TechnologysRefuge.pdf

Liesveld, R., & Miller, J. A. (2005). *Teach with your strengths: How great teachers inspire their students*. Gallup Press.

Lloyd, A., Kennan, A., Thompson, M., Kim, M., & Qayyum, A. (2013). Connecting with new information landscapes: Information literacy practices of refugees. *Journal of Documentation*, *69*(1), 121–144. https://doi.org/10.1108/00220411311295351

Lopez, S. J., & Louis, M. C. (2009). The principles of strengths-based education. *Journal of College and Character*, *10*(4). https://doi.org/10.2202/1940-1639.1041

Lotherington, H., & Jenson, J. (2011). Teaching multimodal and digital literacy in L2 settings: New literacies, new basics, new pedagogies. *Annual Review of Applied Linguistics*, *31*, 226–246. https://doi.org/10.1017/s0267190511000110

Maber, E. J. T. (2016). Finding feminism, finding voice? Mobilising community education to build women's participation in Myanmar's political transition. *Gender and Education*, *28*(3), 416–430. https://doi.org/10.1080/09540253.2016.1167175

MacGillivray, A. (2018). Leadership as practice meets knowledge as flow: Emerging perspectives for leaders in knowledge-intensive organizations. *Journal of Public Affairs*, *18*(1), 1–10. https://doi.org/10.1002/pa.1699

Macrae, H., & Agostinelli, J. (2002). Women and literacy in Australia: A closer look. *Fine Print*, *25*(2), 13–18.

Madison, D. (2012). *Critical ethnography: Method, ethics, and performance* (2nd ed.). Sage.

Maiter, S., Simich, L., Jacobson, N., & Wise, J. (2008). Reciprocity: An ethic for community-based participatory action research. *Action Research*, *6*(3), 305–325. https://doi.org/10.1177/1476750307083720

Mant, A. (1999). *Intelligent leadership*. Allen & Unwin.

Marková, I., Linell, P., Grossen, M., & Salazar Orvig, A. (2007). *Dialogue in focus groups. Exploring socially shared knowledge*. Equinox.

Marquardt, M., & Waddill, D. (2004). The power of learning in action learning: A conceptual analysis of how the five schools of adult learning theories are incorporated within the practice of action learning. *Action Learning: Research and Practice*, *1*(2), 185–202.

Marsh, J., Hannon, P., Lewis, M., & Ritchie, L. (2017). Young children's initiation into family literacy practices in the digital age. *Journal of Early Childhood Research: ECR*, *15*(1), 47–60. https://doi.org/10.1177/1476718X15582095

Marshall, C., & Rossman, G. (1995). *Designing qualitative research* (2nd ed.). Sage Publications.

Martin-Jones, M., & Jones, K. E. (Eds.). (2000). *Multilingual literacies: Reading and writing different worlds* (Vol. 10). John Benjamins Publishing.

Maxwell, J. (2012). *A realist approach for qualitative research*. Sage.

McCaffrey, K. T., & Taha, M. C. (2019). Rethinking the digital divide: Smartphones as translanguaging tools among middle eastern refugees in New Jersey. *Annals of Anthropological Practice*, *43*(2), 26–38.

McClanahan, L. (2014). Training using technology in the adult ESL classroom. *Journal of Adult Education: MPAEA*, *43*(1), 22–27.

Miettinen, R., & Virkkunen, J. (2005). Epistemic objects, artefacts and organizational change. *Organization*, *12*, 437–456. https://doi.org/10.1177/1350508405051279

Milton, M., & Vozzo, L. (2013). Digital literacy and digital pedagogies for teaching literacy: Pre-service teachers' experience on teaching rounds. *Journal of Literacy and Technology*, *14*(1), 72–97.

Miralles-Lombardo, B., Miralles, J., & Golding, B. (2008). *Creating learning spaces for refugees: The role of multicultural organisations in Australia*. National Centre for Vocational Education Research. http://hdl.voced.edu.au/10707/122946

Mockler, N. (2015). From surveillance to formation?: A generative approach to teacher 'performance and development' in Australian schools. *Australian Journal of Teacher Education (Online)*, *40*(9), 117–131.

Morrison, S. (2021). *A modern digital economy to secure Australia's future*. https://www.pm.gov.au/media/modern-digital-economy-secure-australias-future

Murray, D. E. (2008). From marginalisation to transformation: How ICT is being used in ESL learning today. *International Journal of Pedagogies and Learning*, *4*(5), 20–35. https://doi.org/10.5172/ijpl.4.5.20

Murray, D. E., Lloyd, R., & McPherson, P. (2006). *Teacher and learner use of new technology in the AMEP*. National Centre for English Language Teaching and Research.

New London Group. (1996). A pedagogy of multiliteracies: Designing social futures. *Harvard Educational Review*, *66*(1), 60–93.

Nghia, T. L. H., Pham, T., Tomlinson, M., Medica, K., & Thompson, C. D. (Eds.). (2020). *Developing and utilizing employability capitals: Graduates' strategies across labour markets*. (1st ed.). Routledge Research in Higher Education. Routledge. https://doi.org/10.4324/9781003004660

Noguerón-Liu, S. (2017). "Everybody knows your business"/"Todo Mundo Se Da Cuenta": Immigrant adults' construction of privacy, risk, and vulnerability in online platforms. *Journal of Adolescent & Adult Literacy, 60*(5), 505–513. https://doi.org/10.1002/jaal.599

Northouse, P. G. (2010). *Leadership: Theory and practice*. Sage Publications. https://www.proquest.com/books/leadership-theory-practice/docview/1288987790/se-2?accountid=12528

Norton, M. (1994). Literacy work as women's work and other reasons it is undervalued. *Australian Journal of Adult and Community Education, 43*(1), 71–75. https://doi.org/10.3316/aeipt.66072

OECD. (2015). Does having digital skills really pay off? *Adult Skills in Focus, 1*. https://doi.org/10.1787/5js023r0wj9v-en.

O'Grady, M. (2016). Feminism in community: Adult education for transformation. *Action Learning: Research and Practice, 13*(2), 187–190. https://doi.org/10.1080/14767333.2016.1170985

Omerbašić, D. (2015). Literacy as a translocal practice: Digital multimodal literacy practices among girls resettled as refugees. *Journal of Adolescent & Adult Literacy, 58*(6), 472–481. https://doi.org/10.1002/jaal.389

O'Reilly, K. (2005). *Ethnographic methods*. Routledge.

O'Reilly, K. (2009). Rapport. In K. O'Reilly (Ed.), *Sage key concepts: Key concepts in ethnography* (pp. 175–181). SAGE.

Orlikowski, W. (1992). The duality of technology: Rethinking the concept of technology in organizations. *Organization Science, 3*(3), 398–427. http://www.jstor.org/stable/2635280

Orlikowski, W. J. (2007). Sociomaterial practices: Exploring technology at work. *Organization Studies, 28*(9), 1435–1448. https://doi.org/10.1177/0170840607081138

Orlikowski, W. J. (2010). The sociomateriality of organisational life: Considering technology in management research. *Cambridge Journal of Economics, 34*(1), 125–141. https://doi.org/10.1093/cje/bep058

Pangrazio, L., Godhe, A.-L., & Ledesma, A. G. L. (2020). What is digital literacy? A comparative review of publications across three language contexts. *E-Learning and Digital Media, 17*(6), 442–459. https://doi.org/10.1177/2042753020946291

Peromingo, M., & Pieterson, W. (2018). The new world of work and the need for digital empowerment. *Forced Migration Review, 58*, 32–33. https://www.proquest.com/scholarly-journals/new-world-work-need-digital-empowerment/docview/2062902270/se-2?accountid=12528

Perri 6, & Bellamy, C. (2012). *Principles of methodology: Research design in social science*. SAGE.

Pham, T., & Soltani, B. (2021). *Enhancing student education transitions and employability: From theory to practice* (1st ed.). Routledge. https://doi.org/10.4324/9781003168737

Rappel, L. J. (2015). Integrating the personal and the professional. *Adult Education Quarterly, 65*(4), 313–325. https://doi.org/10.1177/0741713615585573

Reed, J., & Payton, V. R. (1997). Focus groups: Issues of analysis and interpretation. *Journal of Advanced Nursing, 26*(4), 765–771. https://doi.org/10.1046/j.1365-2648.1997.00395.x

Refugee Council of Australia. (2019). *Settlement services*. https://www.refugeecouncil.org.au/settlement-services/2/

Refugee Council of Australia. (2020). *How many refugees have come to Australia?* https://www.refugeecouncil.org.au/how-many-refugees-have-come/

Reichel, D., Siegel, M., & Andreo, J. C. (2015). *ICT for the employability and integration of immigrants in the European Union*. European Commission. Joint Research Centre Institute for Prospective Technological Studies.

Richardson, L. (2000). Writing: A method of inquiry. In N. K. Denzin & Y. S. Lincoln (Eds.), *Handbook of qualitative research* (pp. 923–948). Sage.

Ritzhaupt, A. D., Liu, F., Dawson, K., & Barron, A. E. (2013). Differences in student information and communication technology literacy based on socio-economic status, ethnicity, and gender. *Journal of Research on Technology in Education, 45*(4), 291–307. https://doi.org/10.1080/15391523.2013.10782607

Robinson, V. (2001). Descriptive and normative research on organisational learning locating the contribution of Argyris and Schon. *The International Journal of Educational Management, 15*(2), 58–67. http://www.emerald-library.com/ft

Roehl, T. (2012). Disassembling the classroom – an ethnographic approach to the materiality of education. *Ethnography and Education, 7*(1), 109–126. https://doi.org/10.1080/17457823.2012.661591

Rogers, E. E., & Hansman, C. A. (2004). Social and cultural issues in urban communities. *New Directions for Adult and Continuing Education, 2004*(101), 17–28. https://doi.org/10.1002/ace.125

Rose, G. (2016). *Visual methodologies*. Sage.

Rowsell, J., Morrell, E., & Alvermann, D. E. (2017). Confronting the digital divide: Debunking brave new world discourses. *The Reading Teacher, 71*(2), 157–165. https://doi.org/10.1002/trtr.1603

Rowsell, J., & Pahl, K. (2012). *Literacy and education: Understanding the new literacy studies in the classroom*. (2nd ed.). Sage Publications.

Rowsell, J., & Pahl, K. (2015). Introduction. In J. Rowsell & K. Pahl (Eds.), *The Routledge handbook of literacy studies* (pp. 1–16). Routledge.

Roy, L. A., & Roxas, K. C. (2011, October–December). Whose deficit is this anyhow? Exploring counter-stories of somali bantu refugees' experiences in 'doing school'. *Harvard Educational Review, 81*(3), 521–618.

Rudnitski, R. A. (1996). Global leadership theory: Theoretical roots, principles and possibilities for the future. *Gifted Education International, 11*(2), 80–85. https://doi.org/10.1177/026142949601100203

Ryu, M., & Tuvilla, M. R. S. (2018). Resettled refugee youths' stories of migration, schooling, and future: Challenging dominant narratives about refugees. *The Urban Review, 50*(4), 539–558. https://doi.org/10.1007/s11256-018-0455-z

Sanguinetti, J. (1994, April). The sound of babel and the language of friendship: An exploration of critical and feminist pedagogies and their application in teaching ESL and literacy to women. *Australian Journal of Adult and Community Education, 34*(1), 18–38. https://doi.org/10.3316/aeipt.66066

Sanguinetti, J., Waterhouse, P., & Maunders, D. (2004). Pedagogies for life and employability: How generic skills and attributes are fostered in adult and community education. In P. L. Jeffery (Ed.), *AARE 2004 conference: Papers collection* (19 p.). AARE.

Sarros, J. C., Cooper, B. K., & Santora, J. C. (2011). Leadership vision, organizational culture, and support for innovation in not-for-profit and for-profit organizations. *Leadership & Organization Development Journal, 32*(3), 291–309. https://doi.org/10.1108/01437731111123933

Scanlon Institute. (2019, June). *Australia's English problem: How to renew our once celebrated Adult Migrant English Program*. Scanlon Foundation Research Institute. https://scanloninstitute.org.au/sites/default/files/2020-01/June2019_Scanlon-Institute_Narrative-3.pdf

Schwartz, D. (1989). Visual ethnography: Using photography in qualitative research. *Qualitative Sociology, 12*, 119–154. https://doi.org/10.1007/BF00988995

Scott, S., & Webber, C. F. (2008). Evidence-based leadership development: the 4L framework. *Journal of Educational Administration, 46*(6), 762–776. https://doi.org/10.1108/09578230810908343

Scott Jones, J., & Watt, S. (Eds.). (2010). *Ethnography in social science practice*. Routledge/Taylor & Francis Group.

Sefton, R., Waterhouse, P., & Cooney, R. (1995). *Workplace learning and change: The workplace as a learning environment*. Automotive Training Australia.

Selwyn, N. (2002). *Defining the 'digital divide': Developing a theoretical understanding of inequalities in the information age*. Occasional Paper 49. Cardiff University. http://www.cf.ac.uk/socsi/ict/definingdigitaldivide.pdf

Senge, P. (1990). *The fifth discipline: The art and practice of the learning organization*. Doubleday.

Shan, H. (2015, March). Women, gender, and immigrant studies in Canadian adult education: An ethnographic content analysis. *Canadian Journal for the Study of Adult Education, 27*(2 (Special Issue)), 46–63.

Shapiro, S., & MacDonald, M. T. (2017). From deficit to asset: Locating discursive resistance in a refugee-background student's written and oral narrative. *Journal of Language, Identity & Education, 16*(2), 80–93. https://doi.org/10.1080/15348458.2016.1277725

Shariati, S., Armarego, J., & Sudweeks, F. (2017). The impact of e-skills on the settlement of iranian refugees in Australia. *Interdisciplinary Journal of e-Skills and Lifelong Learning, 13*, 59–77. https://doi.org/10.28945/3704

Skinner, E. N., Hagood, M. C., & Provost, M. C. (2014). Creating a new literacies coaching ethos. *Reading & Writing Quarterly, 30*(3), 215–232. https://doi.org/10.1080/10573569.2014.907719

Smith, D. (2001). Texts and the ontology of organizations and institutions. *Studies in Cultures, Organisations and Societies, 7*(2), 159–198. https://doi.org/10.1080/10245280108523557

Smith, D. (2005). *Institutional ethnography: A sociology for people*. AltaMira Press.

Smyser, H. (2019). Adaptation of conventional technologies with refugee language learners: An overview of possibilities. *Language, Teaching, and Pedagogy for Refugee Education, 15*, 125–139. https://doi.org/10.1108/S2055-364120180000015010

Smythe, S. (2018). Adult learning in the control society: Digital era governance, literqacies of control, and the work of adult educators. *Adult Education Quarterly, 68*(3), 197–214. https://doi.org/10.1177/0741713618766645

Snyder, I. (1997). *Page to screen: Taking literacy into the electronic era*. Allen & Unwin.

Snyder, I. (2008). *The literacy wars: Why teaching children to read and write is a battleground in Australia*. Allen & Unwin.

Sørensen, E. (2009). *The materiality of learning: Technology and knowledge in educational practice*. Cambridge University Press.

Sow, M. T., & Aborbie, S. (2018). Impact of leadership on digital transformation. *Business and Economic Research, 8*, 139–148. https://doi.org/10.5296/ber.v8i3.13368

Spillane, J., Halverson, R., & Diamond, J. (2001). Investigating school leadership practice: A distributed perspective. *Educational Researcher, 30*(3), 23–28. https://doi.org/10.3102/0013189X030003023

Starrat, R. J. (2001). Democratic leadership theory in late modernity: An oxymoron or ironic possibility? *International Journal of Leadership in Education, 4*(4), 333–352. https://doi.org/10.1080/13603120110080978

State Government of Victoria. (2021). *Discover Victoria's diverse population*. https://www.vic.gov.au/discover-victorias-diverse-population

State of Victoria. (2018). *The EAL framework*.

References

State of Victoria. (2019). *The future of Adult Community Education in Victoria: 2020–25.* https://www.education.vic.gov.au/Documents/training/learners/learnlocal/Future-ACE-2020-25-Ministerial-Statement.pdf

Street, B. (2009). The future of "social literacies". In M. Baynham & M. Prinsloo (Eds.), *The future of literacy studies* (pp. 21–37). Palgrave Macmillan UK.

Street, B. V. (1984). *Literacy in theory and practice.* Cambridge University Press.

Swain, J. (2018). A hybrid approach to thematic analysis in qualitative research: Using a practical example. In *SAGE research methods cases.* https://www.doi.org/10.4135/9781526435477

Taimalu, M., & Luik, P. (2019). The impact of beliefs and knowledge on the integration of technology among teacher educators: A path analysis. *Teaching and Teacher Education, 79,* 101–110. https://doi.org/10.1016/j.tate.2018.12.012

Thomas, J., Barraket, J., Wilson, C. K., Rennie, E., Ewing, S., & MacDonald, T. (2019). Measuring Australia's digital divide: The Australian digital inclusion index 2019, RMIT University and Swinburne University of Technology, Melbourne, for Telstra. https://doi.org/10.25916/5d6478f373869

Tour, E. (2015). Digital mindsets: Teachers' technology use in personal life and teaching. *Language Learning & Technology, 19*(3), 12–139.

Tour, E. (2017a). Teachers' self-initiated professional learning through personal learning networks. *Technology, Pedagogy and Education, 26*(2), 179–192.

Tour, E. (2017b). Teachers' personal learning networks (PLNs): Exploring the nature of self-initiated professional learning online. *Literacy, 51*(1), 11–18.

Tour, E. (2020). Teaching digital literacies in EAL/ESL classrooms: Practical strategies. *TESOL Journal, 11*(1), n/a. https://doi.org/10.1002/tesj.458

Tour, E., Creely, E., & Waterhouse, P. (2020). Considering the benefits of research participation: Insights from a study of adult EAL educators. *TESOL in Context, 29*(2), 63–84. https://doi.org/10.21153/tesol2020vol29no2art1434

Tour, E., Creely, E., & Waterhouse, P. (2021). "It'sa black hole…": Exploring teachers' narratives and practices for digital literacies in the adult EAL context. *Adult Education Quarterly, 71*(3), 290–307. https://doi.org/10.1177/0741713621991516

Trainor, A., & Bouchard, K. A. (2013). Exploring and developing reciprocity in research design. *International Journal of Qualitative Studies in Education, 26*(8), 986–1003. https://doi.org/10.1080/09518398.2012.724467

Traxler, J. (2018). Digital literacy: A Palestinian refugee perspective. *Research in Learning Technology, 26.* https://doi.org/10.25304/rlt.v26.1983

Tudsri, P., & Hebbani, A. (2015). 'Now I'm part of Australia and I need to know what is happening here': Case of Hazara male former refugees in Brisbane strategically selecting media to aid acculturation. *Journal of International Migration and Integration, 16*(4), 1273–1289.

Turner, M. (2019). *Multilingualism as a resource and a goal: Using and learning languages in mainstream schools.* Proquest.

Tynan, M., Gralton, E., McCredden, J., Gralton, E., Tynan, T. M., Kan, M., & Kennedy, R. (2018). Evaluation of the adult migrant English program new business model. *Social Compass & Department of Home Affairs.* https://immi.homeaffairs.gov.au/amep-subsite/Files/amep-evaluation-new-business-model.pdf

Valadez, J. R., & Duran, R. (2007). Redefining the digital divide: Beyond access to computers and the Internet. *High School Journal, 90*(30), 30. https://link.gale.com/apps/doc/A161127932/AONE?u=monash&sid=bookmark-AONE&xid=48efcda9

van Rensburg, H. J., & Son, J.-B. (2010). Improving English language and computer literacy skills in an adult refugee program. *International Journal of Pedagogies and Learning*, *6*(1), 69–81. https://doi.org/10.5172/ijpl.6.1.69

Vella, J. (2002). *Learning to listen learning to teach: The power of dialogue in educating adults* (Revised ed.). Jossey-Bass: A Wiley company.

Wacquant, L. (2002). Scrutinizing the street: Poverty, morality, and the pitfalls of urban ethnography. *American Journal of Sociology*, *107*(6), 1468–1532. https://doi.org/10.1086/340461

Walstab, A., Volkoff, V., & Teese, R. (2006). *ACE makes a difference: Building pathways, providing opportunities & creating outcomes: Final report - stage 3 – 2006.* Adult Community & Further Education Board.

Warschauer, M. (1999). *Electronic literacies: Language, culture, and power in online education.* L. Erlbaum Associates.

Waterhouse, P., & Virgona, C. (2008). *Working from strengths: Venturing towards strengths- based adult education.* NCVER. https://www.ncver.edu.au/research-and-statistics/publications/all-publications/working-from-strengths-venturing-towards-strength-based-adult-education

Watts, J. (2008). Integrity in qualitative research. In L. Given (Ed.), *The Sage encyclopedia of qualitative research methods* (Vol. 1, pp. 440–441). SAGE.

Welch, D., Grossaint, K., Reid, K., & Walker, C. (2014). Strengths-based leadership development: Insights from expert coaches. *Consulting Psychology Journal: Practice and Research*, *66*(1), 20–37. https://doi.org/10.1037/cpb0000002

Whitley, M. A., Coble, C., & Jewell, G. S. (2016). Evaluation of a sport-based youth development programme for refugees. *Leisure/Loisir*, *40*(2), 175–199, https://doi.org/10.1080/14927713.2016.1219966

Wilkinson, J., & Kaukko, M. (2020). Educational leading as pedagogical love: The case for refugee education. *International Journal of Leadership in Education: Understanding Leadership for Refugee Education. Guest Editors: Khalid Arar, Deniz Örücü, Duncan Waite*, *23*(1), 70–85. https://doi.org/10.1080/13603124.2019.1629492

Williamson, B. (2017). *Big data in education: The digital future of learning, policy and practice.* SAGE.

Wilson, W., & Chaddha, A. (2009). The role of theory in ethnographic research. *Ethnography*, *10*(4), 549–564. https://doi.org/10.1177/1466138109347009

Zaidi, R., & Rowsell, J. (2017). Literacy lives in transcultural times. In R. Zaidi & J. Rowsell (Eds.), *Literacy lives in transcultural times* (pp. 1–14). Routledge.

INDEX

Pages in *italics* refer to figures and pages followed by n refer notes.

ACE *see* Adult Community Education (ACE) Centre
ACTA *see* Australian Council of TESOL Associations
activity-oriented focus group 57
Adult Community Education (ACE) 9–10, 52–53
adult EAL: context 28, 43, 111, 135, 157; education in Australia 35; learners 16, 71–72, 79–80, 82, 88, 100, 103, 109, 111–112, 118, 125, 135, 152–153, 155, 158, 165, 167; organisations 158; programmes 151, 154, 169; sector 16, 29, 131, 149, 151–152, 154, 171; settings 27, 38–39, 131, 162
Adult Migrant Education Services (AMES) 8
Adult Migrant English Program (AMEP): Australian core skills framework 8; challenges 10–12; EAL framework 8; TESOL 9
Agostinelli, J. 55
Alam, K. 6
Alderson, A. 133
AMEP *see* Adult Migrant English Program
AMES *see* Adult Migrant Education Services
Australian Council of TESOL Associations (ACTA) 12
Australian Digital Inclusion Index 7
automated/"zero-touch" technologies 3–4

Barron, A. E. 6
Benseman, J. 50
Blackwell, A. 133
Bracken, S. J. 28
Butorac, A. 133

Campbell, B. 53
CBD *see* central business district
central business district (CBD) 45–46
CEO *see* Chief Executive Officer
CEO of Langfield 1–2; collaboration as the core leadership value 143–144; leadership and vision for change 138–143; situated difficulties of enacting change 144–147; supporting change through strategic provisioning 147–149; transformational leadership 149–152, *150*
Chief Executive Officer (CEO) 39, 48–49, 53, 55–56; at Langfield *see* CEO of Langfield
Clemans, A. 28
Coleman, M. 142
community-based adult EAL sector 149, 154, 169
computer-assisted language learning (CALL) 14
Content and Language Integrated Learning (CLIL) 14
Corman, M. 42
Covid-19 pandemic 4, 169–171

Index

critical ethnography 40
Culturally and Linguistically Diverse (CALD) 26
curriculum and pedagogy 154; development of suitable pedagogies 156–158; digital literacies in EAL curriculum 155; in milieu of digital change 155–156; organisation-wide approach to digital literacies 156

Dawson, K. 6
democratic leadership practices 162–164
desktop computer 2, 24, 49, 62–63, 66–69, 73, 75, 83, 88, 91, 104, 135, 146–147
digital age 21, 115, 131, 162
digital Australia: digital society 5–6; and newcomers 3–5
digital culture 23, 87, 100, 103
digital experiences 6, 67, 80, 85, 90–91, 99
digital landscape 61–62, 159
digital literacies: in adult EAL settings 12–15; basic digital technology language and skills 96–100; deliberate application of strengths 106–107; digital age 20–21; digital cultures 23; digital multimodal composing 100–103; everyday activities 62–65; framework 164–166; importance of 84–87; individualised learning 104–105; Langfield learners *see* Langfield learners' digital literacy practices; literacy studies 22, 24; peer-learning 105–106; possibilities for 109–112; role of 95; socio-cultural framing 24–25; strengths-based practices 25–29; strengths development 107–108; teachers' perspectives on strengths 108–109; within teaching and learning at Langfield *see* Langfield; *Techno-Tuesday see* Techno-Tuesday programme
digital technology 1, 3–6, 13, 16, 19–23, 35, 38, 61–62, 66–67, 69–70, 72, 77, 80–81, 85–86, 90–91, 95–100, 108–112, 115, 117–120, 126, 131, 134, 145–146, 151, 153, 158, 164

EAL *see* English as an Additional Language
EAL educators, relevant teaching resources 166–167
effective leadership *30*; evidence-based approach 31; grounded knowledge 31; inclusive people management 30; laissez-faire leadership approach and style 32, *33*; setting of a vision 30; strengths-based 31–32
emails/Gmail 13, 24, 62, 66–67, 74–75, 78, 91, 100, 103–105, 108, 122, 135, 155, 157

English as an Additional Language (EAL) 2, 26, 48; adult learners/settings *see* adult EAL; framework 13–14; programmes 3, 7–17, 111, 149–151, 153–155, 169
English as a Second Language (ESL) 14, 26
ESL *see* English as a Second Language
ethnographic research: artefacts 57–58; data generation 55; field notes 55–56; focus groups 57–58; individual interviews 56, 58; methodological and ethical issues 167–169; participant observation 55; photographs 55, 58; thematic data analysis 58; video recording 55, 58
ethnography: forms of 40–41; *materiality* of the context 40; origin 40; realism 40; "siteness" of the site 40; social research 39

Facebook 23–24, 64, 155
Figgis, J. 133
focus group participants 62–63, 66, 70, 72, 91, 126, 128
Foley, A. 10

García, O. 23
Godwin-Jones, R. 13
Google 63–65, 67, 101, 124; forms 90, 102; icon 96; translate 53, 74–75, 80, 106, 117
Gormley, G. 42
government-funded EAL programmes 7; Adult Community Education 9–10; Adult Migrant English Program 8–12; digital literacies in adult EAL settings 12–15
Greenleaf, R. K. 142

Hansman, C. A. 50
Hanson-Smith, E. 131
Hart, N. 42
Hayes, E. 28

ICT *see* information and communication technology
Imran, S. 6
Index of Relative Socio-Economic Disadvantage (IRSD) 46
individual organisation 164
information and communication technology (ICT) 3, 21, 29
in-house professional learning 116–118
inner-urban area of Melbourne 38, *45*, 45–46, 49
institutional ethnography 41; conceptual framework 43, *44*; institutional setting 42; relational processes 43; social focus and ontological constitution 41–42, *42*

institutional settings 39, 41–42
internet 3, 6, 13, 46, 49, 62–63, 74, 86, 97, 125, 146, 156
iPads 49, 62–66, 68, 70, 72–73, 76–77, 79, 83, 88, 91, 94, *94*, 96–98, 104, 106, 117, 146, 148
IRSD *see* Index of Relative Socio-Economic Disadvantage

Johnston, J. 42

Kaukko, M. 52
Kearney, G. 42
Kenny, E. 7
Killion, J. P. 110
Kleifgen, J. A. 23
Knobel, M. 21
Kolb, D. 134

Langfield: choice of methodology 58–59; classroom 1 49, *50*; classroom 2 49, *51*; classroom door with welcoming messages 53, *54*; computer room 49, *52*; EAL teachers 48; feminist perspective 53–55; field notes 1–2; governance and funding 48–49; idea of reciprocity 37; inner-urban area of Melbourne 38, *45*, 45–46, 49; learning spaces and access to technology 49–50; methodological approach 37; mission 50–53; negotiation process 38–39, 49; and research participants 46–48, 50, 59n1; sits 38, 46; social housing estate 47, *47*, 49; teachers 53; teaching and learning digital literacies at 83–113; Victorian context 44–46
Langfield learners' digital literacy practices: applying for a job 67; awareness of oneself as learner 69–73; challenging experience of using desktop computer 66–69; everyday activities of mobile phone and iPads 62–65; familiarity with mobile devices 73–74; field notes 60–61, 74–75; home language 75–76; from immigrant, refugee, and/or asylum-seeking backgrounds 79–82; learning with technologies 66; personal networks 76–77; policy of 74; teachers 77–79; writing resume/CV 67
Lankshear, C. 21
leadership 29, 35, 139–141; aspects of democratic 33–34; of CEO *see* CEO of Langfield; effective *see* effective leadership; value 143–144
LinkedIn 24, 155
Liu, F. 6

Lopez, S. J. 27, 111–112
Louis, M. C. 27, 111–112

MacDonald, M. T. 25
Macrae, H. 55
Malinowski, Bronisław 39
Mant, A. 142
materiality 20, 23, 40, 57, 63, 69, 79, 91, 123, 151
Maunders, D. 52
McClanahan, L. 15
Mead, Margaret 39
messenger 64, 91
Mitchell, K. 133
mobile phone/devices 3, 6, 49, 57, 61–69, 73–75, 77, 79–80, 82–83, 88–91, 94, 100, 105–107, 146–147, 156, 158
Mockler, N. 133
Moodle 170
Morrisett, Lloyd 6

National Training Reform Agenda of 1995 10
Noguerón-Liu, S. 134
Non English Speaking Background (NESB) 26
Norton, M. 28

online platforms 67, 113n2, 155, 170
organisation-wide in-house approach 128–129

participatory ethnography 40
peer-learning 122–123
Peromingo, M. 7, 15
Pieterson, W. 7, 15
policy position 164
preferred professional learning 124, *124*
professional learning 158; appreciating learners' strengths 134; deliberations 131–135; digital literacies 159; external 118–122; in-house 116–118; learners' digital landscapes 159; learners' strengths 159; model *132*; new forms of 160–162; organisation-wide approach to 116; participants' collaborative collage *124*; pedagogies for digital literacies 159–160; peer-learning 122–123; sector-wide 166–167; teachers' preferences 123–131; valuing learners' 134

Rappel, L. J. 10
reciprocity 37–39, 41, 43
registered training organisation (RTO) 139–140
relational ethnography 40

research design for adult EAL settings: fluidity of the organisation 38; learning community and institutional setting 39; reciprocity 38; researcher relationship 38; sustainability 39
Richardson, L. 55
Ritzhaupt, A. D. 6
Rogers, E. E. 50
Rowsell, J. 4
Roxas, K. C. 25–26
Roy, L. A. 25–26
RTO *see* registered training organisation
Ryu, M. 25

Sanguinetti, J. 52
Skills for Education and Employment (SEE) programme 8, 17n4
smartphones 18, 20, 53, 62, 89, 98, 127, 135, 156
Smith, D. 37, 41–43
Smythe, S. 3
Snyder, I. 22
socio-material theory (SMT) 18, 57, 63; concept of *19*, 19–20
Son, J.-B. 6, 14

TAFE *see* Technical and Further Education
Teaching English to Speakers of Other Languages (TESOL) 48

Technical and Further Education (TAFE) 48
Techno-Tuesday programme 49, 55–58, 87–88, 117, 122, 133; collegiality 91–95; comprehensiveness 90–91; integratedness 88–90
TESOL *see* Teaching English to Speakers of Other Languages
Todnem, G. R. 110
training needs analysis (TNA) 148
Traxler, J. 15
Tuvilla, M. R. S. 25
Twitter 23

van Rensburg, H. J. 6, 14
Vella, J. 26
Victorian context 44–46
Victorian Government funding 139
Virgona, C. 26

Waterhouse, P. 52
WhatsApp 155, 170
Wilkinson, J. 52

YouTube 63–66, 76, 97

Zaidi, R. 4
Zalo accounts 64
Zoom 170
Zubrick, A. 133